Mexico Faces the 21st Century

MEXICO FACES THE 21st CENTURY

Edited by Donald E. Schulz
and Edward J. Williams

PRAEGER

Westport, Connecticut
London

The Library of Congress has catalogued the hardcover edition as follows:

Mexico faces the 21st century / edited by Donald E. Schulz and Edward
J. Williams.
      p. cm.—(Contributions in Latin American studies, ISSN
1054–6790 ; no. 5)
   Includes bibliographical references (p.   ) and index.
   ISBN 0–313–29518–2 (alk. paper)
   1. Mexico—Politics and government—1988- 2. Mexico—Economic
conditions. 3. Mexico—Social conditions. 4. Mexico—Relations—
United States. 5. United States—Relations—Mexico. 6. Mexico—
Forecasting. 7. Twenty-first century—Forecasts. I. Schulz,
Donald E., 1942- . II. Williams, Edward J. III. Series.
F1236.M4735 1995
972.08'35—dc20   95–4669

British Library Cataloguing in Publication Data is available.

A hardcover edition of *Mexico Faces the 21st Century* is available
from Greenwood Press, an imprint of Greenwood Publishing
Group, Inc. (Contributions in Latin American Studies, Number 5;
ISBN 0–313–29518–2).

Library of Congress Catalog Card Number: 95–4669
ISBN: 0–275–95358–0

First published in 1995

Praeger Publishers, 88 Post Road West, Westport, CT 06881
An imprint of Greenwood Publishing Group, Inc.

Printed in the United States of America

The paper used in this book complies with the
Permanent Paper Standard issued by the National
Information Standards Organization (Z39.48–1984).

10 9 8 7 6 5 4 3 2 1

Contents

    Undocumented Labor Migration   153
    Jesús Tamayo

10. The Zapatista Revolt and Its Implications for Civil–Military
    Relations and the Future of Mexico   165
    Stephen J. Wager and Donald E. Schulz

11. Through a Glass Darkly: On the Challenges and Enigmas of
    Mexico's Future   187
    Donald E. Schulz

    Selected Bibliography   207

    Index   209

    About the Editors and Contributors   217

Preface

Few countries are as important to the United States as Mexico. Sharing a 2,000-mile border and increasingly integrated with one another economically and socially, the two nations have become interdependent to an extent that could hardly have been imagined a decade ago. In the process, Mexico's problems have increasingly become U.S. problems.

Since the early 1980s, Mexico has gone from one of the most stable countries in Latin America to one of the most volatile. Nineteen ninety-four alone witnessed a peasant uprising in Chiapas, two major political assassinations, an upsurge in narcotics-related violence, kidnappings of important business figures, a rollercoaster election campaign, and, at year's end, a traumatic economic crisis. Meanwhile, in the United States, California voters passed Proposition 187, which was intended to cut off most social services to illegal immigrants (mostly Mexicans). The move produced an immediate backlash in Mexico, hinting of worse to come should anti-immigrant sentiment spread to other U.S. states and Congress.

Thus, there is a need to pause and take stock of where Mexico and U.S.–Mexican relations are heading. This book has evolved out of a conference entitled "Mexico Looks to the Twenty-First Century: Change and Challenge," organized by Edward J. Williams and Donald E. Schulz, and held at the University of Arizona, March 4–5, 1993. The papers delivered on that occasion have been updated and strengthened, and several more have been added to make the volume as comprehensive and current as possible. Edward J. Williams did yeoman work in translating the Sepúlveda and Tamayo chapters, and Donald E. Schulz edited and polished the entire volume. Special thanks are due to the University of Arizona and the U.S. Army's Strategic Outreach Initiative for providing the funding and other support that made this project possible.

Abbreviations

ANCIEZ	National Independent Emiliano Zapata Peasant Alliance
ANOCP	National Worker–Peasant Popular Assembly
BECC	Border Environment Cooperation Commission
CEC	Commission on Environmental Cooperation
CIOAC	Independent Central of Agricultural Workers and Peasants
CISN	Center of Investigation and National Security
CITES	Convention on International Trade in Endangered Species of Wild Fauna and Flora
CNTE	National Coordinating Committee of Education Workers
COPARMEX	Mexican Employers' Confederation
CTM	Confederation of Mexican Workers
DDF	Department of the Federal District
DF	Federal District
EAI	Enterprise for the Americas Initiative
EPA	Environmental Protection Agency
EZLN	Zapatista National Liberation Army
FAT	Authentic Labor Front
FDN	National Democratic Front
FESEBES	Federation of Goods and Services Unions
FNDSCAC	National Front in Defense of the Salary and Against Austerity and the High Cost of Living
FSTSE	Federation of State Employees Unions

GAO	U.S. Government Accounting Office
GATT	General Agreement on Tariffs and Trade
GDP	Gross Domestic Product
GNP	Gross National Product
IBEP	Integrated Border Environmental Plan
INE	National Institute for Ecology
INFONAVIT	National Housing Fund Institute
INI	Institute for Indigenous Affairs
INS	U.S. Immigration and Naturalization Service
JMUSDC	Joint Mexican–U.S. Defense Commission
MAP	Popular Action Movement
MSF	Railroad Workers Union Movement
NADBANK	North American Development Bank
NAFTA	North American Free Trade Agreement
NGOs	Nongovernmental Organizations
OCEZ	Emiliano Zapata Peasant Organization
PAN	National Action Party
PEMEX	*Petróleos Mexicanos* (Mexican Petroleum Company)
PFMA	Federal Attorney General for Environmental Protection
PFPA	*Procuraduría Federal de Protección al Ambiente* (Office of the Attorney General for Protection of the Environment)
PGR	*Procuraduría General de la República* (Mexican Justice Department)
PNR	National Revolutionary Party
PRD	Party of Democratic Revolution
PRI	Institutional Revolutionary Party
PROCUP	Revolutionary Workers Clandestine People's Union Party
PRONASOL	National Solidarity Program
PSUM	Unified Socialist Party of Mexico
SDN	National Defense Secretariat
SECDEF	Secretary of National Defense
SEDESOL	Secretariat of Social Development
SEDUE	Secretariat of Urban Development and Ecology
SME	Mexican Union of Electricians
SUTERM	Mexican Electrical Workers Union
SUTIN	Nuclear Industry Workers Union
UOI	Independent Workers' Unit
UU	Union of Ejido Unions

Mexico Faces the 21st Century

1

Crisis or Transformation?
The Struggle for the Soul of Mexico

Donald E. Schulz and Edward J. Williams

> The perfect dictatorship is not communism, not the Soviet Union, not Cuba, but Mexico, because it is a camouflaged dictatorship. It may not seem to be a dictatorship, but it has all the characteristics of dictatorship: the perpetuation, not of one person, but of an irremovable party, a party that allows sufficient space for criticism, provided such criticism serves to maintain the appearance of a democratic party, but which suppresses by all means, including the worst, whatever criticism may threaten its perpetuation in power.
>
> Mario Vargas Llosa[1]

Whither Mexico? During the NAFTA debate, many supporters of the free trade agreement painted a portrait of a country rapidly vaulting into the 21st century, modernizing economically, democratizing politically, creating a more prosperous and equitable society for its citizens while curtailing northward migration, maintaining political stability, and entering a new era of harmonious cooperation with the United States. Then came 1994, the Year from Hell, and suddenly Mexico seemed in danger of wholesale disintegration.

This chapter will examine the origins and development of the Mexican crisis as it unfolded during the six-year term of President Carlos Salinas de Gortari (1988–1994). Although the main focus will be on democratization and political stability, these matters cannot be entirely divorced from the socioeconomic problems afflicting the country or from its relations with the United States. We will leave it to the other authors, however, to provide a detailed analysis of those issues.

ECONOMIC CRISIS AND POLITICAL DECAY: THE DEINSTITUTIONALIZATION OF HEGEMONY

Any evaluation of the prospects for Mexican democracy must begin with an appreciation of the durability of Mexican authoritarianism. In Mexico, the current political system has survived essentially intact for sixty-six years, since the founding of the "official" party (today called the *Partido Revolucionario Institucional,* or PRI) in 1929. Over the years, noncompetitive elections were institutionalized within a formally multiparty, pluralistic framework. Not only was "the perfect dictatorship" disguised as a democracy, but it displayed an extraordinary capacity to regenerate itself through co-optation and reform. In this sense, change served not as an agent of systemic transformation but rather as a means of preserving continuity. Historically, electoral and party reforms were employed as tactical devices to maintain the legitimacy of the system and the hegemony of the governing elite and the dominant groups within it, and their instrument, the PRI.

Nevertheless, since the 1960s—especially since the violent suppression of the student protests of 1968—the Mexican system has been undergoing a process of gradual, accelerating erosion. This disintegration has been marked by cycles of crisis and reform, with each new turn of the latter giving rise (or at least contributing) to a succeeding crisis. Thus, while changing in order to remain the same has been essential to the maintenance of systemic equilibrium in the short-to-intermediate run, the strategy has been unable to prevent long-term decay. Rather than addressing the fundamental problems undermining the system, reforms were designed to buy time through piecemeal adjustment. The result, by the 1980s, was a generalized crisis encompassing the entire system.

By far the most powerful catalyst in this escalating process of political decay was the economic crisis that struck Mexico in 1982. Until then, the legitimacy of the system had been based not only on its capacity to maintain order and security, but on an "economic miracle" that had been able to provide real increases in living standards even in the face of rapid population growth and a highly unequal distribution of wealth. Between 1933 and 1981, the Mexican economy grew at an average annual rate of 6.2 percent, increasing eighteenfold.[2] Politics was a positive-sum game in which people from all socioeconomic classes could benefit, though granted some "won" far more than others.

In August 1982, however, the country plunged into a period of financial crisis and economic stagnation unprecedented since the Great Depression. During the *sexenio* (the six-year presidential term) of Miguel de la Madrid Hurtado, economic growth stagnated while unemployment and inflation soared, real wages plunged, and per capita gross national product (GNP) dropped from U.S. $3,170 (1981) to U.S. $1,860 (1988).[3] Those most vulnerable were hardest hit. Nor was their plight helped by the administration's neoconservative economic strategy, with its emphasis on cutting government spending (especially on social programs) and reducing the size of the bureaucracy. With less wealth to distribute, politics became a zero-sum game in which the lower and middle classes lost while the wealthy continued to prosper. This meant the end of the inclusionary social contract that had brought all classes under the umbrella of the PRI and that constituted one of the crucial legitimizing myths of the regime.

Coming off a period of rising expectations spawned by the oil boom of the late 1970s/early 1980s, the economic downturn seriously undermined the PRI and the political system, causing major divisions within the ruling elite, weakening corporatist controls over society, and giving rise to a growing number of independent popular movements and a formidable political opposition that by 1988 would come dangerously close to toppling the PRI from its hegemonic pedestal. As the regime lost its ability to reward the populace materially, its legitimacy and system of controls weakened. The corporate network of interest group representation became increasingly ineffectual, especially with respect to the middle and peasant sectors. Even the PRI's domination of organized labor—one of the most crucial pillars of its political power—eroded notably, as *oficialista* ("official") labor leaders lost their ability to control the political behavior of the rank and file. At the same time, there occurred a remarkable flowering of civil society, as forces that had previously been co-opted or excluded gave birth to new organizations. By the end of the 1980s, hundreds of independent nongovernmental organizations had been formed, including political parties and business, labor, peasant, and human rights groups, and were joining together in common cause. In 1988, many became active participants in the electoral process.

Meanwhile, the ruling elite was increasingly riven with factionalism and strife. Within the PRI, there was growing tension between the traditional dominant *políticos* (politicians) and the *técnicos* (technicians), who had come to dominate policy making under de la Madrid. In part, this conflict was the product of policy differences. Many old-guard *políticos* viewed the privatization of state enterprises, the reduction of subsidies, and the curtailment of public spending as betrayals of the party's revolutionary heritage. They tended to view political reforms with suspicion, fearing that increased competition would undermine the PRI's hegemony and their own power and lead to political instability. While the division was by no means clear cut (not all *técnicos* are political reformers and some can best be viewed as "technopols"—i.e., as combining technical and political skills and outlooks), in general those who favored traditional economic solutions got frozen out. In October 1987, many left the party to form an opposition movement under the leadership of Cuauhtémoc Cárdenas and Porfirio Muñoz Ledo. Others remained, but their tepid support for the *oficialista* candidate, Carlos Salinas de Gortari, undermined the party's ability to get out the vote.

By early 1988, the PRI's hegemony was crumbling under pressure from diverse political forces both from within and without the party. From the left, dissident former members of the PRI were joining socialists, populists, and nationalists to form a *Frente Democrático Nacional* (National Democratic Front, or FDN) in support of Cárdenas' presidential candidacy. From the right, disgruntled medium and small entrepreneurs, hurt by the economic crisis and resentful of the government's favored treatment of big business, were rallying to the banner of the *Partido Acción Nacional* (PAN) and its candidate, Manuel Clouthier. In contrast to Cárdenas, who had inherited the name and part of the mystique of his revered father (former President Lázaro Cárdenas), and Clouthier, who was a fiery orator, the PRI's Carlos Salinas seemed colorless. His candidacy was unpopular within his own party. He was the representative of the new technocratic generation that was wresting control from the "dinosaurs" in the party apparatus and organized labor. Nor did he have that much support within the government, where many bureaucrats feared for their jobs under an austerity-minded administration.

On July 6, election day, many traditional PRI voters abstained or went over to the opposition. Only through massive fraud was Salinas able to capture a bare plurality. When the early returns showed Cárdenas in the lead, the government's computers went dead. Only after a week's delay were the official results released: Salinas had "won" 50.7 percent of the vote, the narrowest margin of victory in the PRI's history. The opposition had gained almost half the seats in the Chamber of Deputies and four seats in the Senate. This was the first time ever that the PRI had lost a Senate race. The perfect dictatorship, it seemed, was in the process of either being transformed into a democracy or disintegrating.

THE SALINAS *SEXENIO*: "DEMOCRATIZATION" AND THE REINSTITUTIONALIZATION OF HEGEMONY

Thus was born, amidst political turmoil and illegitimacy, the historic *sexenio* of Carlos Salinas. Here there was much irony. During the campaign, Salinas had stressed that his would be a "modernizing" presidency in terms of both economic and political reform. He had called on his colleagues in the PRI to reject their old habits of electoral fraud. The reality of what had actually happened seemed to mock his professed commitment to democracy.

There was another contradiction as well: This most modern of Mexican presidents had come to power at the head of an organization whose social and political bases were in the past. The PRI found its greatest support in the most underdeveloped, backward, and isolated areas of the country—in the poverty-stricken, rural south rather than in Mexico City or the northern border states, among the old, the uneducated, the peasants, and the *caciques* (local bosses). In contrast, Mexico's future—the urban middle and working classes, the educated, and the young—largely voted for the opposition.

The trouble, of course, was that Mexico was changing. Economic development and modernization were transforming the socioeconomic structure in ways that were weakening the traditional culture and the social groups that supported it. A significant proportion of those sectors were already abandoning the PRI and, in conjunction with other, more recently emerged groups, were demanding substantive political reforms. The PRI's hegemony had been broken. The question was whether (or to what extent) it could be restored or whether the leadership would now permit a democratic transition.

In rhetoric, at least, Salinas seemed to opt for the latter. But there was a problem: how to introduce democracy without jeopardizing the power and spoils of the ruling class. No political elite can be expected to preside voluntarily over its own demise. Thus, part of the challenge facing the new president would be to modernize the PRI and the political system in such a way as to enable the former to maintain its dominance under more competitive circumstances.

This was a slippery slope. The danger was that, in the process of introducing reforms, the government might undermine not only the PRI but political stability as well. Salinas was aware of the risk of trying to introduce major economic and political changes simultaneously, and he became even more so as the Gorbachev experiment in the Soviet Union, which tried to do just that, unraveled between 1989 and 1991. How could one maintain order and create new bases of political support while requiring even greater economic sacrifice? His conclusion: Economic and political reform would have to proceed at "different rhythms," with economics having the priority. As for the seeming incompatibility of democracy and continued PRI dominance, "I keep hearing that in Mexico one party has held power for years, but when I think of how one party has long ruled in countries like Japan or Italy, I pay less attention."[4]

Yet the issue could not be ignored. Salinas' economic and political strategies were inextricably interconnected. His goals of maintaining political stability and PRI dominance were dependent on economic recovery and the generation of prosperity. And his economic development strategy was dependent on attracting international support, especially from the United States. The centerpiece of Salinas' economic policy—the North American Free Trade Agreement (NAFTA)—was precariously dependent on the approval of the U.S. Congress. Thus, a concerted political and public relations effort had to be made to cultivate an image of a responsible, modernizing, and democratic Mexico.

The result was something akin to an optical illusion. Political reforms were embraced, but the substance of democracy remained elusive. Electoral reforms were largely meaningless, in some cases even tightening the PRI's grip on power. At the state and municipal levels, fraud continued unabated; indeed, it seemed to be undergoing "modernization," as new techniques (cybernetics) were added to traditional ones. On occasion, when these maneuvers were too blatant or the opposition protested too vociferously and created a public relations problem, Salinas would step in and resolve the dispute. This led to the removal of a number of "victorious" PRI candidates and, in some cases, their replacement by opposition leaders. This gave the appearance of liberalization while defusing embarrassing protests and co-opting some elements of the PAN (which was allowed to acquire three governorships), but it had little to do with democracy. Rather, this was an integral part of the Mexican system of *presidencialismo,* which gave the president almost absolute power during his term of office.[5] This was the hard core of the authoritarian system, and there was no indication that Salinas intended to weaken it. On the contrary, he seemed to be streamlining the system and centralizing even more power in the presidency.

Other reforms met similar fates. In spite of promises to democratize the internal workings of the PRI, little was accomplished. Although early on Salinas launched a highly publicized campaign against corruption, this was mainly due to his need to establish himself as a strong leader. This time-honored tactic, which allowed him to distance himself from the venality of the past and demonstrate his commitment to reform, made no more than a dent in the endemic malfeasance plaguing the body politic. Lured by huge amounts of easy money and a virtual guarantee of impunity, many high-level military and police officers forged ties with narcotics traffickers. At the same time, public funds continued to be diverted to private purposes, including PRI political activities. The government's privatization program provided new opportunities for its business supporters to make financial killings. Judicial reforms further concentrated power in the executive; authoritarian controls over labor were tightened.

Human rights violations also persisted. Prior to 1982, the government had been able to rely largely on economic rewards to maintain political control. But when the economic crisis hit, this was no longer possible, and the regime had been increasingly forced to resort to repression. The turmoil of 1988 had posed a threat to political stability and PRI dominance. So although some small measures were taken to reduce human rights abuses, the basic pattern of violence and impunity remained unchecked. Local labor bosses formed goon squads to kill rivals and terrorize rebellious union locals. Rural strongmen hired death squads to subdue peasants seeking the enforcement of land reform laws. The Federal Judiciary Police arrested, "disappeared," or assassinated human rights activists, labor and *campesino* organizers, and other troublesome elements. Cárdenas supporters, in particular, became a favorite target.

But repression and the facade of reform were not the only means used to restore PRI hegemony. Economic rewards were employed as well. Under Salinas, social spending rose substantially, even as the overall budget was drastically reduced. The centerpiece of Salinas' social policy was the National Program of Solidarity (*Solidaridad*), which provided poor communities with a vast array of public services. This was a fundamentally political program, designed to weaken the nascent alliances that had been created between Cárdenas' newly formed *Partido de la Revolución Democrática* (Party of Democratic Revolution, or PRD) and the urban poor. The intent was to co-opt the latter by incorporating them into the state's distributive network. At the same time, Solidarity would attempt to rejuvenate the PRI by forcing it to establish new political bases. Above all, however, it strengthened Salinas' political standing and the system of *presidencialismo*.

Complementing the president's social development strategy, moreover, were the promise and evidence of economic recovery. Between 1988 and 1990, the gross domestic product (GDP) increased from 1.2 percent to 4.4 percent, and although it declined to 3.6 percent in 1991, per capita gross national income kept rising. Inflation plunged from 159 percent in 1987 to around 23 percent in 1991.[6] Foreign investment flooded the country. While the government's neoliberal economic program benefitted almost entirely the rich and the middle class (which gained ready access to U.S. consumer goods), even the poor could hope for a better future. The capstone of the president's economic strategy—NAFTA—promised to spur growth, create jobs, and raise living standards. In the meantime, Solidarity provided a downpayment; the program became a symbol of Salinas' good intentions.

By midterm, then, a combination of factors had considerably strengthened the position of the president and the PRI. Salinas had proven to be a strong leader, with a vision of the future that appealed to millions of Mexicans. Some had already reaped tangible gains from his policies, and many more had acquired hope that they too might soon benefit. Nor were his accomplishments limited to the domestic realm. By entering into a partnership with the Bush administration to negotiate NAFTA, he had acquired hemispherewide stature. This was a source of nationalistic pride. Salinas was leading Mexico into the 21st century, and he was doing so not as a supplicant but as an equal partner of the United States.

Meanwhile, political reforms provided a facade of democratization even as the PRI continued to enjoy an overwhelming advantage in financing, access to state resources, and news coverage. Critics continued to be subjected to threats and violence. The PAN had been partially co-opted, much of its economic program had already been adopted by Salinas, and some of its leaders had been "tamed" by having been brought into the system. At the same time, the less compliant PRD had become the target of propaganda, intimidation, and electoral fraud, designed to demoralize, isolate, and divide it while siphoning off its political support. During these years, the strength of the Cárdenas coalition ebbed steadily. The PRD proved to be less a coherent party than a conglomeration of diverse groups and ideologies held together by the personalistic leadership of Cuauhtémoc Cárdenas. Without a national election to showcase its strongest political asset, it lost much of its appeal.

Thus were the conditions created for the PRI's dramatic recovery. With a few significant exceptions, the party swept the state and local elections of 1989 and 1990, culminating in a smashing victory in the August 1991 midterm elections. In the latter, the PRI received over 60 percent of the national vote, winning 310 of the 500 seats in the Chamber of Deputies (up from 266 in 1988). The party also won all six of the gubernatorial posts that were contested and all but one Senate seat. It even prevailed (overwhelmingly) in the area of its greatest weakness, the Federal District. To all appearances, PRI hegemony had been restored. Only time would reveal this to be an illusion.

THE SALINAS *SEXENIO*: FROM REINSTITUTIONALIZATION TO CRISIS

On November 17, 1993, the U.S. House of Representatives ratified NAFTA, ushering in a new era in U.S.–Mexican relations, Mexican economic development, and, possibly, Mexican political evolution. This was the high point of the Salinas *sexenio*. The president had established himself as a visionary and a statesman, arguably the greatest Mexican leader of the century. Polls showed him to be widely popular. Economically, the country seemed poised to make the transition from underdevelopment to modernity. Politically, the PRI seemed invulnerable. Given the magnitude of the achievement, how could it fail to consolidate its newly restored hegemony?

Beneath the surface, however, trouble was brewing. Since 1990, economic growth (as measured by GDP) had steadily declined from 4.4 percent in 1990 to 2.6 percent in 1992. In 1993, it grew by only 0.4 percent. By year's end, the country was experiencing negative growth. Added to this were the deleterious effects of the government's economic policies. Although the upper and middle classes had benefitted from many of these measures, the same could not be said for the vast majority of the poor. By now most tariffs, food price controls, and subsidies for food and agricultural inputs had been eliminated; the economy had been opened up to the large-scale importation of food and feed; and credit and technical assistance had been privatized, as had over a thousand state corporations. In early 1992, moreover, Article 27 of the Mexican Constitution, which had provided the legal basis for agrarian reform, had been revised. The government announced a formal end to land redistribution. *Ejido* members[7] who had received land now acquired the right to sell, rent, sharecrop, or mortgage it and to enter into contracts with private entrepreneurs, including foreign investors. In effect, communal landholdings were being privatized.

One can scarcely overstate the potential significance of these changes. In their totality, they seemed to be the beginning of a "silent revolution" at the grassroots of Mexican society. Already hundreds of thousands of workers had lost their jobs as privatized industries slashed their work forces and companies unable to compete with the influx of inexpensive U.S. products cut back their operations or went out of business. The impact was especially traumatic in the countryside. After 1989, only maize and beans continued to receive guaranteed prices. Peasants growing other crops often found it difficult to sell their produce. Under NAFTA, moreover, the situation seemed likely to become much worse as tariffs and import quotas on maize and beans were phased out, along with corn subsidies, over fifteen years. With the reforms of Article 27 now permitting the sale of *ejido* lands, it appeared highly probable that inequality and land concentration would get much worse, as poor peasants came under increasing pressure to sell out to large agro-export producers. How many people would ultimately be affected was difficult to say, but some analysts estimated that 700,000 to 800,000 agricultural workers might be displaced by declining corn prices. Others suggested that as many as 15 million people could be forced out of agriculture as a consequence of NAFTA and other policy changes. A U.S. Embassy political officer predicted that out of the roughly 20 million Mexicans working the land in 1993, only half would be left in 2009.[8]

These worst-case scenarios are subject to debate. Two years after the reform of Article 27, there had still been no massive privatization of communal lands. Nevertheless, there were growing indications that *ejido* social organization was crumbling and that agrarian conflicts were on the rise. Many peasants reacted to the reforms with confusion, suspicion, and sometimes open hostility. As the economy continued to decline—along with the prices for such basic products as wood, coffee, cattle, and corn—desperation grew. Not even the social programs of Solidarity could neutralize declining incomes, rising unemployment, and increasing landlessness.

This was especially the case in the poverty-stricken southern state of Chiapas. There the economic decline had been particularly sharp. Chiapas was Mexico's primary coffee-producing state, but between 1989 and 1994 the international price of coffee had fallen by half. Combined with changes in federal government policy, this led to a 65 percent drop in income for coffee growers.[9] In the face of these kinds of losses, Solidarity could have little effect. Indeed, in some respects it made things worse. Although its expenditures in Chiapas increased substantially, much of this ended up in the pockets of local political bosses. The manipulation and diversion of

Solidarity funds intensified unrest in Indian communities, fueling demands for socioeconomic and political change. As conflict surged, peasants battled other peasants, large landowners and their hired thugs, local security forces, and even the Mexican army. By 1993, press reports of guerrilla activity began to circulate. By now, however, the Salinas administration was in the midst of a fierce struggle for NAFTA and was trying to foster the image of a politically stable Mexico that would be a "reliable partner" for the United States and Canada. Accordingly, the reports were publicly denied. The guerrillas, it was assumed, were a minor problem, easily manageable.

But beyond the declining economy, the spread of social pain, and growing socioeconomic inequality, there was also a rapid proliferation of corruption and criminal violence. Much of this was narcotics related. Mexico was not quite in the process of being "Colombianized," although there was talk to that effect. The danger was not that drug lords would wage war on the state *á la* Medellín, but that they would subvert it through corruption. By now, marijuana was the most important cash crop in Mexico. The country was the leading producer of heroin and foreign marijuana for the U.S. market, and some 50 to 70 percent of all cocaine shipped to the United States passed through Mexico's borders. Much of this occurred with the complicity of Mexican authorities, especially the police. In 1988, drug revenues had amounted to between 1.25 to 4 percent of Mexico's GNP, and roughly 6 to 20 percent of export earnings. And there was no end in sight. Indeed, U.S. intelligence and law enforcement sources reported that Mexican and Colombian smugglers were setting up factories, warehouses, and trucking companies to exploit the increase in cross-border commerce expected under NAFTA.[10]

As opportunities for profit grew, so did drug-related violence. Stepped-up law enforcement led to the suppression of some cartels. By elevating the price of drugs at all stages of production, however, these efforts increased earnings and hence the incentives for trafficking. Thus, the suppression of some cartels only led to a proliferation of competing organizations. By 1993, there were roughly a dozen grand mafiosos and many other minor ones, and they were increasingly engaged in turf wars. In May, the violence hit home when Cardinal Juan Jesús Posadas Ocampo was gunned down at the Guadalajara airport during a shootout between rival gangs.

The Posadas assassination sent shock waves through the body politic. The government's account (the killing was found to be a case of mistaken identity) was greeted with widespread skepticism. By now the administration was caught in a credibility gap. Only the previous year, its report on a gas explosion in Guadalajara that had killed over 200 people had been received with similar disbelief. Public cynicism and suspicion, always substantial with regard to political matters, were spreading fast, in large part propelled by the government's own behavior. Beyond the corruption and violence, the discrepancy between the government's promises of political reform and its actual conduct was increasingly difficult to conceal. In state and local elections, fraud continued unabated. Only eleven days after the U.S. House of Representatives approved NAFTA, an especially blatant instance occurred in the Yucatán, where PRI operatives stole ballot boxes and altered tally sheets to deny the governorship to the opposition.

Nor was Salinas able to remain untouched. In February 1993, he presided over a PRI fund-raising dinner at which more than two dozen of the country's wealthiest businessmen were asked to give $25 million each to the party's 1994 election campaign. The meeting became public knowledge, and a scandal ensued. Most of the diners had either profited from the purchase of privatized state companies, maintained business monopolies with official support, or been given special consideration by the government's NAFTA negotiators. One allowed that he had grown so rich that he might give the PRI as much as $70 million.

After this it became much harder to take Salinas' professions of reform seriously. While the president soon recognized his misstep and announced his willingness to place a cap on individual donations, few believed him. The limit on donations seemed little more than a political maneuver designed to placate critics both in Mexico and the United States. Moreover, in the weeks that followed there was growing evidence that the "dinosaurs" (traditional *políticos*) within the PRI were staging a comeback—or, at least, that the "yuppies" (*técnicos*) around Salinas had accepted the need for a strategic truce during the coming election year. Thus, when the administration proposed new changes in the election laws, the response was skeptical. This was the sixth electoral reform in fifteen years. None of the previous efforts had done much to curb fraud, and critics charged that these measures would be no different.

In perspective, the reforms were a first step. They placed some restrictions on fund raising, reduced the government's control over electoral authorities, and gave the opposition more access to the news media. Congress also approved constitutional amendments to assure other parties' greater representation in the Senate and ease a prohibition on the election to high office of Mexicans whose parents were foreign born. The latter, however, was not scheduled to go into effect until 2000, which meant that the PAN's strongest candidate would not be eligible in 1994. How meaningful the other measures would be depended on their enforcement, but the country's past record was not encouraging.

On November 28—the same day as the fraud-drenched balloting in the Yucatán—Salinas engaged in the traditional *destape* or "unveiling" of the PRI's presidential candidate. The ritual had more than a little symbolic significance. For all Salinas' assurances that Mexico was on the path of democratization, the decision had been made by distinctly undemocratic means. Neither party caucuses nor primary elections had been used; rather, the instrument was the *dedazo*—figuratively, the pointing of the presidential finger at the chosen one. Clearly, Salinas had no intention of diluting the near-absolute power of the president to select his successor. The PRI had never lost an election at this level, so it had to be assumed that the nomination of Luis Donaldo Colosio, the minister of social development, was tantamount to his election.

THE YEAR OF LIVING DANGEROUSLY: THE REVOLT IN CHIAPAS AND THE COLOSIO ASSASSINATION

On January 1, 1994, a guerrilla group calling itself the Zapatista National Liberation Army (Ejército Zapatista de Liberación Nacional, or EZLN) seized four cities and a number of villages in the impoverished southern state of Chiapas. The assault took the Mexican government and military completely by surprise. For twenty-four hours, the rebels held San Cristóbal de las Casas—a city of 90,000 inhabitants—before retreating. As the army counterattacked, casualties mounted. In the days that followed, at least 145 people, many of them noncombatants, were killed.

The violence traumatized the country. The government's initial reaction was to crack down hard and look for scapegoats. Within a matter of days, however, Salinas recognized that a more conciliatory approach would have to be adopted. The conflict was receiving intense public attention both in Mexico and the United States. Almost overnight, it had shattered the carefully constructed image of Mexico as a modernizing society that was rapidly making the transition into the First World. Now the facade had been stripped away, revealing something far less attractive.

This was not the message that Salinas wanted to send. Massive violence would not only frighten away investors and damage the prospects for economic recovery, but it might create a backlash that could destroy NAFTA. Moreover, this was an election year. Already there was growing criticism of the PRI and the government for their political domination and inability to halt the socioeconomic deterioration that was occurring. The Zapatistas' demands spoke directly to these issues, and many Mexicans were rallying to their cause. It seemed unwise politically to reject negotiations. A peaceful solution was much preferred to a bloodbath.

Thus it was that on January 10 Salinas fired his hard-line minister of the interior, appointing in his place a distinguished jurist and human rights ombudsman, Jorge Carpizo MacGregor. At the same time, he asked Foreign Minister Manuel Camacho Solís to lead an effort to reach a negotiated settlement. A unilateral ceasefire was announced and an amnesty issued; the governor of Chiapas was replaced; and the controversial bishop of San Cristóbal de las Casas, Samuel Ruiz, was invited to join the mediation.[11]

Chiapas was a catalyst for the release of broader frustrations. Popular sentiment in favor of the rebels now grew rapidly. Their spokesman, a charismatic ski-masked commando calling himself Subcomandante Marcos, quickly took on the aura of a folk hero. Not everyone agreed with the rebels' actions or all of their demands, but a broad segment of Mexican society clearly believed that many of the latter were justified. Even the government acknowledged as much, and this lent the rebels' cause even greater legitimacy. Soon other groups began to take up the cry. In Mexico City, demonstrations were held and bombs set off. In Chiapas and elsewhere, *campesinos* seized hundreds of thousands of acres of agricultural land.

Under growing pressure from the rebels, the opposition parties, and some elements within his own political circle and anxious to keep the crisis from spreading, Salinas agreed to institute more reforms. In February, the government accepted that foreign observers be allowed at Mexican polling stations. The opposition was promised greater access to the media. The Federal Electoral Institute was to be put under nonpartisan direction and voter rolls subjected to more rapid and intense auditing. A new assistant attorney general specializing in electoral affairs would be empowered to prosecute fraud. Laws would be revised to include new election-related crimes. Campaign spending and fund raising would be limited. Efforts would be made to prevent government resources from being used for the benefit of any particular party.

Meanwhile, the PRI presidential candidate, Colosio, began to distance himself from Salinas, criticizing his mentor for focusing on macroeconomic issues at the expense of the poor and concentrating "excessive" power in the presidency. The country's profound social problems, he proclaimed, could no longer be ignored. Democratization had to be effectuated. From now on, the PRI would receive no special favors from the state.

Whether—or to what extent—these various hints, promises, and reforms would actually be carried out was, of course, an open question. Certainly, the measures that were enacted were a significant improvement over those of the previous year. They could not, however, stop the violence that was tearing at Mexican society. On March 3, several people were killed in a shootout between federal and state judicial police in Tijuana. A week later, Alfredo Harp Helú, a billionaire confidant of President Salinas, was kidnapped. The following month, in an almost identical incident, another prominent businessman was seized.

But the greatest shock was yet to come. On March 23, Luis Donaldo Colosio was gunned down at a campaign rally. Coming on top of the killing of Cardinal Posadas, the revolt in Chiapas, the kidnapping of Harp Helú, and other violence, the murder raised the specter of national disintegration. Efforts by the authorities to reassure the public had precisely the opposite effect. Initially, it was suggested that the killing had been done by a single, deranged individual. By early April, however, six other suspects had been identified, and the special prosecutor was spinning theories of a grand conspiracy. But evidence proved elusive, and the authorities eventually returned to their original hypothesis. Meanwhile, attorneys general came and went with blinding regularity (three new ones since the beginning of the year); a special commission named by the president to launch an independent investigation resigned; and a Tijuana police chief, who had called into question the "lone assassin" theory, was murdered amidst reports that someone had tampered with evidence that he had collected. These developments further undercut the administration's credibility and fueled all sorts of rumors, including speculation that Colosio had been done in by reactionary elements in the PRI.

By now the Mexican stock market was teetering. In an effort to restore confidence and stabilize the economy, the United States extended Mexico a $6 billion line of credit. But even so, private investors were taking their money out of the market and putting it into dollars so fast that the stability of the peso was threatened. By mid-April, some $6 billion had fled the country.[12]

Nor was the economy the only thing that was hemorrhaging. Even before the assassination, the PRI was deeply divided. The selection of Colosio as the party's presidential candidate had alienated not only many "dinosaurs" but some modernizers. Most prominent among the latter was Manuel Camacho Solís. As mayor of Mexico City, Camacho had built a reputation as a conciliator and reformer. He had expected to be chosen as Salinas' successor and had been furious when the latter had opted for Colosio. To placate him, the president had appointed him foreign minister and, when Chiapas exploded, special envoy to negotiate an end to the conflict.

But Chiapas had given Camacho a new lease on his political career. He had jumped into the fray with enthusiasm, quickly becoming, like his Zapatista counterpart Subcomandante Marcos, a national celebrity. The two men received so much attention that they overshadowed Colosio, who found it difficult to get his campaign off the ground. Along the way, Camacho began staking out an independent position, pressuring Salinas and Colosio to go further in their commitments to reform than they might otherwise have gone. In his dialogue with the Zapatistas, Camacho allowed the agenda to be broadened to include basic issues of democracy and human rights that went far beyond the limited confines of Chiapas. At times, he even made veiled threats to enter the presidential race himself.

While the prospect of a Camacho candidacy caught the imagination of millions of Mexicans, not everyone was pleased. Within the Colosio camp, the outrage was palpable. A Camacho candidacy would split the PRI, undermining Colosio's chances and perhaps paving the way for a Cárdenas victory. Accordingly, pressure was applied on Camacho to get him to withdraw from the political scene. After some wavering, the erstwhile candidate acquiesced.

Two days later, Colosio was assassinated. There was no small touch of irony here. The PRI was now without a presidential candidate. Yet a Camacho candidacy no longer seemed feasible. His threat of a breakaway campaign had so alienated Colosio's followers that any attempt to succeed the fallen candidate might have shattered party unity. The problem was that the alternatives were not very appetizing. The most likely prospect seemed to be the former budget and education minister, Ernesto Zedillo Ponce de León, who was cut from the same technocratic mold as Salinas and Colosio. But Zedillo was virtually unknown to party workers and the public. He was a colorless personality, with few political skills and no following. Aside from some big businessmen and foreign investors, few could generate much enthusiasm over his candidacy.

The most obvious alternative was the PRI president, Fernando Ortiz Arana. Ortiz was the favorite of most of the party bosses. He seemed likely to attract broader support than Zedillo. But he would have represented a sharp break from the highly trained professionals who had dominated the Salinas administration. He had no background in economics and was not a member of the president's inner circle, and it was by no means clear that he could be trusted to continue Salinas' program. In the days that followed, the various factions began lobbying for their favorites. So intense was the infighting that at one point Ortiz Arana had to ask his followers (who had taken to booing Zedillo and even Salinas) to restrain themselves.

In the end, Salinas chose Zedillo. Neither the decision nor the process was popular. Many PRI leaders had been pressing for a primary election, or at least a secret vote among themselves. Salinas, however, was determined to preserve the powers of the presidentialist system. The result—rather than an opening up of the selection process or the introduction of an element of democracy—was another *dedazo*.

Finally, there was Chiapas. Prior to the assassination, Camacho had appeared on the verge of a breakthrough. A draft peace agreement had been drawn up, addressing most of the rebels' socioeconomic demands. Promises of roads, housing, schools, health clinics, and aid to farmers seemed likely to improve the daily lives of the populace. New laws would outlaw racial discrimination and recognize indigenous customs. Except for issues relating to Indians, however, the accords focused almost entirely on Chiapas. There were no tangible concessions on democratization and electoral reform on the national level, and even those on local political arrangements fell well short of the rebels' demands for regional autonomy. Demands that Article 27 be implemented as originally intended—to give land to all peasants who worked it—were rejected (although provision was made to continue redistribution in Chiapas). As for NAFTA, the government promised to study its impact on the state and consider job retraining programs and other measures.

To most observers, these looked like generous concessions. But the rebels had more ambitious objectives; moreover, experience had taught them to be wary of government promises. Commenting on the draft, Subcomandante Marcos dismissed it, saying that he had no authority to negotiate. The proposals would have to be submitted to the grassroots communities in the areas under EZLN control. Peace was still far away.

There matters stood at the time of Colosio's assassination. In the wake of the killing, the talks were suspended. Efforts by the Zapatista leaders to submit the draft to their followers proved cumbersome and time consuming. As the weeks passed, Chiapas faded from the headlines, overshadowed by the assassination and the growing public focus on the political campaign.

But the Zapatistas had not disappeared. They still had their weapons. Although the ceasefire seemed to be holding, a provocation by either side could ignite new fighting, with massive bloodshed and the possible spread of war to other states. To make matters worse, a dangerous backlash was occurring. In the face of widespread land seizures, cattle rustling, town hall occupations, and kidnappings, some ranchers, PRI militants, and other locals were already responding with violence. In Chiapas, force and illegality had always been the weapons of the powerful. Those who were newly threatened let it be known that if the military could not maintain order, they would do so—by any means necessary.

THE YEAR OF LIVING DANGEROUSLY: THE CAMPAIGN

Something extraordinary was happening. A political system that for decades had been one of the most stable in Latin America had become, seemingly overnight, volatile and unpredictable. One could no longer take the PRI's hegemony for granted. Nor could one make any assumptions with regard to political stability. The ruling party was now precariously dependent on a political amateur, Ernesto Zedillo, whose lackluster personality made him an unattractive presidential candidate. Moreover, Zedillo would be forced to rely heavily on the PRI Old Guard. In a campaign in which corruption was a major issue, this was an embarrassment: Among the first to jump on Zedillo's bandwagon were several former PRI governors who had been forced to resign because of graft or electoral fraud.

In the beginning, it was assumed that the most serious challenge would come from the PRD's Cárdenas. But Cárdenas' campaign never got off the ground. Desperately short of funds, it was undermined both by PRI efforts to portray the candidate as a radical, who would endanger the country's political stability and prosperity, and by some PRD militants whose penchant for civil disobedience only lent credence to the charges. On top of this, Cárdenas turned out to be an ineffective campaigner. In mid-May, he gave a disastrous performance in Mexico's first nationally televised presidential debate. Speaking in the same deadpan manner that he used at campaign rallies, Cárdenas "tranquiliz[ed] the audience with his characteristic low, monotone drone."[13] Almost overnight, he plunged to third place in the polls, behind Zedillo and the PAN's Diego Fernández de Cevallos.

A few days later, moreover, Cárdenas traveled to Chiapas, hoping to gain some favorable publicity by demonstrating solidarity with the rebels' cause and basking in Subcomandante Marcos' charisma. Instead, Marcos publicly humiliated him by subjecting him to a series of lectures by skeptical guerrilla commanders. Marcos himself accused the PRD of following the same economic policies and undemocratic practices as the PRI. In the end, the "photo opportunity" turned into a nightmare and reinforced the disastrous impression of the debate.

The real surprise of the campaign, however, was Diego Fernández. Prior to his televised appearance with Cárdenas and Zedillo, the PAN candidate had commanded less than 10 percent support in the polls. But his two wooden opponents provided him with perfect straight men for his acerbic sound bites. In response to Zedillo's proud claim to have authored Salinas' economic program, Fernández quipped that "as far as we are concerned, your National Development Plan has produced 40 million poor people."[14] It was a brilliant performance and led to a wave of popular support that shot him into the lead in the polls. For weeks thereafter, he and Zedillo ran neck and neck.

Yet Fernández was an unlikely candidate. As head of the PAN's congressional delegation, he had voted with the PRI on a wide range of legislation. He had publicly praised Salinas as the best president in Mexican history. Indeed, given that the PAN's economic program had been co-opted by the PRI, some wondered what Fernández would do differently from Zedillo if he were elected. He was, moreover, a quixotic personality, capricious, abrasive, and lacking in diplomacy. In early July, he virtually stopped campaigning and sequestered himself in preparation for the anticipated second debate with his opponents. When the debate failed to materialize—Zedillo was far too smart to subject himself to *that* again—Fernández was deprived of the one trump card he had left. As the weeks passed and he began slipping in the polls, an air of fatalism engulfed his campaign. By early August, the handwriting was on the wall.

Meanwhile, political stability and democratization remained fragile. In June, the credibility of the electoral process was threatened when Salinas' interior minister, Jorge Carpizo MacGregor, resigned. Carpizo had become a symbol of the government's commitment to a fair election. He had brokered negotiations that had produced some of the most important political reforms. Mexican officials had repeatedly invoked his name to convince foreign governments and investors that Mexico was serious about democratization. Now, citing the opposition of "many people in the most diverse sectors" of politics, Carpizo described himself as "disillusioned" and "indignant." His calls for fair elections had been met with "more lies, more calumnies and more hypocrisy."[15]

This crisis, at least, was short lived. After two days of talks with the president, Carpizo withdrew his resignation, and the election campaign continued apace. The same could not be said, however, about the negotiations on Chiapas. On June 10, the Zapatistas announced that the government's peace proposal had been rejected by 97.88 percent of their supporters. This ended any hope that a settlement might be attained in time for the August elections. It also finished Camacho Solís as peace commissioner. In the wake of the rejection, public bickering broke out between Camacho and Zedillo, with the former resigning in a huff. The peace process was now put on hold, as attention was focused on the approaching elections.

During these months, the rebels seemed increasingly out of touch with both their Chiapan constituents and the Mexican public. A combination of government socioeconomic programs and improved public relations and the Zapatistas' own authoritarian behavior was eroding their popular support. They had now virtually abandoned their socioeconomic demands on behalf of Chiapas' impoverished Indians in favor of a sweeping appeal for democracy and liberty on a national basis. Rejecting the government's reforms, the insurgents called for a National Democratic Convention to form a transitional government that would produce a new constitution and organize honest elections.

The upshot was a kind of "Woodstock in the Jungle." In early August, thousands of supporters from all over Mexico flocked to Chiapas to attend the Zapatista-organized convention. Denouncing the PRI as the "common enemy of us all," the delegates vowed to engage in massive civil disobedience if the August 21 vote proved fraudulent. Addressing the audience, Subcomandante Marcos promised that the guerrillas would not resume the war unilaterally, but he also said that they would not surrender their arms and would be ready to use them if that was the will of the people.

The National Democratic Convention enabled the Zapatistas to regain the initiative momentarily. It upstaged Zedillo and the PRI, injected the rebels directly into the election campaign, and increased the pressure on the government to guarantee the integrity of the balloting. This was, however, a fleeting triumph. Marcos' threat to resume the fighting masked the fact that the EZLN was in a desperately weak position militarily. It had lost the critical advantage of surprise and was virtually surrounded by the much larger, better equipped, and better trained Mexican army. (The only escape route was over the Guatemalan border.) Nor did it seem likely that the Zapatistas could be saved by their supporters in the cities or in other rural areas. Armed groups, where they existed, appeared too inconsequential to be much help.

It had been for precisely this reason that the Zapatistas had early on shifted from a military to a political strategy. Yet they seemed unlikely to attain their most ambitious objectives. Their popular support had eroded.

The only presidential candidate acceptable to them was Cárdenas, and he was far behind. August 21, it appeared, would be a moment of truth.

It was. On election day, the Mexican people voted for Ernesto Zedillo and the PRI. Zedillo won slightly over 50 percent of the vote—almost exactly what Salinas had officially received in 1988—but in contrast to that contest, no opposition candidate was close enough to claim victory. (Fernández received about 27 percent of the vote and Cárdenas 17 percent.) Although there were numerous irregularities, most Mexican and foreign observers attested that the balloting was fairer than in the past. Although Cárdenas claimed foul, the massive violence feared by so many Mexicans never materialized.

Elsewhere, the PRI swept to victory in election after election, winning solid majorities in both the Chamber of Deputies and Senate. The only really sour note was in Chiapas, the only state in which a gubernatorial race coincided with the presidential contest. There the PRI's Eduardo Robledo Rincón defeated the Zapatista-supported PRD candidate, Amado Avendaño Figueroa, in an election seriously marred by fraud. Whether these irregularities were enough to have altered the outcome was debatable, but the EZLN threatened to take up arms if Robledo were inaugurated.

In perspective, the elections, although flawed, were probably about as good as could reasonably have been expected. They were fair enough that the country did not explode in violence, which was not an unimportant accomplishment. They were also a milestone on the long road to democracy. On the whole, they probably reflected the will of the Mexican people fairly well. In this year of crisis and insecurity, the public was simply not willing to risk further instability by turning power over to the opposition.

THE YEAR OF LIVING DANGEROUSLY: THE TRANSITION

Between the August elections and Zedillo's inauguration in early December, two developments occurred which cast shadows over Mexico's future. The first was the assassination in late September of PRI Secretary General José Francisco Ruiz Massieu. This was the second major political killing in a half year, and it rudely shattered the relief that Mexicans felt at having avoided a violent election. Clearly, the crisis was not over; the situation remained volatile. Investigators quickly established that the killer was a hired assassin and linked him to a larger conspiracy supposedly involving dissident elements in the PRI and narcotics traffickers. Salinas' reforms, it was said, had infuriated powerful individuals, who had amassed huge fortunes by using the party's labor and peasant organizations and big-business connections to extort payoffs, secure government contracts, and open Mexican territory to drug cartels. The threat of reform within the PRI—the possibility that the party might be cut loose from the government and that more serious anticorruption drives might be launched—had been "tantamount to a declaration of war." Tens of billions of dollars were at stake annually.[16]

Ruiz Massieu was to have been the leader of the PRI caucus in the Chamber of Deputies. He had been expected to play a crucial role in brokering the reforms planned by Zedillo. At the time of his assassination, he was already lining up party delegates behind the president-elect's program. Thus, his death appeared to be a warning of what could be expected should Zedillo push ahead with his plans.

But Ruiz Massieu was also the brother of deputy attorney general Mario Ruiz Massieu, who in recent weeks had presided over a wave of high-profile drug raids, including the arrest of members of the powerful Gulf of Mexico cartel. Mario Ruiz had vowed to jail the country's largest drug lords by the time Salinas left office. Accordingly, government investigators suspected that the killing was also intended to "send Mario a message to back off." In a radio interview, Ruiz declared that the "most solid hypothesis" was that the traffickers had conspired with "a group of resentful or archaic politicians who don't want change or modernization of political life." Other reformers had also been targeted. Among those implicated were a former PRI leader in Tamaulipas and a current federal legislator from that same state. Ruiz indicated, however, that higher figures were also involved.[17]

Ruiz never completed his investigation. In late November he resigned, accusing the attorney general and the PRI's president and new secretary general of obstructing the investigation. At the same time, he issued a report identifying twenty-nine people as being involved in the assassination, almost all of whom had ties to Tamaulipas, where the Gulf cartel was based. Ruiz announced that he would send the evidence to an independent notary to be safeguarded until Zedillo took office.

Whether anything would come of the investigation was hard to say. Ruiz himself noted that the investigation was entering a "political" phase. The PRI elite, he suggested, was "stronger than the president's determination and [had] overruled the president's call for justice and truth." Although he had identified those who had obstructed his efforts, they "will surely obtain a government position on December 1."[18]

Subsequently, there would be serious questions raised about Mario Ruiz's reliability. At the time, however, it was hard to escape the impression that the struggle for the soul of Mexico was intensifying and had entered a new and potentially more violent stage. During these weeks, too, Colosio's assassin was sentenced. While the presiding judge found the defendant solely responsible for the killing, millions of Mexicans continued to believe—rightly or wrongly—that the candidate had been the victim of a conspiracy. Nor was this conviction lessened by the fact that, the verdict notwithstanding, three members of Colosio's security detail who had been arrested on suspicion of being involved in the assassination were not released.

The second major development during the transition took place on November 8, when the voters of California overwhelmingly approved Proposition 187, which would deny education, welfare, and nonemergency health care to illegal immigrants. The vote produced an immediate backlash in Mexico, where president-elect Zedillo warned that the measure could have dangerous political consequences if it led to the violation of the human rights of Mexicans living in the United States. In Mexico City's fashionable Zona Rosa, several dozen protestors ransacked a McDonald's restaurant, while others burned the U.S. flag in the Zócalo.

This was a foreshadowing of what might be expected should the anti-immigrant/anti-Mexican fever spread to other states and to the U.S. Congress. It suggested that the U.S.–Mexican honeymoon that had accompanied NAFTA might presently give way to a more conflict-ridden relationship. Relations between the two countries would be closer than ever before, but closeness would not necessarily mean harmony.

Also significant was something that did not happen: Despite the Zapatistas' threats to resume the war in Chiapas if the PRI governor-elect were inaugurated, on December 8 Eduardo Robledo was sworn in without a resurgence of the fighting. Instead, there was a bit of guerrilla theater. A few hours after Robledo's inauguration, a parallel ceremony was held for his opponent, Amado Avendaño, who promised to form an itinerant government. Wisely, federal and state authorities refrained from interfering. Both Robledo and Zedillo adopted conciliatory stances, the former offering to resign if the Zapatistas turned in their weapons. (The new governor also appointed a member of the PDR secretary of government.) For his part, Zedillo pledged to continue the ceasefire.

THE YEAR OF LIVING DANGEROUSLY (CONCLUSION): THE ZEDILLO PRESIDENCY—A BEGINNING BOTH PROMISING AND OMINOUS

The question, of course, was where would Mexico go from here. During the campaign, Zedillo had pledged to deepen democratization by distancing the government from the PRI and curbing the powers of *presidencialismo*. The state's massive assistance to the party, he said, would be ended; the latter's candidate-selection process would be opened up by the introduction of primary elections; the *dedazo* would be abandoned; and more power would be given to Congress and to state and local authorities. In his inaugural address, moreover, he went even further, criticizing Salinas for tolerating graft and lax law enforcement and for neglecting the poor. He promised more efforts on behalf of electoral reform; a new fight against poverty; and a wholesale revamping of the corruption-ridden judicial system. Acknowledging widespread dissatisfaction with the investigations of the Colosio and Ruiz Massieu assassinations, the new president pledged to step up efforts to solve those cases. Signaling his willingness to cooperate with the opposition, he brought a member of the PAN into his cabinet as attorney general, the first time ever that such a move had been made.

Zedillo was saying all the right things, and he seemed poised to move fast. Four days after taking office, he launched his first major legislative initiative, a constitutional reform designed to overhaul the Supreme Court, strengthen the independence of the judiciary, achieve a better balance between the branches of government, and improve law enforcement. The Supreme Court reform, especially, had potentially profound implications and gave that institution for the first time the power of judicial review.

Yet in spite of these hopeful signs, doubts remained. Salinas too had pledged to promote democratization—and then had largely forgotten it until the Zapatista revolt, the Colosio assassination, and other pressures of this crisis-ridden election year forced him to address the issue. Would history repeat itself?

During the second half of December, moreover, the bottom dropped out of the peso. The precipitator (though not the basic cause) of the crisis was the Zapatista threat to resume war if the PRI governor-elect took office in Chiapas. Stock investors, unsure of Zedillo's ability to handle the problem, began exchanging their pesos for dollars. Between mid-November and mid-December, at least $4 billion fled the country. On December 19, Subcomandante Marcos announced that the rebels had occupied thirty-eight municipalities. The claim soon proved false. (There were some demonstrations outside the Zapatista-controlled Lacandona which gave the impression that the rebels had broken out of the army's cordon, but this turned out to be more guerrilla theater.) Nevertheless, the impact on the economy was immediate: The peso plunged, the stock market shuddered. The rapid depletion of Mexico's hard currency reserves forced the government to devaluate and, when that failed to stem the flow, to float the peso. Even an $18 billion international credit line (half of which came from the United States) and an Economic Emergency Plan to cut government spending and generate new revenue could not halt the decline. By mid-January, the value of Mexican currency had dropped 40 percent, and the stock market had fallen 21 percent.

The collapse exposed the continuing fragility and volatility of the economy, with its overpriced peso and dependence on foreign investment, and raised serious questions about the future. Investor confidence lay shattered; the country was caught in another round of inflation and declining real wages; and a recession seemed all but inevitable. The credibility of Mexico's leaders and their economic strategy had been badly damaged, and no one could say how long it would take to mend. When at year's end Popocatépetl, the long-dormant volcano southeast of Mexico City, began to spew huge clouds of steam and ash, forcing the evacuation of over 70,000 people, it seemed somehow symbolic—a fitting end to a Year from Hell.

WHITHER MEXICO?

But the crisis did not abate. International efforts to stabilize the economy proved slower and less effective than anticipated. As the peso and stock market continued to fall, along with investor confidence, the specter of a full-scale panic grew. Some $28 billion in short-term Mexican treasury bills were due in the months ahead. If Mexico were forced to default, it would likely plunge into a depression, with ominous implications for political and social stability. In turn, a Mexican default could trigger massive capital flight from other developing countries and come back to hit the United States, which depended on those areas for about 40 percent of its exports.

With this in mind, the Clinton administration and the international bankers stepped in. When his efforts to win approval for a $40 billion loan guarantee package ran into congressional opposition, President Clinton acted on his own authority to offer Mexico $20 billion in U.S. government short-term loans and loan guarantees. Along with some $30 billion in commitments from the International Monetary Fund, the Bank for International Settlements and other sources, this brought the total commitment to Mexico to around $50 billion.

But even this did not halt the slide. Political turmoil continued, and by early March the peso had fallen to around eight to the dollar, less than half what it had been worth on December 20. After weeks of indecision, the Mexican government announced a tough new stabilization plan. Already there had been 250,000 lay-offs in 1995, and official forecasts suggested there would be at least half a million more in March and April. The government now raised its estimate of inflation for the year to 42 percent and predicted a 2 percent decline in the GDP. Many more businesses were expected to go bankrupt. Interest rates of 90 percent or higher on mortgages, credit cards, and car loans were driving many families into insolvency. In addition, the country seemed headed for a full-scale banking crisis.

The upshot was a wave of public anger directed at those held responsible for the disaster—especially Carlos Salinas. While for the moment Mexicans seemed to accept Zedillo's protestations of innocence (he had, after all, inherited the problem), it seemed only a matter of time before he too became the target of public frustrations. Already, he was having to deny charges that U.S. loan guarantees contained political conditions. More dangerous yet, for both Zedillo and the United States, was a requirement that Mexican oil revenues be channelled through the Federal Reserve Bank of New York in order to guarantee repayment in the event of loan defaults. Petroleum had long been one of the most sacred symbols of Mexican independence. The danger of a nationalistic backlash was palpable and seemed likely to haunt both countries for the foreseeable future.

Yet, even amid all this turmoil there were occasional rays of light. In mid-January, the government and the PRI reached an accord with the opposition to conclude "definitive" reforms of federal and state election laws and guarantee the integrity of elections. They also agreed privately to campaign spending limits, equal access to the media, the ending of government support for the PRI, and other measures. Two items, however, were especially noteworthy: It was agreed that (1) an election would be held for mayor or governor of Mexico City, a key political post filled by presidential appointment, and (2) new elections would be held in Chiapas and Tabasco.

The agreement held out hope that the crisis might be brought under control. If the opposition could be drawn into the democratization process and their support obtained for the Economic Emergency Plan and the resolution of the turmoil in Chiapas and Tabasco, then the political and economic situations might stabilize. But the moment proved fleeting. In Tabasco, where PRD demonstrators were laying siege to the oil industry and the new state government, PRI stalwarts, infuriated by reports of Zedillo's concessions, took to the streets. The PRD protestors were routed. Only after the government began to back away from its pledge of new elections did the situation begin to return to normal.

By early February, Zedillo was under growing pressure to resolve the crisis in Chiapas one way or another. He had become convinced that it was a "cancer" on his presidency, and this view was reinforced by hardliners who urged him to use military force to end the rebellion. At the same time, he was increasingly frustrated by the Zapatistas' intransigence. The economy continued to spiral downward. Elections in the key state of Jalisco were approaching, and polls showed the PAN far in the lead. To make matters worse, the president was rapidly acquiring a serious image problem. His ineffectual handling of the economic crisis smacked of weakness and vacillation. He needed to assert his authority and prove that he was a strong leader.

And so on February 10, Zedillo went on the offensive. In a nationwide address, he complained that the Zapatistas had rebuffed his overtures. Rather than negotiate seriously, he said, they were preparing to renew the violence. He announced that the government had uncovered the identity of Subcomandante Marcos—allegedly Rafael Sebastián Guillén Vicente, a Jesuit-trained former college professor from Tampico—and several other EZLN leaders, and that he had ordered the military to assist the attorney general's office in arresting them. The army immediately moved against the guerrillas, capturing two of the purported leaders (but not Marcos). For their part, the Zapatistas remained defiant, and they were supported by hundreds of thousands of people who took to the streets to protest the offensive. The PRD denounced the government for unilaterally breaking the truce and declared the previous month's accord on democratization null and void.

If Zedillo had hoped that military action would strengthen his (and the PRI's) political position, he was soon disabused. On February 13, the PRI suffered its worst electoral defeat ever, as the PAN won landslide victories in gubernatorial and mayoral elections in Jalisco and Guadalajara, respectively. This was the first in a series of important state elections scheduled in 1995. To many, it seemed a foreshadowing of things to come.

By now, the offensive in Chiapas was under growing counterattack from critics, who were convinced that it would lead to a bloody denouement. As charges of human rights abuses proliferated, they spread to the United States, where human rights activists and congressional critics urged the Clinton administration to intervene with Zedillo to stop the offensive. Moreover, despite some $50 billion in loan guarantees, the Mexican economy showed few signs of recovery. With investors wary and the Mexican stock market depressed, pressure mounted on Zedillo to resolve the Chiapas crisis via negotiations rather than risk the continuing economic turmoil that more violence might offer.

Thus, the day after the elections Zedillo reversed course once more. The military was ordered to halt its offensive; a new appeal for dialogue was issued. At the same time, Eduardo Robledo, the new governor of Chiapas, stepped down. While this concession could not in itself resolve the crisis, it held out hope for a negotiated solution. Unfortunately, it also reinforced the impression of presidential weakness and vacillation. To many observers, the president appeared to be twisting in the wind, swaying this way and that with every new gust that came his way.

Even so, Zedillo sometimes showed signs of real leadership. During these weeks, he spoke candidly to the Mexican people about the depth of the economic crisis and the need for sacrifice. He promised to follow through on his pledge to weed out corruption and pursue the Colosio, Ruiz Massieu, and Posadas assassination cases wherever the evidence might lead. No one, he insisted, was above the law. In late February, Attorney General Antonio Lozano announced that two more suspects had been arrested and charged in the Colosio case. New videotape evidence, it was said, revealed collusion between several people: There had apparently been a second gunman; evidence had been tampered with and mishandled. Salinas administration officials had either bungled the investigations or engaged in a deliberate cover-up. In the process, important witnesses had been ignored and key suspects allowed to go free.

A few days later, Carlos Salinas' older brother, Raúl, was arrested in connection with the Ruiz Massieu assassination. According to the authorities, Raúl had been the intellectual co-author of the killing and had facilitated the escape of the renegade legislator, Manuel Muñoz, who was thought to have done the actual planning. Subsequently, the prosecutor in the case went even further, hinting darkly that both Salinas brothers might have had financial or political reasons for eliminating Ruiz Massieu. Still others speculated that the killing may have been the product of personal animosity between Raúl Salinas and Ruiz.

So ended the political career of Carlos Salinas de Gortari. Only a few weeks earlier, he had been widely popular; indeed, many had considered him one of Mexico's greatest presidents. Now his reputation lay shattered, ravaged first by public disclosure of his responsibility for the economic crisis, then by these more ominous hints and revelations. While he tried to go public in his own defense—denying charges that he had obstructed the Colosio investigation, attacking Zedillo for mismanaging the economic crisis, and even engaging in a bizarre, short-lived hunger strike—it was no use. By now, most Mexicans were thoroughly disillusioned with him. His former protégé had abandoned him. In truth, Salinas provided the new president with a convenient foil to deflect popular outrage and establish his own credentials. During these weeks, Zedillo and his aides wasted few opportunities to remind the public that the economic crisis was Salinas' doing. He, Zedillo, had tried to warn Salinas of the need to devalue, but the latter had been too busy running for the presidency of the World Trade Organization to pay heed. In the short run, at least, the tactic worked. The president's standing in the polls soared.

These episodes also had larger significance: They violated the unwritten rules of the Mexican political game, whereby ex-presidents did not criticize sitting presidents and in return received, along with their relatives, impunity for their own previous sins. Beyond this, one could not but wonder where all this was leading. Zedillo had now publicly committed himself to real investigations. If he backed off, he would lose what credibility he had gained and his presidential image would be damaged even further. On the other hand, if he followed through it meant threatening some of the most corrupt and violent elements in Mexico, and that could be dangerous. One could not escape the impression that Zedillo was placing his own life in jeopardy.

As if all this were not enough, in early March Mario Ruiz Massieu was arrested at Newark airport, trying to flee Mexico one step ahead of the law. Mexican authorities quickly charged the former prosecutor with having intimidated witnesses and falsified evidence in his investigation of his brother's assassination. Apparently, he had been trying to protect Raúl Salinas. Subsequently, it was disclosed that some $10 million had been found in various U.S. bank accounts under Ruiz's name. Where all this money had come from was unclear, but the most obvious hypotheses (aside from kickbacks from federal police commanders) were drug traffickers and elements who wanted to keep Raúl Salinas' name out of the investigation.

A few days later, Carlos Salinas left Mexico for the United States and virtual exile. While there were denials that the former president had been asked to leave, various Mexican officials confirmed that this had indeed been the case. How this would affect the investigation into the Ruiz Massieu assassination remained to be seen. When he was in office, Mario Ruiz had repeatedly briefed Salinas, and it seemed unlikely that the latter had been unaware of his brother's involvement. While there had allegedly been no deal made in exchange for Salinas' departure, several officials noted that, given the extreme sensitivity of the matter, they would proceed against the former president only if they were certain of his complicity.

The fall of the families Salinas and Ruiz Massieu underscored yet another dilemma facing Mexico and the United States. How in today's Mexico could one tell the good guys from the bad? For years, U.S. policy had been predicated on the assumption that Carlos Salinas and the *técnicos* represented the forces of virtue. Now, it appeared, the "modernizers" were also prone to dishonesty. By the same token, these developments called into question the integrity and reliability of *any* government investigation into the corruption and violence that were plaguing the country. For the moment, it was in President Zedillo's political interest to reopen the Posadas, Colosio, and Ruiz Massieu investigations. But whether truth and justice would ultimately triumph was still very much in doubt.

NOTES

1. *Proceso,* No. 723, September 10, 1990, p. 53.
2. Instituto Nacional de Estadísticas, Geografía e Informática, *Estadísticas Históricas de México* (Mexico, D.F.: INEGI, 1986), p. 311.
3. International Bank for Reconstruction and Development, *World Tables 1992* (Baltimore, Md.: The Johns Hopkins University Press, 1992), pp. 4–5.
4. Quoted in *Newsweek,* December 3, 1990.
5. The most important restriction on the president's power was that he could not succeed himself. He could, however, determine his successor by designating the PRI's presidential candidate.
6. Forecast International/DMS, "Mexico (Data)," *DMS Market Intelligence Reports: Latin America and Australasia,* June 1994, p. 4; International Bank for Reconstruction and Development, *World Tables 1993* (Baltimore, Md.: The Johns Hopkins University Press, 1993), pp. 9, 25; Political Risk Services, "Mexico Update," December 1, 1992.
7. *Ejidos* are communal landholdings composed of properties redistributed during the agrarian reform.
8. Interview, August 23, 1993. According to the Mexican undersecretary of agriculture, Luis Téllez, it was the government's intention to encourage the emigration of over 13 million people from rural areas by the turn of the century.
9. Luis Hernández Navarro, "The New Mayan War," in *NACLA Report on the Americas,* Vol. 27, No. 5 (March–April 1994), p. 9.
10. Tim Weiner and Tim Golden, "Free-Trade Treaty May Widen Traffic in Drugs, U.S. Says," *New York Times,* May 24, 1993; Peter Reuter and David Ron-

feldt, "Quest for Integrity: The Mexican–U.S. Drug Issue in the 1980s," *Journal of Interamerican Studies and World Affairs,* Vol. 34, No. 3 (Fall 1992), p. 91.

11. The latter was in accordance with rebel demands. Many in the Chiapas power elite considered Ruiz a Zapatista.

12. Foreign Broadcast Information Service (FBIS), *Daily Report: Latin America,* April 19, 1994.

13. Tod Robberson, "Mexican Candidate's Support of Rebels Gets Him Little in Return," *Washington Post,* May 20, 1994.

14. Tim Golden, "Mexican Party's Long Rule Threatened by Conservative," *New York Times,* May 29, 1994.

15. FBIS, *Daily Report: Latin America,* June 27, 1994.

16. Tod Robberson, "Probe Underlines Split in Mexico's Long-Ruling Party," *Washington Post,* November 20, 1994.

17. Sallie Hughes, "Politicians and Drug Lords Said to Have Plotted Mexican Assassination," *Washington Post,* October 7, 1994.

18. FBIS, *Daily Report: Latin America,* November 25, 1994.

2

Striving for Mexican Democracy: The PRI and the Opposition

Roderic Ai Camp

The typical observer describing the general context of party politics in Great Britain or the United States fills his or her narrative with constant references to the Conservatives, Labor, Democrats, and Republicans. In Mexico, the same conversation would normally begin with the terms *PRI* and the *opposition*. This seemingly insignificant distinction suggests important features about Mexican party politics, including major structural differences from the U.S. and British democratic models as well as differences in self-image.

Great Britain deserves much of the credit for developing the crucial practice of a "loyal opposition," legitimizing and institutionalizing a party or parties out of power. Yet in England, the balance in electoral strength among two or more parties, and their constant exchange in holding power, led to a mentality which stressed individual parties rather than merely lumping them together into a semipermanent category of "opposition." By contrast, the six-and-a-half-decade dominance of Mexico's Institutional Revolutionary Party (PRI) and its antecedents and the weakness of opposing parties generally (including some with long, institutional lives) have led to the latter's collective categorization as mere opposition parties, implying a second-class status.

It could be argued that for Mexican democracy to flourish and for party and electoral politics to contribute positively to its evolutionary process, the country's political parties need to extend their status beyond this opposition mentality. Their inability to do so explains, from an electoral angle, the incomplete quality of Mexican democracy, as well as the major obstacle to achieving it.[1]

Mexico has no real history of party politics. In the nineteenth century, two movements or sets of ideas, subsumed under Liberal and Conservative labels, emerged. Their confrontation was often violent and uncompromising, provoking long periods of civil war. In the period of relative stability which followed—known as the *Porfiriato* (1876–1911)—several factions emerged. (One, known as the *Científicos,* is sometimes referred to as an antecedent of Carlos Salinas' technocrats.) Yet no enduring political parties developed. The same can be said for the immediate postrevolutionary era. Although many incipient parties were founded during the prerevolutionary and revolutionary decades, they were short lived and lacked any significant organizational structure. Although some of these organizations might have been able to survive beyond their leaders' political careers, most were regional in nature and were easily squelched by the emergence of the government-controlled National Revolutionary Party (PNR) in 1929.[2] Thus, Mexico had little historical experience prior to 1988 with party competition.

Mexico's conceptualization of the nature and role of political parties distorts theorists' traditional definition of party functions. In democracies, parties are established to obtain political power. In Mexico, in contrast, *the* party was established to retain (not acquire) political power. This simple fact, which suggests that the PRI does not truly qualify as a political party, redefines the role of political parties in Mexico and affects democratization.

Most analysts have stressed, of course, that the PRI was founded by incumbent office-holders, therefore altering its functions, weakening it as a significant, independent political institution, and assuring it a role tangential to the political process. These points will not be belabored here.[3] At the same time, however, the government party's characteristics defined those of the opposition. In other words, all other parties were automatically relegated to the category of "opposition." Those parties—at least the ones genuinely in opposition to government leadership—and the "official" party (the PRI) attempted to function along the lines of parties found outside of Mexico: They were trying to seize political power through the electoral process. The Mexican reality was inappropriate to their function.

Mexico created a peculiar, unique political environment. The "official" party carried out its tasks as a representative of an incumbent political leadership. Only rarely were there fair and open elections. The opposition parties, on the other hand, attempting to function as if this were an ideal-type electoral environment characterized by the usual democratic trappings, found, for the most part, their efforts stymied. Over time, the most successful of these parties came to recognize that it was necessary to play by the unique rules of the Mexican political game rather than by the democratic electoral principles found elsewhere.

THE MEXICAN POLITICAL SYSTEM IN FLUX

It is within this larger, historic framework that the parties presently find themselves. Conditions which have long governed the party process generally—and the relationship between the PRI and the opposition, in particular—are currently undergoing significant changes. Many factors account for these developments and will affect both the opposition's and the PRI's future roles. Among the most important questions to be asked about these changes are the following:

- To what degree are the functions of elections changing in Mexico, and how does this affect the role that parties will play?
- To what extent is the political system's institutional structure changing, and how might it alter party competition?
- How has the concept of the state changed since 1988, and will it affect the relationships in the party process?
- What is the source of democratization in Mexico? Will the parties bring about competition? Will democratization increase opposition strength?
- How extensive are external influences on Mexico's democratization process generally, and its competitive party system specifically?
- Do mass political values offer a welcoming environment for democratization and party competition? Or are they obstacles to opposition growth?

As I have argued elsewhere, the electoral context in Mexico, as in any other polity, determines the function of parties.[4] Parties reinforce the democratization process, which typically must incorporate the concept of party competition and an exchange of power if elections are to determine who governs. If elections only provide a means to legitimize government leadership, without allowing for much change in actual leaders, then parties can contribute little to democratization. It is fair to say that the 1988 presidential elections forced Mexico's leadership to face a choice in the role that elections should play, placing in flux the function of the electoral process.

Mexican leaders since the late 1960s have wavered between (1) making the electoral process more competitive by initiating electoral reform and (2) immediately reversing themselves by suppressing opposition successes. The 1988 electoral contest mirrors both of these strategies.[5] Mexico's political establishment thus appears divided over two political paths: (1) *democratic,* a belief that given a fully competitive system the political establishment can still, for the most part, win on its merits; and (2) *priocratic,* a belief that the PRI deserves to govern, and if it is necessary to engineer results to accomplish that goal, then that is an acceptable strategy.

The decision about whether to become more democratic or to retain authoritarian features from the past usually has been left to the incumbent leadership. Sometimes Mexico's political leaders have responded to perceived strengths within the opposition camp. Sometimes they have decided to enhance the opposition in order to legitimize their own political position. In 1987, confident of its ability to prevail, the government proclaimed that presidential and congressional elections would be clean and competitive. What began as a campaign against a disparate, insignificant collection of leftist parties and the right-of-center National Action Party (PAN) ended in a surprising showing by an alliance of parties, which coalesced around the candidacy of Cuauhtémoc Cárdenas.

Cárdenas' dramatic success ties into the changing concept of elections in two important ways. First, Cárdenas' alleged or near victory over Carlos Salinas de Gortari demonstrated that, given the right political conditions and in the absence of widespread fraud, elections could perform the tasks assigned to them in a democratic context. Second, it is important to emphasize that Cárdenas had left the incumbent leadership; moreover, within that leadership, he had represented those who believed that the PRI could win on its own merits, provided that it campaigned on a platform reversing some of the economic policies of the de la Madrid administration (1982–1988).[6]

The elections since 1989 illustrate not only the ability of the PRI to make a comeback but also the belief of the establishment leaders that they must resort to traditional electoral practices to determine the outcome.[7] It is true that one opposition party, PAN, achieved several notable victories on the state level, winning gubernatorial offices in Baja California (1989) and Chihuahua (1992). Although these victories suggest PAN's regional strength, it is important to note that PAN is the only party other than PRI to win such elections. Since 1989, moreover, the dominant elements in the leadership have negotiated with the PRI and essentially accepted, at least for the moment, Salinas' rules of the game. Many former PAN leaders have recently abandoned the party, arguing that this collaboration is shortsighted. The party, it is said, has settled for selected electoral victories in lieu of a long-term, confrontational strategy supportive of full, electoral democratization.[8] [Editors' note: This chapter was completed prior to the 1994 elections, which were relatively clean by Mexican standards. For an analysis of those elections, see chapter 1.]

Although electoral reforms and the degree to which the government has committed itself to enforcing them impacts directly on opposition party strength, certain institutional structures influence the electoral process and the growth of opposition parties.[9] The most important of these are the relationship between two of the three federal branches, the executive and the legislative, and the relationship between the national and local governments. These features impact directly on the Mexican party system.

It is important to remember that historically, Mexico's legislative branch exercised very little influence over policy making. The Congress has had neither the same political strength nor the legitimacy of executive institutions. All past political reforms involved the distribution of party strength in the legislature. It is no accident that the only national representation achieved by any opposition party occurs within this branch.

What is the function of legislative institutions in Mexico? Interestingly, they parallel electoral functions. The legislative branch has been used as a vehicle to legitimize executive branch decisions. Occasionally, when a controversial policy issue arises, such as the reform of church–state relations, deputies will debate the issue publicly. Contrary to the impression they might give, deputies and senators do not create legislation; rather, it is handed to them by the executive branch.[10]

The legislative branch's weakness is not only evident in policy terms, but equally important (especially in relationship to electoral politics) in its role in developing political leadership. Because Mexico's Constitution does not permit consecutive reelection of deputies and senators, these representatives, regardless of party, are unable to establish any form of constituency relationship with their district or state. Thus, the executive branch can further enhance itself at the expense of the legislature, and legislative careers are undervalued, both for policy-making roles and as upwardly mobile channels to influential national office.

Legislative bodies, much more so than national bureaucracies, are essential to functioning democracies. Diversity within a political system's leadership typically is expressed within the Congress. That diversity is further translated into negotiated legislation. Mexico's leadership not only controls the legislative branch, but the executive exercises absolute command over legislative policy and the composition of congressional leadership.[11]

One of the explanations for why Mexico's legislative branch has been devalued, and the executive branch has remained dominant, is the state's significance in the Mexican and Latin American context. The Spanish colonial heritage provided Mexicans with important roots favorable to a strong state. The Mexican Revolution did not weaken the concept of the state; indeed, if anything, the state reemerged from the revolutionary violence stronger than in 1910.[12]

An expectation exists in Mexico for the state to exercise an important role in the lives of its citizens. Given the fact that Mexicans have dealt with a largely authoritarian regime, their image of the state works against legitimizing democracy. The state's authoritarian nature has been reinforced strongly by two interrelated characteristics: (1) confusion between loyalty to the state and loyalty to the nation, and (2) a similar confusion between the state as a broad concept of government vis-à-vis the government and the dominant political party, the PRI, combined.

Mexico's political leadership effectively encouraged the confusion between state and national loyalty, painting those critical of the state as un-patriotic. This can be illustrated in several ways. Observers have pointed to the Salinas administration's strategy in accepting some important PAN victories on the state and local level while rejecting any gubernatorial victories of Cárdenas' Democratic Revolutionary Party (PRD). There are a number of reasons for this behavior. One is a visceral feeling on the part of government loyalists that Cárdenas and his strongest supporters—many of whom deserted the PRI to organize an opposing party—are traitors. They are thought of not only as traitors to the PRI, for which some rationale exists, but as traitors to the nation and the state. This emotional reaction has affected the government leadership's ability to negotiate reasonably with the PRD and to recognize the latter's genuine, electoral successes.

The other arena in which the Mexican concept of the state influences democratization's impact, fueling the confusion between patriotism and dissent, is the state's role as a censor of the fourth estate (the press). The role of the press in Mexico is based on an authoritarian, rather than a libertarian, notion. This relationship between the print and electronic media has become so entrenched that, in addition to implied or threatened state censorship, self-censorship is even more common.[13] The effects of censorship on electoral politics, and on policy debates, is dampening.[14] For example, study after study of both the national and regional media illustrate the degree to which newspapers give coverage to the PRI versus the opposing parties, thus generating a tremendous distortion in publicity available to the competing parties.[15] Furthermore, the state constantly uses its resources to buy coverage, subsidizing journalists, articles, and press coverage. Many publishers, anticipating government reaction, censor their own reporters, as in the recent case of the English language publication *The News* (Mexico City), which fired reporter Zachary Margoulis for his revelations about the PRI's candidate for governor of Puebla.[16]

A more common abuse, one which the political leadership has refused to recognize, is placing the PRI under the umbrella of the government itself. Not only have government funds, as distinct from party funds, supported electoral activities, but the PRI awarded itself special privileges through its relationship to government leaders. This is most notably illustrated by the fact that PRI presidential candidates have borrowed a group of military officers and enlisted men to organize and implement some of the logistics of their campaigns.[17] Such use of military personnel by civilian authorities is strictly forbidden under military and civil law.

In response to repeated criticism of the PRI–government connection, the establishment leadership has begun to make modest changes. Among the most interesting during the Salinas administration was the public disclosure that the PRI, under the leadership of its finance secretary, Miguel Alemán, Jr., was exploring alternative means of independent financing. In 1993, the

Chamber of Deputies adopted new electoral reforms, including controls over campaign financing. Since then, the PRI has allegedly severed its economic ties to the state.

THE SOURCES OF DEMOCRATIZATION

Democratization can take many forms. The origins of the process are multitudinous, and many influences could be described. Yet in the context of party competition and electoral politics, a major development issue is the primary source of democratization. Mexico presently is characterized by a semiauthoritarian political system, whose powers lie primarily within the executive branch, in the hands of the president. Opposition parties, primarily the PAN and the PRD, ensure constant pressure to democratize the system. But until very recently, the president has been unwilling to respond to these pressures, or when he has he has done so through presidential fiat. Thus the president, in general, has been a weight on the democratization process.

President Salinas has made economic reforms, and these are considered by many to be liberalizing measures, the hallmark of his administration. Although his rhetoric supports political reforms, he has made it abundantly clear, in word and deed, that economic change takes priority over political liberalization. More importantly, the president has not only slowed the implementation of radical political reforms but has reinforced traditional institutional prerogatives.

Since 1989, most party competition has occurred at the local and state level. The PAN's victory in Baja California established the simple precedent that the government might recognize a genuine electoral success if certain conditions pertained. Without enumerating these conditions, the victory gave hope both to PAN leaders elsewhere and to the PRD. These parties began to learn, following the example of the late Salvador Nava (an independent political activist for four decades in San Luis Potosí), that civil disobedience might be the most effective strategy.[18]

Given the increased interest in Mexico from abroad, the importance of the country's political image to its investment goals, and the anticipated agreement between Mexico, Canada, and the United States, opposition public protests and marches on the capital proved to be viable political strategies. Interestingly, the Salinas administration legitimated these new strategies between 1989 and 1992 by directly intervening in gubernatorial elections. This is significant for three reasons. First, the national government (through the president) made clear the function of gubernatorial elections. Elections (the casting of votes), at least at the state level, did not determine who would win power. Rather, elections set the stage for other forms of political behavior. If the opposition could demonstrate through *post*election means that it was unfairly deprived of victory, or that fraud was excessive (even if it would not have actually won the election), the president would intervene. Second, election laws themselves were meaningless in resolving political disputes between the contending parties. Third, and most important, all parties began to look to the president to solve these disputes, introducing other de facto structural and institutional variables into the process.

President Salinas fed this process. He intervened in Guanajuato (1991), replacing the winning candidate (a PRIista) before taking office with an interim PAN member; in San Luis Potosí (1991), where he removed the two-week-old incumbent PRI governor, replacing him with an important national PRI political figure; in Tabasco (1992), where he replaced the incumbent governor after extensive charges of fraud in local elections; and in Michoacán (1992), where he replaced a recently installed PRI candidate with an interim governor.

On January 1, 1994, opposition parties received an unexpected boost in their demands for free elections from an indigenous uprising in the highlands of Chiapas. A guerrilla army, calling itself the Zapatista Army of National Liberation, attacked several cities. Although the government initially harshly repressed the guerrillas with military force, it suddenly reversed its policy and pursued a strategy of negotiation. The Zapatistas, whose primary complaints are local in origin and stem from long-standing exploitation and poverty, also made an important demand for clean presidential elections in August 1994. The uprising itself, and the guerrillas' specific demands, further delegitimized Salinas' political and economic strategies, strengthening the groundswell of support, national and international, for fair elections.

Not all influences on democratization rise from internal sources, structural, institutional, cultural, or otherwise. No country could claim to share a 2,000-mile border with a political culture and an economy as different from its own as the United States without receiving some influences. The international movement toward economic liberalization and economic blocs has definitely favored Mexico's economic reforms.[19] Many analysts have argued that these reforms will, in the long run, favorably influence a trend toward democratization. The argument, in its simplest form, is that economic competitiveness promotes a culture of democratic decision making. The approval of NAFTA, if such arguments are valid, will enhance the influence of American and Canadian economic values on those liberalization processes.[20]

Politically speaking, the influence of the United States is more subtle and difficult to measure. Its very proximity has contributed to regional differences in its southern neighbor. It is no accident that the PAN thrives in the outer reaches of Mexican national territory, whether in the north or in the gulf. Studies of northern Mexico, in particular, have demonstrated the United States' influence on the political culture of those regions.[21]

The presence of the United States and the recent agenda of bilateral re-lations between the two countries have encouraged many other influences, some of which have impacted on political party behavior. One of the most interesting of these is the realization of Mexican opposition leaders, as well as government leaders, that the United States is one of several significant political constituencies. Not only are Mexican politicians appealing to American government officials, but since 1988 they have become far more sophisticated in their appeals to influential academics and universities, to the American media, and even to the Mexican community in the United States.[22]

Opposition leaders have also successfully sought out other international organizations located in the United States. Party leaders have tried to reduce or eliminate electoral fraud by forcing the Mexican government to bring in outside observers. Although they were initially unsuccessful, independent democratic groups were able to bring in international observers, including members of the experienced Carter Center observation team, which over-saw the Nicaraguan elections. Finally, during the 1994 election campaign, the government reversed its position, authorizing foreign observers.

Equally important, although more indirect in its impact, is the increased visibility given to human rights abuses in Mexico. Many of these violations are related to opposition political leaders or to investigative reporters fo-cusing on government corruption. Although Americas Watch and Amnesty International reports have not prevented continued abuse, including the assassination of opposition party members, their added scrutiny and un-favorable publicity have made for a more favorable environment for dissent than otherwise would be the case.[23]

The continued growth of political parties in Mexico requires more than a severe economic crisis. Although the difficult situation of the 1980s, which is far from over, appears to have been the primary cause of oppo-sition support in the 1988 elections, the average voter will have to take a greater interest in political activism.[24] The stage is set for such a change. Voters in the United States and Mexico are both more willing to take other routes to demonstrate their support for or rejection of government policies. (The recent uprising in Chiapas generated a wave of nonviolent protests.) Few Mexicans, however, are willing to devote themselves to organizing politically. Considerable cynicism exists toward elections. Although in-creased commitment to political organizations, including parties, would likely help to push the electoral process in the direction that it theoretically should go, the lack of electoral integrity imposes a large barrier. For ex-ample, a 1993 poll in the Federal District reported that only 14 percent of the respondents had much confidence in the electoral process, and 40 per-cent had little or no confidence.[25]

Survey data make clear that much latent support exists among Mexicans for basic elements of democratization, including a competitive political system and multiple political parties. But these same surveys also suggest that many Mexicans may not yet understand the meaning of political opposition and the need for tolerance toward dissenting views. This is surely, in part, a byproduct of the historical position of lumping "the opposition" into a less than worthy category, as though it did not inherently have as much legitimacy as the party in power. Although many Mexican observers attribute citizen intolerance to the Catholic culture, empirical research in the United States suggests that this is a spurious relationship.[26]

CONCLUSION

What will the future bring in terms of party competition, opposition growth, and democracy? First, is the function of elections likely to change? On this score, the Salinas administration had a mixed record. On the one hand, the two electoral victories in Baja California and Chihuahua gave the opposition, for the first time, the ability to demonstrate its administrative skills at the state level. Those elections did, in effect, determine who governed. In the case of Chihuahua, the outcome was less clear given the fact that the PAN victory was recognized by the president, who congratulated the PAN candidate *before* the vote count was completed. Continued widespread use of fraud suggested that Mexican elections on the whole had not gone beyond their traditional function of legitimating the party in power. Within the larger context of NAFTA, the opposition would be able to press more effectively for implementation of cleaner elections, especially in the north. It remained to be seen, however, whether the results of this pressure would equally benefit other regions and presidential elections. Nevertheless, the PRI presidential candidate, Ernesto Zedillo, pledged that the August 1994 balloting would be fair, and the legislature approved technical changes in the Federal Electoral Institute, which is responsible for certifying the ballots, thus establishing independent control for the first time.

A change in the institutional structure received a shot in the arm with the results of the 1988 election, in which opposition party representatives accounted for nearly half of the seats in the lower house, Mexico's primary legislative body. Given the fact that Mexico requires a two-thirds vote of approval for any constitutional legislation, the importance of the legislature's composition increased dramatically. Unfortunately, the opposition was not able to sustain its level of representation after the 1991 congressional elections. Salinas was actually able to increase the level of executive-initiated legislation, further reducing the policy influence of the lower house. Nor did the results of the August 1994 elections seem likely to bring much change. Though Zedillo won barely 50 percent of the vote, this was not reflected in Congress, where the PRI gained solid majorities in both houses. To all appearances, the governing party would need only minimal opposition support to make constitutional changes.

Perhaps the greatest area of change—and one which offers the most hope for the future—was in the concept of the state. The state, at least in terms of its economic control, decreased in size. However, it is important to offer the caveat that a decrease in size does not necessarily correspond to decreasing influence. Indeed, the argument could be made that the Mexican state was stronger in 1994, at the end of Salinas' term, than it was in 1988.[27] Some progress, however small, had been made in separating the PRI from the government, and therefore from the state. Pushing the PRI toward financial independence from the government is an important first step in making the parties more competitive. The system could be democratic with the presence of an influential state, but it cannot be democratic if only one party is identified with, and retains control over, state resources.

President Salinas introduced many changes during his administration, some of them extraordinary compared to his predecessors and what was expected at the time of his inauguration. Some of those political or social changes can be described more accurately as modernizing, as distinct from democratic. The most pronounced examples were constitutional reforms involving church and state. While it is true that these changes eliminated religious human rights abuses, it is forgotten that the state retains the right to interpret who qualifies as legal religious associations. At the same time, however, the new laws encouraged the Catholic Church to pursue a more active political role, adding its voice to those demanding democratization and fair elections.

Although the president's record on direct electoral reforms was mixed at best, he encouraged (if not intentionally) democratic principles even within his own party. These principles have yet to be implemented in practice, but thousands of party officials are seriously committed to a larger voice in party decision making. Still, presidential intervention in state elections made it clear that national executive processes, not the elections, often determined the outcome. Local PRI leaders felt abandoned and ignored, as the national leadership contradicted their efforts. As if to recognize the serious consequences of this strategy, Salinas intervened in the Tamaulipas elections in the fall of 1992. Instead of kowtowing to opposition protests, he ordered his subordinates to sustain results favorable to the PRI. (This was accomplished through a series of threats and blackmail against the opposition candidate and his family.) The president also replaced his government minister with the governor of Chiapas, an individual known for his uncompromising position and hard-line politics. (Subsequently, however, the Zapatista uprising forced a reversal of Salinas' strategy. The president fired his new minister, appointing a former Supreme Court justice and human rights leader as secretary of government.)

External influences also offered continued hope in effecting democratization. Stronger ties between the United States and Mexico seemed more likely to increase the liberalization trend, although not necessarily through U.S. government actions. The recent history of the Reagan and Bush administrations demonstrates how American governmental pressures, and their consequent effects on Mexican electoral politics, can vary. Rather than predicting the influence of a given administration, it is more important to suggest that a variety of groups and individuals will take greater interest in Mexico. Various American sectors, affected beneficially or adversely by a free trade agreement, will not be timid about focusing on noneconomic Mexican issues, including government corruption, electoral fraud, human rights abuses, and authoritarian practices in general. Thus, external influences are likely to offer a constant and somewhat increasing pressure favorable to expanded democratization, and opposition parties will broaden their contacts among U.S. interest groups.

Finally, although mass political values are slow to change, the political culture is definitely in a state of flux. Citizen values, on the whole, offer an ambience favorable to increasing democratization. It has not been demonstrated, however, that political reform is necessarily uppermost in the minds of most Mexicans. At this state of their development process, Mexicans (as Salinas correctly guessed) are more concerned about their economic future. If they link their economic future to political liberalization, or perceive the latter to be a requirement for continued political stability, then pressure for more rapid political change will occur. The expansion of nongovernmental organizations has been phenomenal in Mexico in the last six years. These forms of expression, as well as changing attitudes toward more activist forms of participation, seem likely to encourage the growth and strength of political parties, as well as structural changes in the electoral process.[28]

EDITOR'S POSTSCRIPT

Since the PRI's sweeping victory in the August 1994 general elections, the Mexican crisis has intensified. This requires some brief modification of the preceding analysis. The socioeconomic disaster that struck in December, beginning with the devaluation of the peso, has severely damaged the PRI's legitimacy. The opposition's political position has improved considerably, as the Zedillo administration has become increasingly sensitive to the political concerns of the United States and other foreign economic donors and the Mexican public has vented its anger at the PRI by giving the PAN overwhelming victories in gubernatorial elections in Jalisco and Guanajuato and the mayoral race in Guadalajara. At the same time, the PRI "victor" in the disputed gubernatorial election in Chiapas has stepped down, and a new balloting has been promised.

Clearly, the constraints on fraud have grown. President Zedillo seems more inclined than his predecessor to cooperate with the opposition and allow them their share of victories. On the other hand, he is also in a much weaker political position than Salinas, and hence more vulnerable to countervailing pressures from "dinosaurs" within his own party. When, in January 1995, he promised new elections in Tabasco, where a disputed balloting had occurred a few weeks earlier, the local PRI machine launched a full-scale rebellion. Party stalwarts blocked highways, closed down hundreds of businesses, and took over the state television network to broadcast attacks on Zedillo. In the end, the president backed off. In May, moreover, he recognized a questionable PRI victory claim in a fraud-tainted gubernatorial election in the Yucatán.

In short, the situation is fluid. There are both currents and crosscurrents at work, and these contending pressures can be seen in Zedillo's own behavior. Thus, he has opened up the Supreme Court to opposition membership and appointed a member of the PAN attorney general. But he has also brought "dinosaurs" into the cabinet and, in January, even increased their representation. Similarly, that same month the government reached an accord with the opposition and the PRI to conclude "definitive" reforms of the federal and state election laws. But then, almost immediately, Zedillo ordered a short-lived military offensive against the Zapatistas, outraging the opposition and effectively torpedoing the agreement.

Thus ambivalence, rather than the staunch pursuit of democracy, may be the defining feature of the Zedillo administration. This is a president who has pledged to guarantee the integrity of the electoral process, yet who allowed the PRI machine in the Yucatán to run its business as usual, buying votes and coercing voters. Whether he can ever entirely free himself from these parochial interests is very much in doubt. (One indication may be his response to recently uncovered evidence of PRI campaign finance violations in the Tabasco gubernatorial race. Will he now reconsider his recognition of the PRI "victor"?)

This being said, on the whole recent developments seem to justify a somewhat more optimistic prognosis for democracy than was the case when Professor Camp was writing his chapter. In addition to those factors already noted, President Zedillo has moved to empower the traditionally rubber-stamp legislature with real oversight responsibilities, and the economic crisis seems likely to make congressmen (including members of the PRI) more inclined to challenge the executive. Moreover, the PAN now has two potentially strong presidential candidates in the recently elected governor of Guanajuato, Vicente Fox Quesada, and the current attorney general, Antonio Lozano Gracia, either of whom might give the PRI candidate a run for his money in the next election. Granted, that is a long way off, and a lot can happen between now and then. There will be many state elections over the next five years, and their results will bear close watching.

Finally, one may doubt whether it can any longer be argued that the

Mexican state is stronger than it was in 1988. This may have been true even as recently as a few months ago, but today the signs of decay are such that one must seriously consider the possibility that the structure may be crumbling.

—Donald E. Schulz

NOTES

1. For other variables important to both the democratic transition and the maintenance of democracy in formerly authoritarian polities, see Larry Diamond et al., "Building and Sustaining Democratic Government in Developing Countries: Some Tentative Findings," *World Affairs Journal*, Vol. 150, No. 1 (Summer 1987), pp. 5–19; James Malloy, ed., *Authoritarians and Democrats: Regime Transition in Latin America* (Pittsburgh: University of Pittsburgh Press, 1987); and Terry Lynn Karl and Phillipe Schmitter, "Modes of Transition in Latin America, Southern and Eastern Europe," *International Social Science Journal*, Vol. 128 (1991), pp. 269–81.

2. For the most comprehensive history of the PNR, see Luis Javier Garrido's *El Partido de la Revolución Institucionalizada, la Formación del Nuevo Estado en México (1928–1945)* (Mexico, D.F.: Siglo XXI, 1982); in English, the best work is Dale Story's *The Mexican Ruling Party, Stability and Authority* (New York: Praeger, 1986).

3. One of the most interesting recent analyses of the party's evolution is that by James W. Wilkie, ed., "The Six Ideological Phases of Mexico's 'Permanent Revolution' Since 1910," in *Society and Economy in Mexico, Statistical Abstract of Latin America Supplement Series*, Vol. 10 (Los Angeles: UCLA Latin American Center Publication, 1990), pp. 1–58.

4. Roderic Ai Camp, "Battling for the Voter: Elections, Parties and Democracy in Mexico," paper presented at the Research Conference on Deepening Democracy and Representation in Latin America, Center for Latin American Studies, University of Pittsburgh, April 1993.

5. For discussion of the Mexican leadership's perspective within the 1988 presidential succession, see Peter H. Smith, "The 1988 Presidential Succession in Historical Perspective," in *Mexico's Alternative Political Futures*, edited by Wayne A. Cornelius et al. (La Jolla: Center for U.S.–Mexican Studies, University of California, San Diego, 1989), pp. 391–416.

6. The point can be made that Cárdenas, through his father, the source of his popularity, provides a link to earlier trends in political liberalism, although as Hank Schmidt correctly argues, not economic liberalism. See Schmidt's insightful comments in "Toward the Innerscape of Mexican Historiology: Liberalism and the History of Ideas," *Mexican Studies*, Vol. 8, No. 1 (Winter 1992), p. 129.

7. They have also resorted to a sophisticated economic strategy, short of buying the votes in the election itself. As a consequence, in part, of the privatization program, the government has used immense sums of money to finance grassroots projects throughout the country. Critics charge a direct correlation between the foci of such allocations and poor PRI showings in the 1988 elections. Such efforts are not new, but the visibility of this program, known popularly as Solidarity, sets it apart

from prior agencies, given the president's personal interest and involvement. See Alan Knight's illuminating discussion in "Solidarity: Historical Continuities and Contemporary Implications," paper presented at the National Latin American Studies Association Meeting, Los Angeles, September 1992.

8. The defections have included an influential group of figures, including ex-party presidents and presidential candidates, among them Pablo Emilio Madero, José Gonzáles Torres, Jesús Gonzáles Schmal, and Bernardo Bátiz. This leaves the path open for the so-called Neo-PANismo wing to dominate the leadership and policy direction of the party.

9. For an excellent discussion of the 1990 reforms and their implications, see Ruth Berins Collier, *The Contradictory Alliance, State–Labor Relations and Regime Change in Mexico* (Berkeley: International and Area Studies, University of California, 1992), pp. 142ff.

10. Interview with a deputy who prepared the PRI position on church–state legislation, Mexico City, August 4, 1992.

11. In an interesting case study of the Representative Assembly of the Federal District, an attempt to grant nearly one-fifth of Mexico's population some semblance of self-government, one analyst concluded that Mexico's leadership had used the Assembly to broaden its own legitimacy and strengthen authoritarian rule. See Clifford J. Wirth, "Democracy in Mexico City: La Asamblea de Representantes del Distrito Federal," paper presented at the Latin American Studies Association, Los Angeles, September 1992, p. 21.

12. For background on the state's postrevolutionary evolution, see Nora Hamilton, *The Limits of State Autonomy, Postrevolutionary Mexico* (Princeton: Princeton University Press, 1982).

13. See my discussion of this in *Intellectuals and the State in Twentieth-Century Mexico* (Austin: University of Texas Press, 1985), pp. 193ff.

14. In a recent study reported in Jesús Orozco Zablah, "Olimpíadas o Tlatelolco, 1968 in el Memoria," *Este País,* October 1992, pp. 26–29, one-third of the respondents still believe they cannot speak freely about the events of the 1968 student massacre, a remarkable figure given the date of this event and the relatively strong level of freedom of speech in Mexico.

15. For example, see Raúl Trejo Delarbe, "Campaña y Elecciones en la Prensa de la Ciudad de México," in *Así Se Calló el Sistema: Comunicaión y Elecciones en 1988,* edited by Pablo Arrendondo Ramírez et al., (Guadalajara: Universidad de Guadalajara, 1991), pp. 79–127. For equally well-documented data on television news, which is more directly under the control of government censors, see Arrendondo's chapter, in the same collection, "Opacidad en la Ventana Electrónica: el Proceso Electoral de 1988 en los Noticeros Televisivos," pp. 129–83.

16. The *Mexico Report* claims that the government forced the owner to fire Margoulis, January 13, 1993, p. 10. See *Proceso,* December 7, 1992, p. 10, for more details.

17. See my *Generals in the Palacio: The Military in Modern Mexico* (New York: Oxford University Press, 1992), p. 82. For other abuses, see Luis Javier Garrido, "De Verde Olivo," *La Jornada,* October 1, 1992.

18. For the best description of the procedures for making electoral protests, see Arturo Núñez Jiménez, *El Nuevo Sistema Electoral Mexicano* (Mexico: Fondo de Cultura Económica, 1991).

19. For the argument that "international pressures, not the will of state managers, were instrumental in patterning the evolution of the economic restructuring program," see Judith Eichman, "The Mexican State and the Political Implications of Economic Restructuring," *Latin American Perspectives* (Spring 1992), p. 89.

20. See, for example, Luis Rubio, "Political Origins and Effects of Economic Reform in Mexico," in *Political and Economic Liberalization in Mexico: At a Critical Juncture?*, edited by Riordan Roett (Boulder, Colo.: Lynne Rienner, 1993). For arguments both pro and con, see Peter H. Smith, "The Political Impact of Free Trade on Mexico," *Journal of Interamerican Studies and World Affairs*, Vol. 34, No. 1 (Spring 1992), pp. 1–25.

21. Edward J. Williams, "The Resurgent North and Contemporary Mexican Regionalism," *Mexican Studies*, Vol. 6, No. 2 (Summer 1990), pp. 299–323.

22. See Carlos Gil, *Hope and Frustration, Interviews with Leaders of Mexico's Opposition* (Wilmington, Del.: Scholarly Resources, 1992), especially the chapter on "Cuauhtémoc Cárdenas and the Rise of Transborder Politics," pp. 287ff.

23. The extensiveness of these abuses is well documented in Alicia Ely-Yamin and María Teresa Jardí, "Justice Corrupted, Justice Denied: Unmasking the Untouchables of the Mexican Federal Judicial Police," Mexico Project, World Policy Institute, New School for Social Research, New York, November 1992. The study concluded that many of the prominent offenders were reassigned to new posts in other states, where they continued to torture and kill their victims. See also Americas Watch, *Human Rights in Mexico, A Policy of Impunity* (New York: Human Rights Watch, 1990).

24. As Charles Davis and John Speer point out in their recent analysis of survey data, Mexicans have not engaged in politics simply because of economic needs. Other variables, including their expressive orientation toward politics, affect behavior. They also suggest that once a minimum threshold of economic security is reached, economics may not be such a powerful motivating force. See "The Psychological Bases of Regime Support Among Urban Workers in Venezuela and Mexico: Instrumental or Expressive?" *Comparative Political Studies*, Vol. 24, No. 3 (October 1991), pp. 335–36.

25. Ricardo de la Peña and Rosario Tolendano Laguadia, "Capitalinos: El 55%, Insatisfechos con Nuestra Democracia," *Etcétera*, February 11, 1993, p. 20.

26. See Andrew M. Greeley, *The Catholic Myth, the Behavior and Beliefs of American Catholics* (New York: Collier Books, 1990).

27. In fact, in his insightful comparison between Mexico and Brazil, Ben Schneider makes this argument explicitly. He contends that "making the state more effective—rather than ideology, foreign encouragement, or partisan gain—has primarily inspired Mexican privatization" and strengthened the developmental state. See "Partly for Sale: Privatization and State Strength in Brazil and Mexico," *Journal of Interamerican Studies and World Affairs*, Vol. 30, No. 4 (Winter 1988–1989), p. 105.

28. On the other hand, it can be argued that civic-action groups have not led to increasing democratization, and that authoritarian structures can modernize without becoming democratic. See especially Viviane Brachet-Márquez, "Explaining Sociopolitical Change in Latin America: The Case of Mexico," *Latin American Research Review*, Vol. 27, No. 3 (1992), p. 112.

3

Mexico's Political Transition: The Emergence of Civil Society

Isidro Sepúlveda

As the turn of the century approaches, Mexico moves to a transition from a traditional, corporatist regime to a more modern configuration characterized by a market economy and increasing political pluralism. Economic modernization defined the Mexican project during the *sexenios* of Presidents Miguel de la Madrid Hurtado (1982–1988) and Carlos Salinas de Gortari (1988–1994). Social and political reform must focus the agenda of President Ernesto Zedillo Ponce de León (1994–2000).

De la Madrid inherited an economy threatened both from within and without. In the international context, that economy suffered from negative influences like falling petroleum prices and rising interest rates. In addition, it had been damaged by the administrative incompetence of the previous regime. De la Madrid rescued the country from impending economic collapse and inched toward economic restructuring, and Salinas moved measurably beyond that by significantly redefining the economy.

By 1995, the Mexican economy looked dramatically different than it had in 1982. International commercial policy advanced from protectionism to free trade when Mexico affiliated with the General Agreement on Tariffs and Trade (GATT) in 1986 and NAFTA in 1994. Privatization changed the economy from a system dominated by state-owned industry to a configuration of private companies. The banking system, the communications monopoly, copper mines and smelters, steel mills, airlines, and hundreds of other enterprises moved from state to private ownership. De la Madrid and Salinas slashed government regulations and reduced subsidies. They cut corporate and individual income tax rates but expanded coverage to new vocations and clamped down on tax evasion.

Both presidents also moved hesitantly toward social and political reform, but their measures proved less comprehensive and far less energetic. De la Madrid expanded the size of the Chamber of Deputies, facilitating more representation for minority parties. Salinas copied the essence of that measure for the Senate. Other legislation sponsored a comprehensive renovation of the national voting list, added new penalties for manipulation of the electoral system, and attempted to depoliticize the administration of elections. As for social reforms, Salinas introduced his "Solidarity" program amidst great fanfare. The program targeted the poor and promised improvements in education, housing, and basic infrastructure.

The commitment to sociopolitical reform evolved in clearer profile during the last years of the Salinas regime. The PRI selected as its presidential candidate the minister for social development, Luis Donaldo Colosio Murrieta. Colosio's campaign emphasized sociopolitical reform before his assassination in early 1994. Subsequently, Zedillo's dedication to reform flagged a bit, but the rebellion in Chiapas combined with the requirements of campaign rhetoric to press the issue on him. As Zedillo launched his *sexenio,* the necessity for sociopolitical reform crowded him. It is the imperative of his presidency.

This chapter analyzes the Mexican political system in transition. It includes a discussion of the challenges to and changes within the traditional corporative system; an analysis of the role of the 1988 election in redefining politics and pushing the major parties toward transitional redefinition; and an argument that the evolution of pressure groups in Mexico anticipates the formation of a civil society, the cradle for the nurturing of an authentic democracy.

MEXICO IN POLITICAL TRANSITION

The date that defines Mexico's hesitant transition toward a more participatory political system defies exact specification and varies with differing analytical emphasis. In a general way, the outset of the Revolution of 1910 signifies a watershed in modern Mexican history. The educational reforms of the 1920s pioneered by José Vasconcelos contained the seeds of political change, as did the industrialization process that began about 1940. More recently, the government's brutal repression of student protestors in 1968 seared the Mexican soul, triggering an agonizing reappraisal of Mexico's political order.

The 1988 Elections and the Transition

Several factors converged to make the 1988 elections and their aftermath a watershed in the history of the Mexican political system. The aftermath includes the policies and programs of the Salinas administration, the ongoing reorientation of the major political parties, and the 1994 elections.

Table 3.1
The Percentage of the PRI Vote in Presidential Elections 1958–1994

Year	Percentage
1958	90
1964	88
1970	86
1976	99
1982	74
1988	51
1994	50

Source: The PRI and Mexican Democracy (Mexico, D.F.: Partido Revolucionario Institucional, 1994), p. 34.

The 1994 elections carry their own significance, but they also reflect the ongoing transition signaled by the 1988 contest.

Both 1988 and 1994 mark profound changes in the socioeconomic substructure of the country (see Table 3.1). In a general way, the ambitions of the Revolution had borne fruit. The Mexican people had gained sophistication. The educational system had expanded, and literacy rates had improved. Better transportation and communications put millions in touch with a larger universe. The Mexican "economic miracle" had made for a richer population. The context in 1988 (or 1994) looked dramatically different from 1908 or 1918.

Beyond the immediate circumstances, the electoral record reflected a steady decline of the PRI's influence, suggesting eroding political support that continued into 1988. The trend was crystal clear. With the exception of 1976, when the PAN failed to field a candidate, the PRI percentage of the vote declined in every succeeding presidential election after 1958.

Within that larger historical context, several other economic and political influences served as immediate catalysts for change. Most important, Mexico's economy lay in shreds during the de la Madrid *sexenio*. Gross national product decreased; almost all Mexicans lost economic ground. People were poorer in 1988 than in 1982. That relative economic deprivation struck unusually hard since the country had enjoyed extraordinary economic growth in the postwar era. For more than four decades, from 1940 through 1982, the economy had expanded by more than 6 percent a year. The economy had doubled every twelve years.

In the political realm, the PRI had decreased in organizational coherence and electoral vigor. Indeed, the party suffered a perilous schism in 1987 when the *Corriente Democrático* (Democratic Current) bolted the PRI to coalesce with other (mostly leftist) forces to form an electoral *Frente* (Front) to contest the elections. Moreover, the selection of the candidates foretold problems for the PRI. The official party chose Salinas, a lackluster *técnico* at the time, no matter what his reputation may be in the annals of history. The opposition front nominated Cuauhtémoc Cárdenas, a dignified man with a quiet charisma and bearing the name of his revered father, Lázaro Cárdenas.

The election crystallized important realities, signaling the beginning of a political transition. The shaky consensus tying the elites to the maintenance of the corporative system hung in mortal jeopardy. Important social forces in Mexico now stood ready to compete against the official party. The system cried out for repair, revision, and renewal.

Readings of public opinion before and after the election lent credence to the point. A 1986 *New York Times* survey based on a national sample indicated widespread and profound dissatisfaction in Mexico. Of those questioned, 83 percent judged that the country was traveling a "bad road"; 88 percent characterized the "condition of the national economy" as "bad" or "very bad"; fully 83 percent anticipated no improvement in the dismal economic situation.[1] Beyond this, 63 percent agreed that "the Mexican political system should be changed so that candidates of other parties will be able to win more often." Again, 63 percent held that the government worked to promote its own interests rather than to benefit the majority. It is no wonder that the elections placed the PRI in jeopardy.

A national survey conducted two years after the election by Mexico's secretariat of government confirmed the need to move toward reform. Seventy-nine percent of the respondents called for a change in the political system.[2] It is also significant that the same survey reflected a desire for a revised order growing from consensus, not imposition from above.

Although developments in the longer term spotlighted the Salinas administration's incomplete move toward a middle ground approaching consensus, the initial steps showed some promise. The economic project defined the context. Economic growth sought to coax the masses away from Cárdenas and the newly formed PRD. At the other end of the political spectrum, the neoliberal economic reforms seduced many in the private sector and the PAN and moved them toward a newly defined middle, fashioned by the president and his followers. More directly and even more dramatically, Salinas tried to curry favor from both left and right in 1989 when he jailed a powerful labor union chief and a leading member of the stock exchange, both for corruption.

President Salinas also manifested his conciliatory search for consensus in the area of state elections. In a precedent-shattering gesture in 1989, he sanctioned the election of PANista Ernesto Ruffo Appel to the governorship in Baja California. Thus, Ruffo became the first opposition governor in Mexico since the founding of the official party in 1929. In 1991, the president again reached out to the PAN and the independent opposition when he overturned PRIista governors-elect in Guanajuato and San Luis Potosí. In Guanajuato, a PANista assumed the interim position; in San Luis Potosí, an independent PRIista became interim chief executive. Francisco Barrio's triumph in Chihuahua in 1992 placed a third PANista in a gubernatorial post.

The government's initial response to the rebellion in Chiapas again reflected a conciliatory posture toward political change. While subsequent events added increasing complexity to the relationship between the government and the Zapatistas, Salinas reached out to the rebels in early 1994, promising important reforms. He recognized the legitimacy of their grievances and dispatched one of his most esteemed advisers, Manuel Camacho Solís, to negotiate with the dissidents. Equally important, Salinas officially regularized the mediation of Chiapas Bishop Samuel Ruíz García, one of the few people in positions of authority who had the trust of the Zapatistas and their followers.

In sum, the post-1982 period witnessed significant transitional changes that became especially important as Mexico looked toward the 21st century. De la Madrid, Salinas, and Zedillo overhauled the economy and inched toward social and political reforms. Demands from an increasingly sophisticated Mexican society spurred the process forward. As the political parties realigned, many anticipated the evolution of a Mexico defined by new sociopolitical patterns.

The Parties in Transition

From another perspective, the ongoing internal perturbation and redefinition of Mexico's political parties also reflects the system's transition. The *Corriente Democrático*'s exit from the official party created the basis for the foundation of the PRD, but it also facilitated a new departure by the PRI. Spurred by Salinas and his fellow *técnicos,* the PRI repudiated its orientation toward state leadership in the economy. The party reduced the influence of its labor sector and attracted more adherents from the business community. It also disavowed its traditional nationalistic gringo baiting, welcomed U.S. investment, and embraced the United States in NAFTA. It moved from the moderate left of the political spectrum toward the right.

However dramatic the PRI's ideological and policy shifts, it has scored far less success in moving toward internal democracy. In truth, the redefinition of the ideology and official policy posture has been achieved so effortlessly because the party continues to be an authoritarian organization designed to receive the word from the top. Since Salinas assumed office, PRI reform initiatives have been aborted several times. Colosio may have been genuinely committed to such change, but his time passed too rapidly. President Zedillo appears disinclined to inaugurate meaningful reform within the party, at least for the moment. Thus, as of the mid-1990s, the official party continued to be a mixture of traditional corporate interests in juxtaposition with hesitant and unsure reformers. Revisionist impulses persist, but the direction of the party's movement remains uncertain. It is unequivocally in transition.

The PAN also is in transition. Reflecting a reaction to the PRI's reorientation as well as other influences, the PAN began to redefine its political posture during the early years of the Salinas administration. The major controversy within the party concerns its relationship to the PRI and the neoliberal economic initiatives of the de la Madrid, Salinas, and Zedillo administrations. One faction counsels collaboration with the government and the PRI; neoliberalism, after all, encompasses important elements of the policies and programs advocated by the PAN since its foundation in 1939. The other major current advocates that the PAN remain in opposition because the government and the PRI are still corrupt and authoritarian institutions, continually transgressing human rights and perpetuating electoral fraud. According to this line of thought, collaboration with the Zedillo government and the PRI invariably contaminates the PAN and threatens its long-range political fortunes.

The PAN's internal struggle exploded in 1993 when a prestigious group of former party leaders left the PAN to form the *Foro Doctrinario y Democrático* (Doctrinarian and Democratic Forum). The excellent showing of PAN candidate Diego Fernández de Cevallos in the 1994 presidential elections confirms the position of the collaborationists within the party, but the division continues to corrode party unity. Like the PRI, the PAN continues in transition.

The same can be said about the PRD. After it failed to live up to early optimistic predictions in the 1994 elections, the party continued an anguished argument about its future course and leadership. From the outset, the PRD has suffered from ideological and organizational incoherence, reflecting the disparate factions that compose it. Like many movements of the left, many PRDists take their ideology seriously and often divide on its formulation and implementation, placing the party in almost constant jeopardy of division.

In sum, the elections of 1988 (and of 1994, to a lesser degree), the programs of President Salinas, and the continuing redefinition of the nation's three major parties represent significant components of the Mexican system in transition. Moreover, the picture takes on even greater clarity in view of several other dimensions of the polity.

THE EROSION OF TRADITIONAL CORPORATISM AND THE ADVENT OF CIVIL SOCIETY

If the Mexican transition eventually moves toward a more authentic participatory democracy, two prerequisites loom indispensable: (1) Mexico's traditional authoritarian and top-heavy, state-dominated corporatism must be transformed into a more democratic, societal form of corporatism or be discarded altogether; and (2) concomitantly, a "civil society" characterized by freely derived grassroots participatory organizations informed by tolerant and cooperative operational norms must evolve. In the first instance, society must be independent of the state. Moreover, it must be capable of producing material and nonmaterial benefits and of resolving disputes without the intervention of the coercive elements of the state.

The first of these participatory prerequisites appears to be underway and is fairly easy to describe and analyze. The second, the emergence of a civil society, is less clear and poses more analytical difficulties.

The Erosion of Corporatism

Mexican corporatism has fallen on difficult times for several reasons. Most important, the Mexican people have outgrown it. The state corporatist apparatus that evolved in the 1920s, 1930s, and 1940s/1950s did so in the aftermath of a brutal and destructive civil war (the Revolution), on the cusp of a threatening economic recession in the 1930s, and in the midst of a compulsive and headlong drive to industrialization in the 1940s/1950s.

Those were difficult times characterized by high levels of poverty, ignorance, and insecurity. Under those circumstances, a corporatist system proved relatively easy to impose. Some even argue that it may have been appropriate to the sociopolitical and economic milieu of the times. Those times and conditions have long since passed. The Mexican population in the mid-1990s boasts a relatively high degree of sophistication, wealth, and personal security. Hence, a corporatism fashioned under differing circumstances is no longer appropriate.

On another level, corporatism is no longer either desirable or viable from the perspective of those who have defined the structure of the state and its policies. Pedro Aspe, Manuel Camacho Solís, Colosio, de la Madrid, Salinas, Jaime Serra Puche, Zedillo, and their collaborators and minions who have framed policy since the early 1980s repudiate the economic implications of corporatism as inefficient and unproductive and despise the sociopolitical characteristics as shameful and embarrassing to national dignity.

State power has waned in the mid-1990s. The comprehensive regulatory and manipulative accoutrements of traditional corporatism are more difficult to muster as the state shrinks and the private sector swells. The economic competence of the state recedes almost daily. In the early 1980s, it held and operated a vast array of enterprises, not only the "peaks" of the economy, like the banks, but also a fair number of far less consequential valleys, like candy factories.

But by the mid-1990s the profile of the Mexican economy looked strikingly different. De la Madrid and Salinas had privatized the nation's banking system, its communications monopoly, copper mines and smelters, steel mills, and literally hundreds of other economic enterprises. Other compa-

Table 3.2
Declining State Influence in the Mexican Economy: Three Indicators

	1982		1992	
% of Private and Public Investment	Private:	55%	Private:	80%
	Public:	45%	Public:	20%
Expenditure of Public Sector as % of GDP	1988:	40%	1994:	25%
Number of State-Owned Companies	1982:	1155	1991:	269

Sources: "Cae Gasto del Sector Público . . . ", *Reforma* (Mexico, D.F. 30 de Marzo, 1994, p. 29A; "Investment," *Latin American Weekly Report*, March 10, 1994, p. 104; and "State-Owned Companies, 1930–1991," Review of the Economic Situation of Mexico, México, D.F., Banco Nacional de México, June 1991, p. 231.

nies and operations, like the nation's ports and railroads, while formally owned by the state, were actually controlled or heavily influenced by both the national and foreign private sector through leasing and subcontracting arrangements. Even *Petróleos Mexicanos,* the hallowed oil monopoly, has been significantly decentralized and subcontracted in increments that moved it increasingly beyond state control.[3]

Table 3.2 presents data on several economic indicators measuring the relative influence of the private and public sectors in Mexico's economy. In every case, they demonstrate the balance of power shifting away from the state toward the private sector. The latter accounts for the lion's share of new investment; state expenditures account for less in the overall GDP; and the state controls significantly fewer economic enterprises.

The state's relative withdrawal from the economy reduces the pervasive characteristics of the stifling, authoritarian corporatist order. The Mexican people are becoming too sophisticated and independent to countenance the continuation of an outmoded system; political elites recognize its inefficiency and its repressive implications; and economic modernization has eroded the comprehensive control exercised by the state prior to the 1980s.

The breakdown of the symbiotic relationship between government and organized labor offers a cogent example of the decline of Mexico's traditional corporatism.[4] The government-labor connection is evolving from a well-established patron-client relationship traditionally characterized by a dominant government and a dependent labor sector within a corporatist relationship. The Mexican labor movement reaped benefits from its intimate relationship with government, but it also paid a price. What the federal government gave, it could also take away—or at least manipulate. In the process, the government molded a highly political union movement controlled by the national elites and formally directed by a compliant cadre of leaders.

That defined the situation as the 1980s and 1990s unfolded, and the de la Madrid and Salinas governments fashioned innovative departures in socioeconomic and political policies. The new policies implied a revision of the traditional advantages enjoyed by organized labor in its corporate arrangement with government. The latter purged dissident union leaders, disciplined friendly ones, and extracted painful economic and social sacrifices from working men and women.

The logic of the affair was relatively straightforward. The government sought to create a socioeconomic and political environment conducive to an increase in private foreign investment and the repatriation of Mexican flight capital. Whatever the economic virtues of that strategy, it has significantly revised the patron-client relationship between government and organized labor. The post-1982 departure set in motion a transitional period in the corporate relationship, marked by increasing stresses and strains.

The crux of the matter is elementary. The patron-client partnership that defined a key dimension of the corporate system survived for decades, nurtured by a mutually advantageous quid pro quo that no longer functions or, at least, reflects a shadow of its former brilliance. The traditional flow featured organized labor delivering votes, fielding "popular" demonstrations, imposing discipline, and lauding the government. In exchange, the latter granted wage raises and social services for union members and security and political positions for the labor leadership.

But on the brink of the 21st century, neither government nor labor can (or will) continue to fulfill its traditional obligations. Organized labor can no longer deliver the votes. Indeed, massive numbers of union members supported Cuauhtémoc Cárdenas in 1988 and 1994, and measurable numbers defected to Fernández de Cevallos in 1994. The government has forsaken organized labor in its support of foreign and domestic investors. Hence, the coalition's raison d'être has vanished; the patron-client relationship is near collapse; a crucial dimension of Mexico's traditional corporatism fades away.

The Emergence of a Civil Society

The emergence of a civil society in Mexico is at once more important and less obvious than other changes discussed thus far. The erosion of traditional corporatism, the transition of the political parties, and the reform of the economy all loom large in contemporary Mexico. All contribute to and interact with forces nurturing the embryo of a civil society.

The classic definition of the Civic Culture spoke of a "political culture of democracy and the social structures and processes that sustain it."[5] Society's developmental level reflects its independence before the state. It also reflects society's will to make its presence felt in its integration into politically relevant structures and processes and the exercise of political power.

Social organization forms a crucial element in the process of political transition. A well-constituted democracy in Mexico presupposes and evolves from a context in which individuals, families, and communities operate freely and responsibly, abiding by the laws of the land and sharing the values and objectives that define the democratic process.

Highlighting one aspect of their study of Mexico's civil society more than a generation ago, Almond and Verba praised the "aspirational aspect of Mexican political culture," noting that it "suggests a potentiality for a civic culture."[6] More than thirty years later, the nation's reality reveals a plethora of profound changes. The society is more diversified and increasingly complex. Multiple social forces thrive and defy being co-opted by bureaucratic organizations. The organization of interest groups beyond the pale of corporatist schemes has multiplied.

The social expression of interests grows both more specific and extended. Exact figures are impossible to come by, since groups form and reform daily, but some estimates suggest that Mexico now has more than 36,000 registered sociocultural associations. These organizations fill the spectrum from traditional, religiously oriented societies through neighborhood associations to environmental groups.

Official governmental policies furthering decentralization have both reflected and stimulated these changes. At the most formal level, for example, the Salinas government established the autonomy of the Bank of Mexico, separating it from direct authority of the presidency and permitting it more freedom of activity. Furthermore, a measure of educational decentralization has expanded the influence of the states by devolving some powers from the central government to the state level.

The reform of the *municipio* (township) during the de la Madrid regime strikes even closer to this theme. In revising Article 115 of the Federal Constitution, the reform chipped away at the top-heavy authority of the Mexico City government, offering important new powers to the *ayuntamiento* (municipal government). These powers include increased financial autonomy to the *municipio* as well as expanding sources of revenue. An implicit goal was an increase in political autonomy evolving from growing financial independence.[7]

The government's privatization of the media also speaks to the need for more vibrant and better informed groups within society. During the Salinas years, newspapers, radio stations, and an important television outlet were sold to the private sector. The new ownership provides the capability for more varied informational fare. It also suggests the potential for expanding coverage of subjects necessary for creative debate and discussion. The formation of *Televisión Azteca* and its 1994 cooperative arrangement with the National Broadcasting Company of the United States illustrates the sort of evolving media alternatives needed to nurture a civil society. In a similar vein, Mexican journalists are inching toward more independence, an indispensable component of an aspiring civil society.

Although it has been interpreted as a negative move by some, President Salinas' revision of the church–state relationship also offered more flexibility to sociocultural relations. Locked in a mutually destructive standoff harkening back to the 1920s, neither church nor state enjoyed space for creative policies and programs. In 1991, an amendment stripped away most of the antichurch stipulations of the Constitution of 1917. The new regime recognized churches as legal entities, allowed public celebrations of religious ceremonies, and permitted churches and religious officials to offer primary and secondary education.

The regime granted the right to vote to priests, nuns, ministers, and rabbis, although it did continue to bar practicing clerics from holding public office. Even so, the reform constituted a significant step forward in breaking through the archaic, rigid, and counterproductive church-state relationship that had dragged on for more than seventy years. As for its implications for civil society and democracy, the reform decreased government regulation of an important community, expanded the number of potential voters, and endowed them with facilities for exercising their rights of petition, press, and speech.

Like Salinas' rapprochement with the Catholic Church, the government's National Solidarity Program cuts both ways for the evolution of civil society. The program was launched in 1989 to provide a cushion for lower socioeconomic groups, which were bearing the brunt of the dislocations wrought by the economic restructuring. By 1992, the program's budget had grown to more than $2 billion, and its impact had multiplied throughout the republic as thousands of Solidarity committees formed at the grassroots level to define projects and administer funds funneled from Mexico City.

The significance of the program for authentic popular participation turns on the issue of the formation and operation of the local committees. Critics correctly charge that they usually fail on several accounts. In the first place, they are frequently controlled by the state and/or municipal governments. In a slight variation of that relationship, local committees are often no more than another offshoot of the official party. Finally, the Mexico City bureaucracy lodged in the secretariat of social development exercises significant influence over the committees because it controls the budget and selects the programs to be funded. In that sense, the committees are thrice cursed and find it difficult to operate as an autonomous agent of local governance.

With those negative pressures duly recorded, it is also necessary to recognize Solidarity's potential contributions. The funding and empowerment of thousands of local committees constitutes enormous potential for moving toward a more pluralistic society. Although the situation of the mid-1990s encompasses more future promise than present reality, the latent potential of the committees suggests an important new force that may contribute significantly to the development of a civil society characterized by various loci of autonomous authority.[8]

Groups that form and thrive independently of government provide even more important evidence of the growth of civil society. Business groups and environmental organizations are splendid examples. Business associations have never been comfortable in the traditional corporatist order, and Mexico's business community has become increasingly independent in the 1980s and 1990s. In 1975, the *Consejo Coordinador Empresarial* (Businessmen's Coordinating Council) established an important precedent for independent organization beyond government-sanctioned groups. The semisecret Mexican Council of Businessmen is even more significant and enjoys even more independence.

As in the United States, Mexico has also seen the flowering of environmental groups. Sparked by the extreme air pollution and lack of water in Mexico City, the ecology movement took root in the early 1980s. Although some groups, like the Mexican Ecological Movement, are criticized as being too close to the government, most of the country's thirty or so organizations have been able to maintain their independence. The *Grupo de Cien* (Group of 100), composed of many leading intellectuals, assumes a particularly independent posture, often openly critical of the government and the political system. According to Homero Aridjis, one of the group's leading spokespersons, "the problem of pollution in Mexico reflects the pollution of the political system."[9]

A few recent examples of popular mobilization complement this picture of a society decidedly more independent than in the past. In 1991, in Guanajuato and San Luis Potosí, popular mobilizations protested electoral fraud and forced President Salinas to overturn PRI victories in gubernatorial races. In Jalisco in 1992, a devastating explosion in Guadalajara's sewer system catalyzed popular protests. Again, citizen outrage forced the resignation of the governor. Popular mobilization and protest also compelled the government to move against *Petróleos Mexicanos* (PEMEX), a sacred cow of the political system. Combined with other influences, the Guadalajara debacle contributed to a thoroughgoing reorganization of the petroleum monopoly.

Finally, recent survey data lend credence to the hypothesis that citizens are repudiating the political vehicles of old and embracing more innovative modes of sociopolitical participation. Two surveys undertaken in the early 1990s make the point. The first of these found a higher level of participation in groups like environmental organizations, neighborhood associations, and the National Solidarity Program (PRONASOL) committees than in political parties or labor unions. Moreover, those participating in the newer organizations placed a higher value on their participation. Fully 88 percent claimed they had gained something from their affiliation and participation, compared to only 65 percent for members of more traditional organizations.[10]

CONCLUSION

As Mexico approaches the 21st century, political change is everywhere. Economic growth and restructuring and social transformation form the context. In the post-1940 era, the economy grew by leaps and bounds, molding a semi-industrialized condition from an agrarian society. In the post-1982 era, the economy shifted from state dominated to private oriented. In the sociocultural sphere, projections foretell a Mexican population of more than 100 million by 2000. Beyond quantity, the quality of the people has advanced due to higher levels of awareness and sophistication wrought by educational reform and the expansion and improvement of transportation and communications.

In the process, the Mexican people have called for political reform. Corporatism, conceived in the 1930s and perfected in the 1940s and 1950s, no longer serves to discipline and channel participation. The major political parties seek new ideas and methods of activity. The old is clearly in jeopardy, but the new is in no sense well defined. The economy and society move inexorably toward more democratic forms, but the political system appears uncertain about its direction.

The argument made here for the development of a civil society carries considerable logic. The heavy hand of the government seems less ominous than in the past. The state owns less and intrudes less. Individuals, groups, and communities wax more spontaneous and freer than before. The space of economic, social, religious, and cultural freedom expands. Sociocultural norms increasingly embrace political change. In a study of recent survey data, Rod Camp concludes (with some reservations) that since the early 1980s there has been a strong shift in Mexican values in a direction supportive of democratic behavior.[11]

But this analysis constitutes an imperfect and incomplete picture of Mexico's contemporary situation. Other evidence provides less ground for optimism. While Salinas may have reduced state power in the economy, for example, the institution of *presidencialismo* waxed ever more powerful during his *sexenio*. President Zedillo appears headed in a similar direction. Moreover, the kidnappings that ravaged Mexico during the mid-1990s can hardly be characterized as "civil" behavior. Rather, they document a troubling inclination toward lawlessness reflected in other dimensions of society as well. Trends toward even more maldistribution of wealth suggest the growing relative impoverishment of lower socioeconomic groups even as Mexico's billionaires multiply. All of these signs and trends militate against the evolution of an authentic civil society.

The future cast of Mexico's society and polity remains uncertain. Some indicators point to a more open, democratic, and participatory Mexico with the dawn of the 21st century, but enough negative evidence clouds the landscape to give pause.

NOTES

1. *New York Times Poll: Mexico Survey*, October 28, November 4, 1986. Mimeographed. Questions 1, 3, 5, 16, 18.

2. *Encuesta Nacional de Cultura Política* (Mexico, D.F.: Secretaría de Gobernación, 1990).

3. On PEMEX, see "Crude Talk," *El Financiero Internacional*, May 30–June 5, 1994, p. 12.

4. See Edward J. Williams and John T. Passé-Smith, *The Unionization of the Maquiladora Industry: The Tamaulipan Case in National Context* (San Diego: Institute for the Study of the Californias, San Diego State University, 1992), pp. 21–29.

5. Gabriel A. Almond and Sidney Verba, *The Civic Culture* (Boston: Little, Brown and Company, 1965), p. 1.

6. Ibid., p. 364.

7. See Victoria E. Rodríguez and Peter M. Ward, *Policymaking, Politics, and Urban Governance in Chihuahua* (Austin: Lyndon B. Johnson School of Public Affairs, 1992), pp. 65–68.

8. For the discussion, see Ted Bardacke, "Solidarity Comes Home to Roost," *El Financiero Internacional*, September 21, 1992, p. 13.

9. Quoted in Tom Barry, ed., *Mexico: A Country Guide* (Albuquerque, N.M.: Inter-Hemispheric Education Resource Center, 1992), p. 275.

10. See Enrique Alducín Abitia, *Los Valores de los Mexicanos* (Mexico, D.F.: BANAMEX, 1990), Tome II; and Saba Consultores, *Estudio Sobre el Perfil Electoral en 1991* (Monterrey, 1991).

11. Roderic Ai Camp, *Politics in Mexico* (New York: Oxford University Press, 1993), p. 71.

4

The Mexican Military Approaches the 21st Century: Coping with a New World Order

Stephen J. Wager

In speculating about the future of the Mexican military, a clear understanding of the past can prove invaluable. As with most institutions, the role of the military will evolve in some form from its previous missions. The history of the army in the 20th century, like that of the nation in general, has centered first and foremost on the Mexican Revolution, which ravaged the country for ten years (1910–1920) and cost the lives of close to 2 million people. The army played a critical role in both the revolution and its outcome. It forged most of the political institutions that subsequently emerged and that provided Mexico with the relative economic and political stability it has enjoyed since the 1920s.

Ironically, the country's political leaders—most of whom were military in the two decades immediately following the Revolution—worked to eliminate the army's direct role in politics as a way of promoting stability. The formation of an official political party in 1929 legitimized a formal role for the military in this *sui generis* system. The founding of this predominant party, known today by the initials PRI, began the process of institutionalizing civilian political power. The civilianization of power took away the army's direct role in political decision making, and the country's new civilian leaders assigned the military the role of guarantor of the overall system. Since the 1920s, the army hierarchy had inculcated in its younger officers an ideology replete with values such as loyalty, a revolutionary heritage, and patriotism. That unique ideology contributed significantly to the enthusiastic acceptance by army leaders of their new mission, which the military has proudly and jealously guarded to this day.[1]

Historical events helped Mexico's new political elite consolidate its preeminent position. As early as 1940, the armed forces had begun to shift all their energies toward the traditional military functions of protecting national sovereignty and preparing for war. In the aftermath of World War II, Mexico elected the first in an unbroken line of civilian presidents and dashed any military hopes of regaining political power. Consequently, the army turned its attention toward civic action and crisis management, where it has remained focused to the present day. As the year 2000 approaches, it only makes sense to draw on this history when conjecturing about the army's future missions, structure, and influence.

THE ROLE OF THE MEXICAN ARMY

The army's mission has generally remained the same since the publication of the military's first organic law in 1926. That law, the legal raison d'être of the institution, defined its mission as follows: "to defend the integrity and independence of the fatherland, to maintain the rule of the Constitution and its laws, and to conserve internal order."[2] That mission remained in effect, although in modified form, until the publication of a new organic law in 1971. The new law eliminated the maintenance of constitutional rule, replacing it with the task of aiding the civilian population in public emergencies and helping with social projects contributing to national progress.[3] This new code simply legalized the civic-action role that the army had been performing as far back as the 1920s. A subsequent change in 1986 added greater specificity to that mission by subdividing it into three separate tasks: (1) providing aid to the civilian population in public emergencies, (2) performing civic action and social works contributing to national progress, and (3) in the case of natural disasters, helping in the maintenance of public order and providing support to the affected population and its property.[4]

Recent changes that have given a greater importance to civic action do not portend any diminution of that mission in the near future. On the contrary, greater emphasis will be placed on it as the military moves into the next century. More specifically, the national development plans of presidents de la Madrid and Salinas called on the army to increase activities that relate to the welfare of the community.[5]

The army's future role in civic action grows clearer when examined in the context of Mexican national security. In 1989, Mexican and U.S. experts met in Mexico City to discuss the concept of Mexican national security. As a result of this conference, most Mexican analysts concluded that their top political leaders did not have a precise definition of the term. Instead, the Mexican government had long confused national security with internal security. These analysts attributed this confusion to the fact that the powers of both government and nation have resided in one person, the president of the Republic. For that reason, Mexican presidents have been more attentive to internal security and have usually viewed the two concepts as synonymous. Such an approach has historically helped reinforce the government's control of the country.[6]

Not surprisingly, the army has adopted a national security philosophy similar to that practiced by top government leaders. In 1980, then secretary of national defense (SECDEF), General Félix Galván López, defined national security as "the maintenance of social, economic and political equilibrium guaranteed by the armed forces."[7] The definition sounded very much like the definition of internal security. Despite growing debate over the meaning of national security and the formation of a National Security Cabinet in 1988, the army will most likely continue to direct its attention to internal rather than national security. With the end of the cold war, the armed forces no longer feel themselves squeezed between the United States and the former Soviet bloc. Reinforced in part by the current international situation and increased domestic tensions, the Mexican government continues to see the major threats to its stability as emanating from within the country, not from some external source. Accepting such a premise, the Mexican army, in its role as guarantor of the political system, will most likely focus the brunt of its effort on internal security. Consequently, at times civic-action tasks may be performed under the guise of national security.

Mexican officers have been trained to respect the country's revolutionary heritage and attach special importance to nationalism and patriotism. These values have buttressed the army's civic-action role for decades. Civic action has been the preferred role of the leadership because it has enhanced the institution's image among the Mexican people. Political leaders, however, have felt compelled to call on the army for assistance in infrequent but highly volatile crises. Since the 1940s, there has been a clever crafting of the military that has ensured compliance with the directives of the ruling elite, no matter how unpleasant. This has led to the army's participation in crisis management, which has almost always marred its reputation. Nevertheless, because it is an integral part of the ruling system, the military has been unable to extricate itself. Through the years, the juxtaposed roles of civic action and crisis management have, at times to the chagrin of its leaders, *impugned* the military's image. In 1968, for instance, soldiers were transformed from patriotic nation-builders into the "butchers of Tlatelolco." Since the 1940s, there has been an underlying struggle within the military to remain focused on civic action, while political leaders at times have felt the need to channel army efforts into crisis management.

The military's active participation in crises has been fairly restricted over the past fifty years. The army has four general sets of defense plans, which carry the classifications of DN-I, DN-II, DN-III, and DN-IV. Plan DN-I encompasses war plans aimed at defending the nation against a foreign enemy. Plan DN-II focuses on eliminating internal security threats; DN-III provides for disaster relief. Recently, Plan DN-IV was added to the inventory for the purpose of organizing and legitimizing the army's role in the antidrug campaign.[8]

With the exception of World War II, Mexico's foreign policy, guided mainly by the principles of nonintervention, respect for self-determination, and a general disdain for military solutions to international problems, has virtually eliminated foreign military involvement or membership in alliance systems. Not surprisingly, therefore, the army has channeled most of its energies toward preserving internal security. Political and military leaders have long associated civic action with that mission. The army had been performing its traditional role of civic action, or *labor social* as Mexicans call it, when World War II forced it back into what the Constitution of 1917 had assumed would be its principal role—defending the nation against a foreign enemy. The execution of that task proved to be an aberration. After the war, political leaders favored the army's resumption of civic action in hopes of distancing its officers from politics.[9]

The army has a rich tradition of rendering assistance to the civilian population. As far back as the early 1920s, it engaged in such tasks as building roads, constructing irrigation works, and repairing railroad and telegraph lines. The 1926 organic law formally made civic action a part of the army's mission. Article 81 provided for the use of military resources in the construction of communications networks and public works that had some correlation with the overall needs of the institution. President Cárdenas (1934–1940) assigned the army a role in *forjando la patria* (nation-building) in an attempt to depoliticize it in the late 1930s. He envisioned the military as an instrument for expanding the central government's control in Mexico's more isolated regions. As an added advantage, civic action kept officers busy, leaving them little time to mingle in politics. The Mexican army became an army of workers that plowed fields and built roads, and its size and organization were regulated accordingly. By the 1940s, the formal adoption of this role had contributed substantially to the governing civilian coalition's ability to edge the military gradually out of the political limelight.

The army's revolutionary heritage has also given legitimacy to its civic-action mission. The military has labored, especially in the country's more remote areas, to bring to fruition the principles of economic and social justice, which many patriots sacrificed their lives for during the Revolution. Civic-action programs have been the principal tools employed in the ongoing mission of maintaining internal peace. The attention the army has given these programs has coincided neatly with its visibly nationalist philosophy.

The lack of an external threat has also facilitated commitment to civic action, and the army's social role has evolved gradually since the 1920s, becoming dominant as the need for a strictly military role declined precipitously after World War II. In an interview with the author, a high-ranking politician from the Echeverría administration (1970–1976) underscored the significance of civic action. Instead of sustaining a static defense, he said, the military adopted a more dynamic approach "to preserve the peace."[10] That decision has brought a good deal of prestige to the army. The small defense budgets resulting from the absence of an external menace and the implicit strategic defense by the United States have made the military's increasing focus on civic action a natural evolution.

In developing civic-action programs, the army's priorities adapted to the changing complexion of the nation. In the 1920s, the military devoted considerable effort to building roads and schools, but by the late 1940s road construction had been contracted out to civilians, with the army relegated to building secondary roads in outlying areas. While the military has continued to build small rural schools, its role in road construction and repair has largely disappeared. By the 1970s, its literacy campaign, which had reached its apex in the 1940s and 1950s, had little impact within either the military or civilian society. In the 1950s, the army had a major role in the eradication of livestock plagues and epidemics, but the evolution of medical science has now eliminated that mission. Social brigades employing military medical personnel to offer basic medical care to individuals living in isolated regions reached their apex in the 1970s. Since then, their effect has been considerably reduced.

Despite the gradual exclusion of certain civic-action duties, the army has continued to perform many important roles. Reforestation, a concern since the 1930s, gained new impetus in the late 1970s and 1980s due to growing national attention to environmental issues. In the Federal District alone, soldiers have planted over 11 million trees. It is safe to assume that the army will continue to play an active role in improving the environment, and in more ways than simply planting trees. The military may eventually contribute to major environmental clean-up projects. In recent years, disaster relief has been a major responsibility. The army established a program for providing such relief in 1966, and this became a formal mission in the new organic law of 1971. The military will continue to play a key role in this area well into the future. However, based on the events surrounding the relief dispensed during the 1985 earthquakes in Mexico City, it would appear that the military's contribution will be principally in rural areas, where soldiers will have less visibility and will not give any hint of martial law.

Protection of government installations is another task that will carry over into the next century. For decades after the Revolution, the army furnished escorts for railroads and government pay agents. By the 1970s, however, it had abandoned those duties and begun providing security at vital installations, such as petroleum refineries and airports. For a short time, it extended its security role to banks threatened by the short-lived guerrilla movement of that period. Finally, it became committed to a water distribution program in the early 1970s and has since been delivering potable water to many of the country's arid and drought-stricken regions. Both the security and water distribution duties will continue past the year 2000.[11]

The most visible role that the military will play during the present decade and beyond is in the antidrug campaign. The significance that army leaders have attached to this mission can be seen in their decision to create a new category of defense plans (DN-IV) to deal with the problem. This task has historically been considered a civic-action function, since it has a direct correlation to internal security. In more recent years, it has assumed political dimensions, given the expanding severity of the problem and the growing number of accusations of government corruption. The issue has also had an adverse effect on Mexican relations with the United States. There has been a misconception that the army did not get involved in antidrug operations until the United States began to pressure the Mexican government in the late 1960s. In fact, the army had reported drug eradication activities in Durango as early as May 1946.[12] The following year, the U.S. Embassy received instructions from the State Department to urge the Mexican government to prevent the cultivation of illegal drugs. Ambassador Walter Thurston advised Washington that he had learned that the Mexican attorney general's office had been planning an extensive program aimed at impeding the cultivation of poppy fields. In 1948, Mexico launched a major antidrug campaign in the northwestern part of the country, including occasional raids into heavy drug-producing areas. Army personnel assisted agents from the attorney general's office in locating and eradicating poppy fields. The campaign has continued at different levels of intensity to the present.[13]

Although virtually nothing has been written about the army's role in the antinarcotics campaign during the 1950s and 1960s, the military worked with agents from the attorney general's office to locate and destroy drug crops in some of the more rugged regions of the country. Official army sources reported the destruction of crops and the apprehension of traffickers in Chihuahua, Durango, and Sinaloa during the 1950s.[14] Subsequently, these operations expanded slightly. The army conducted joint search-and-destroy missions in eight different states and increased the surface area coverage over the previous decade.[15] But despite some improvement, the overall intensity of the effort remained relatively low until the 1970s.

Mexico's Permanent Campaign Against Drug Trafficking picked up considerably toward the end of 1969 as a result of pressure from the United States. The latter implemented Operation Intercept along the U.S.–Mexican border in October, ostensibly to induce Mexico to devote more resources to antidrug activities. U.S. officials believed the drug problem had reached crisis proportions and placed considerable blame on Mexico as a major supplier. Operation Intercept prohibited Mexican goods from entering the United States as a means of coercing Mexico to destroy drug crops chemically. That policy eventually proved counterproductive, but U.S. pressure did seem to affect the amount of resources Mexico would later commit to the campaign.[16] The new emphasis Mexican officials began to place on antidrug efforts had a major effect on the army's participation. Military leaders, on orders from the president, immediately assigned more troops to the war against drugs.

Operation *Cóndor* proved to be the army's most prominent contribution to the permanent antidrug campaign. By the mid-1970s, growth in the drug trade forced the military to take more definitive action against growers and traffickers. Shortly after becoming SECDEF in 1976, General Galván López directed the general staff to formulate a plan aimed at curtailing drug cultivation. The general staff of the national defense secretariat (SDN) subsequently developed *Plan Cóndor* to deploy troops to the country's heaviest drug-producing area on a permanent basis. The army set up headquarters outside the town of Badiriguato, Sinaloa. The plan called for approximately 3,000 soldiers to locate and destroy marijuana and poppy plants in an area comprised of the confluence of the states of Chihuahua, Durango, and Sinaloa. The task force that served in the region drew troops from all over the Republic. The first force reported for duty on January 16, 1977. A new task force has since replaced the previous one every six months up to the present.[17]

The army hierarchy had established a *Plan Canador* in the early 1970s, which directed each military zone to conduct antidrug operations within its area in accordance with the extent of the threat. Drug cultivation occurred with greater frequency in the coastal states, and the military zones in those regions began to devote a substantial portion of their resources to eradication. The land-locked states tended to earmark less resources for the campaign and were able to focus more on other civic-action programs. Richard B. Craig, who did considerable research on Mexico's antidrug campaign, pointed out a number of problems that the army encountered. He described an unfavorable ratio of soldiers to land surface. He also noted that the army lacked sufficient resources and equipment (especially helicopters) to do a thorough job. Craig acknowledged the presence of corruption among some of the zone commanders as well as some interagency friction. Most commanders resented being ordered about by what they perceived to be incompetent federal agents, and as the army became more involved this duty grew more unpopular. Officers viewed the mission as a no-win situation, which carried with it the potential for damaging the military's reputation because of charges of corruption. In spite of these impediments, the army has posted considerable success. Its destruction statistics have been especially impressive and far outdistance the contributions made by any other federal agency.[18] The antidrug campaign continued to command an increasing portion of army resources throughout the 1970s and 1980s.

The advent of the Salinas administration in 1988 added to the significance of the military's role in the antidrug campaign. The administration defined narcotics trafficking as a threat to national security. Although certain "experts" envisioned the drug scourge as a problem of public order rather than national security, Salinas gave the problem high priority.

Shortly after taking office, President Salinas directed the army to move against Miguel Angel Félix Gallardo, a major drug trafficker. Gallardo and his organization operated extensively in the West Coast state of Sinaloa. The army subsequently captured him and one of his lieutenants. In October 1989, Salinas told the U.S. Congress that Mexico intended "to eradicate drug trafficking at its roots."[19] Even the army, previously considered a "sacred cow," has not escaped close scrutiny. New incidents, implicating top-level officers in drug trafficking, received widespread attention in both Mexico and the United States. In one case, an army general, alleged to have offered protection to drug flights from South America, was relieved of his command and reassigned to Defense Headquarters, ostensibly to place him under supervision. In another incident, Salinas ordered the National Commission on Human Rights to investigate the killing of seven narcotics agents by soldiers at a remote landing strip. The incident occurred in November 1991, and two army generals and three other officers were detained and subsequently imprisoned. These types of responses suggest that the government takes narcotics trafficking seriously. Even though the army already devotes considerable resources to the campaign, it will be expected to do even more until greater responsibility can be transferred to law enforcement agencies.

There is another critical consideration with regard to the army's antidrug role. Within the context of U.S.–Mexican relations, the drug issue could prove to be a major impediment to economic integration. It takes on an added dimension when discussed in connection with NAFTA. Signs or perceptions of a soft counterdrug policy in Mexico could jeopardize future trade with the United States. A few years ago, then California Senator Pete Wilson wrote that an inadequate response to drug trafficking could pose the greatest threat to improved U.S.–Mexican relations, the implication being that Mexico's antidrug policies might have a major impact on the country's prosperity.[20] All this points toward the Mexican army continuing this role as it moves toward the 21st century.

The military's civic-action programs have not only highlighted the social consciousness of the Mexican government but have also eased socioeconomic tensions. Consequently, civic action is likely to remain the army's predominant mission. The rationale is simple: The government has correlated national security with internal security. Civic action contributes directly to the maintenance of internal order. Moreover, the responsibilities that the military has assumed in this role leave little time for political adventurism, a benefit political leaders find especially valuable.

THE STRUCTURE OF THE MEXICAN ARMY IN THE 21st CENTURY

The army's mission will be the principal factor in determining its future structure. Other elements that will have a bearing include available funding, U.S. and regional defense policies, and the general political climate in Mexico. The present uncertainty with regard to the army's structure and organization centers on the still unmeasured influence that each factor will have on the final outcome.

After the 1968 student demonstrations, during which hundreds of protestors had been killed or injured at Tlatelolco, the army experienced its first significant increase in size since World War II, mandated by the desire to preclude a recurrence of civil strife. The oil boom in the late 1970s was instrumental in planning a large-scale modernization program. The economic crash, which followed on the heels of that short-lived resurgence, disrupted those plans. As a result, since the early 1980s, the army's modernization has proceeded fitfully, the direct result of a shortage in funds.

Midway into the de la Madrid administration (1982–1988), the national defense secretariat (SDN) proposed a major reorganization of the army that shifted the focus away from political considerations and more toward operational features. This new plan proposed reorganizing the long-standing military zone system into a more tactically suited corps organization. Although this reorganization sought to reshuffle the thirty-six military zones into seven corps, by the time de la Madrid left office, only one corps could be considered fully functional, while another two had only a skeleton headquarters in place. The new SDN administration (1988–1994) remained committed to the reorganization, but it made minimal progress in implementing the planned changes. It seems likely that the restructuring will carry over into the Zedillo administration (1994–2000). On the positive side, this reorganization points toward a more operationally functional army by the year 2000. It appears doubtful that the military hierarchy—or political leaders for that matter—will sanction any new structural changes while the institution finds itself in the throes of a partially completed reorganization. Nor is it feasible to expect that vast amounts of funds will be available to support a structure different from the corps system.

The continued emphasis on mobility is another trend that will continue to receive attention. One of the first stages in the modernization program started in the early 1980s with the motorizing of cavalry units, which had previously relied exclusively on horses. The SDN followed that reform in the late 1980s by purchasing six C-130 troop transport planes from the United States. The Mexican airborne brigade added those planes to its inventory to provide rapid response for emergencies,[21] often a requirement of the internal security mission.

President Salinas responded to a less than successful presidential campaign and a questionable popular mandate by setting out to project an image of a "no-nonsense" president. Almost immediately after assuming office, he flexed his muscles by ordering the military to apprehend the corrupt leader of the national petroleum workers' union, Joaquín Hernández Galicia (*La Quina*). The force launched a surprise attack in January 1989 against the union leader's well-fortified compound, seizing *La Quina* and a large cache of weapons. Shortly thereafter, the president employed army forces in a countrywide dragnet aimed at capturing the nation's leading drug trafficker, Félix Gallardo, which they eventually did. A few months later, he ordered troops to take control of the historically renowned Cananea copper mine as a preemptive measure against striking workers, who might have used violence to gain their demands. The increased "political visibility" of the military at the outset of Salinas' term sent a strong message to the administration's opponents and helped the new president gain the solid political footing that set the tone for the first five years of his presidency.

These successful operations would not have been possible without the recently added mobility of the army. In the early 1990s, the military began purchasing a fairly large number of U.S. surplus jeeps and small cargo vehicles to replace and upgrade its increasingly outmoded inventory. Mexican officers had been extremely impressed with the effectiveness of U.S. forces during Operation Desert Storm. The U.S. success reinforced the perception in the upper echelons of the Mexican military command that self-contained, highly mobile, rapid-response forces were the future direction of the armed forces.[22] In light of the general demilitarization occurring across the globe, a growth in the size of the armed forces seems to be an impractical approach, especially for a traditionally pacifist country like Mexico. However, added mobility can act as a force multiplier if employed effectively.

The changing situation in the countryside also calls for greater mobility. The gradual abolition of the *ejidos* probably signals the end of the *guardias rurales* (rural guards). This paramilitary force has traditionally served as the "eyes and ears of the army" in isolated areas. The military provided many *ejido* members with a rifle and a modest work uniform, and they in turn would help maintain order in the countryside. Commanded by a small cadre of active officers, the *rurales* have not only served as an important source of intelligence, but also as a key link between the army and the peasants.[23] As privatization takes root in the agricultural sector, the *rurales* will most likely disband, leaving the military with less warning of potentially volatile situations. Consequently, the ability to respond rapidly to a developing crisis should become even more critical.

The future structure of the armed forces will also be influenced in part by U.S. military policy. Although the United States will almost certainly remain a regional power, the reduction in U.S. forces will be felt throughout Latin America. The end of the cold war has made demilitarization the preferred policy. In the past, Mexican political leaders have not reacted to the asymmetry between the two countries' armed forces. The prevailing climate both regionally and worldwide is not likely to alter that asymmetry fundamentally, although it will probably be reduced somewhat over the next few years, given the large cuts in U.S. forces. The military budget as a percentage of Mexico's GDP has experienced very minor fluctuations over the past fifteen years. This trend most likely will continue, and the funds allocated to the army should allow it to complete its reorganization under the corps system by the beginning of the 21st century.

THE FUTURE INFLUENCE OF THE MEXICAN MILITARY

Given the military's influence in Latin America during the 20th century, many outsiders have assumed that the Mexican military has played a more significant political role than has actually been the case. Most of the political influence it has attained since World War II has derived from its crisis-management role, which has been fairly limited. However, that role has more often been a double-edged sword than the distinct advantage some have posited. Since the unfortunate incidents during the student uprisings in 1968, military leaders have been reluctant to participate in crisis situations, preferring to leave police actions to local and state authorities. The irony is that only by defending the state in a major crisis can the army substantially augment its power and prestige within the Mexican system.

The army has only infrequently manifested its physical presence in a major way since World War II. Over the past thirty years, it has responded to only three critical challenges to internal security: the student movement in 1968, the rural insurgency in the early 1970s, and, more recently, the continuing struggle against narcotics growers and traffickers. [Editors' note: The Zapatista revolt is a fourth, more recent instance, and will be discussed later.] The first episode seriously tarnished the army's paternalistic and patriotic image. The "Tlatelolco Massacre" discouraged the army's involvement in large-scale social demonstrations, in which soldiers might be forced to repress the populace. Otherwise, the military has maintained a relatively low physical profile. Although its visibility increased when Salinas engaged in what one historian called "Mexican Thatcherism," those surges in influence were fleeting, given the limited duration of the actions.[24]

This strategy of "Thatcherism," named after the former British Prime Minister, refers to the state's use of excessive resources or force to control certain social groups. The government action at the Cananea mine is a good example. In that instance, the army played a prominent role, and it yielded favorable results by subduing a potentially volatile conflict. But because its role in such episodes has tended to be short lived, its leaders have not been able to convert their contributions into long-term gains for the institution. Instead, the hierarchy seems content to continue its traditionally cautious approach, because the institution's growing presence in the antidrug campaign places it in a more precarious position with regard to image, given the propensity for increased allegations of corruption. As with the Cananea incident, the flare-ups in the war on drugs also tend to be evanescent and not conducive to augmenting the army's influence.

In short, "Thatcherism" is more of a political phenomenon aimed at increasing the influence of the ruling party. Although political leaders seem willing to call on the military to support the status quo, they do not necessarily want it to gain added stature within the system. As they guide the country into the next century, they will most likely try to ensure a continuing low public profile for the armed forces. To do otherwise might suggest an inability to maintain control.

There are also other factors inhibiting a substantial growth in military power. One is the public perception of the military. Since the bloodletting of the Revolution, there has always been an undercurrent of antimilitary sentiment in Mexico. The public has viewed the armed forces as a necessary vice, something that has to be tolerated but little more. Through the years, this veiled discontent has been a psychological impediment to a military accretion of power. A recent example emerged in the unlikely form of new history textbooks. In September 1992, the Education Ministry announced the publication of new history books for Mexico's public school system. A mild furor arose over the treatment of the 1968 student movement. The new official history described the military as having repressed the students. Military leaders took exception, and the president moved quickly to assuage them. Nonetheless, the incident may help foster a negative view of the armed forces.

The economic integration that NAFTA promises for Mexico and the United States ostensibly suggests a closer military-to-military relationship as well. Closer military ties would offer opportunities to develop a more professional institution, thereby enhancing the stature of the armed forces. However, a strong argument against such a relationship can also be presented.

One analyst with close ties to the army has related that high-ranking military leaders are not entirely in favor of NAFTA. The agreement has aroused suspicion about U.S. motives. Historical fears of U.S. infringement on Mexican sovereignty have been resurrected, although now such violations would occur through economic duplicity rather than political or military means.[25] Although Mexicans have long viewed the United States as a potential enemy, the mission of the armed forces has never been de facto to defend against foreign incursions. Realistically, if the United States ever decided to invade, the Mexicans could only hope to impede the invasion for a limited time. The army has always focused on preserving internal security, which has never required extensive equipment purchases from the

United States. The end of the cold war further obviates the need for so-phisticated hardware and thus removes one reason for developing closer ties.

Since 1990, there has been little appreciable improvement in military-to-military relations. Although cordiality has increased, the status of major issues such as joint training exercises and joint defense plans has witnessed virtually no change.[26] Military leaders from both countries formed the Joint Mexican–U.S. Defense Commission (JMUSDC) during World War II to serve as a forum for discussing defense issues. Since the 1960s, however, Mexican leaders have virtually neglected that forum. Although the United States has attempted to reinvigorate the JMUSDC on various occasions, Mexico has opted to use the commission almost exclusively for organizing symbolic ceremonies and social activities. At present, there are no indications that the JMUSDC will reassume its original charter anytime soon.

Since the 1930s, presidents have come to play the predominant role in Mexican politics. Nevertheless, although they, their policies, and their programs change every six years, the military as an institution has retained a great deal of continuity. The army does not place a high value on change. Military leaders have relied heavily on traditional values and principles, rather than on innovative approaches to old problems. The Constitution of 1917 designated the armed forces as the protector of national sovereignty, and the military will continue to perform that mission in the years ahead. In so doing, it will try to assure that there will always be a "safe distance" from the powerful neighbor to the north.

As for generating increased influence from within the military, the prospects seem slim. Here again, traditional values play a critical role. Unwavering loyalty to the Revolution and the system begotten by it has been a cardinal feature of the Mexican armed forces. One insider has suggested that, in a sense, the system has bought the military's loyalty. Certain benefits accrue to officers, especially as they advance in rank. For example, they have access to low-interest loans for homes and cars. Benefits such as these, which can also include scholarships to private universities for offspring, can increase an officer's salary more than 30 percent. More significantly, these perquisites further commit officers to the army and make them more dependent on the institution as the primary means of fulfilling their financial responsibilities.[27] These benefits make them staunch supporters of the system and much less willing to risk expulsion by deviating from the highly centralized decision-making process. Strict compliance with the commander's directives ensures continued benefits. Because most officers believe that civilian government has shown concern for their needs, there will be no sudden groundswell to alter the system drastically.

The issue that always generates a lively debate is the likelihood of a military coup. After the unexpected 1973 coup in Chile, there has been a general reluctance to use the word *never* when discussing the Latin American armed forces. Nevertheless, the probability of a coup in Mexico in the near future is virtually nil. Aside from the loyalty that the military has traditionally displayed, officers collectively lack the requisite political skills for the efficacious management of government. More important, the army has direct ties only with the state. It lacks strong links to any major interest group that could fortify a move to take power.[28]

Moreover, the military has no forum within which it could exert its influence and energize key groups to support a coup. The one area in which it might have such influence is with regard to national security. However, under Salinas a national security cabinet was formed to manage these issues. Although the SECDEF is a member, the president exerts tight control and determines what constitutes a security issue. Thus, although the military may contribute input on vital security matters, its principal role has been to carry out presidential directives.[29]

Perhaps more important, tradition will continue to play a major role in the military's behavior. Army leaders have long considered their institution to be a pillar of the system that emerged from the Revolution. In fact, they nurtured the system in its formative years. A military president founded the PRI, which has been the country's sole ruling party. These precedents have solidified the army's position as an integral part of the "revolutionary" system. Since the 1950s, it has worked hard to cultivate the image of a paternalistic and responsible institution dedicated to improving the welfare of the Mexican people. Notwithstanding a few untoward incidents, in the more than sixty years following the Revolution the army has been able to create an image that has set it apart, in a favorable way, from the vast majority of its Latin American counterparts. Military leaders have been intent on maintaining that benign posture, perhaps influenced in part by the widespread political failures of their regional counterparts.

SOME FINAL THOUGHTS

The general deemphasis on the military that has taken place worldwide over the last few years has also had an effect on the Mexican armed forces. Although Mexico has shown little tolerance for fat military budgets, the lack of even a remote external threat in the post–cold war era offers even less reason to enlarge the already "meager" budget. Since the mid-1980s, military leaders have talked about an ongoing modernization process, but they have also emphasized that this program will stress quality over quantity. In other words, bigger does not necessarily equate to better, and that reinforces speculation about continued modest budgets.

While analysts search for reasons that might indicate changes within the military, there is probably nothing on the horizon. Traditionally, the armed forces have been adverse to change. Since the 1950s, they have relied on political leaders for guidance in such matters. A strong partnership has been established between the government and the military, and the former will continue to look after the army's interests and needs because it wants to keep the military in its corner. If the government, dominated by the PRI, continues to retain a healthy consensus, it should have no problems maintaining the army's support. One long-time expert has written that the centralized authority employed by the government nurtures stability.[30] Military leaders have long been cognizant of that reality and felt comfortable with the political system. That should not come as too much of a surprise since their predecessors founded it.

Structurally, the Mexican army of the 21st century will stress greater mobility and quicker reaction. Given the further reduced threat of foreign interference in internal affairs, streamlined, mobile, quick-reaction forces will be best suited for confronting the government's most pressing challenges, which most likely will come from social disturbances emanating from economic problems and from increasingly brash drug lords. The current structural transformation of the "corps system" will probably be accomplished by the turn of the century. At some point over the next decade, this new system will supersede the traditional military zone structure, making the army less politically sensitive to disruptions within individual states. It is still too early to predict the long-range political ramifications of this new remodeling. On the surface, the corps organization would seem to reduce the political influence of military zone commanders. However, it might also have the effect of converting seven or eight corps commanders into major power brokers within the regions under their purview.

As for the future of U.S.–Mexican military relations, they are likely to remain cordial but distant. As guardians of the nation's sovereignty, the Mexican army works to preserve its image of independence and self-reliance. Most armed forces adhere fervently to tradition, and the Mexican military is no exception. It has found no justification for significantly altering its traditional policy of maintaining a safe distance from the United States. The latter was unsuccessful in establishing a military base or conducting joint exercises during World War II and the cold war, and security interests in the United States no longer justify the need for such policies. Civic action or *labor social* has been the constant mission of the Mexican military in the postrevolutionary period. This has always been the underpinning of the army's role in society. Through civic action, the military, as a national institution, has reaped its greatest rewards. Nothing on the horizon suggests that it will reduce or abandon this responsibility. On the contrary, most of its leaders would like to devote greater effort to that mission, believing that they can best enhance the army's prestige by performing such tasks.

Finally, counternarcotics will remain a key mission. In this case, however, many commanders cringe at the thought. In recent years, allegations of military corruption in the drug wars have impugned the army's reputation.[31] At the same time, the government has shown signs of bolstering civilian security services to allow law enforcement agencies to play a larger role. The military will become less influential in this area as the attorney general's office and federal and state police forces augment their assets. This partial shifting of responsibility may relieve the military of some of the allegations of wrongdoing that it has been subjected to in the past. Although this change may take away some of the army's influence in the political arena, it will not affect the army's role as a loyal servant of the Mexican people and an ardent supporter of the legitimate government.

NOTES

1. See chapter 3 of Stephen J. Wager, "The Mexican Army, 1940–1982: The Country Comes First" (Ph.D. dissertation, Stanford University, 1992) for a detailed analysis of this ideology.

2. *Ley Orgánica del Ejército y Armada Nacionales,* March 15, 1926.

3. *Ley Orgánica del Ejército y Fuerza Aerea Mexicanos,* March 18, 1971.

4. *Ley Orgánica del Ejército y Fuerza Aerea Mexicanos,* December 8, 1986.

5. Luis Herrera–Lasso and Guadalupe González, "Balance y Perspectivas en el Uso del Concepto de la Seguridid Nacional en el Caso de México," in *En Busca De La Seguridid Perdida,* edited by Sergio Aguayo Quezada and Bruce Bagley (Mexico City: Siglo Veintiuno Editores, 1990), pp. 400–401.

6. Sergio Aguayo Quezada, "Los Usos, Abusos y Retos de la Seguridad Nacional Mexicana: 1946–1990," in ibid., pp. 114–23; and Herrera Lasso M. and González, "Balance y Perspectivas," in ibid., pp. 397–99.

7. Roberto Vizacaíno, "La Seguridad del País, Fin Primordial del Estado," *Proceso,* September 22, 1980.

8. Raúl Benítez Manaut, "*Las Fuerzas Armadas Mexicanas y su Relación con el Estado, el Sistema Político y la Sociedad,*" paper presented at the Consejo Latinamericana de Ciencias Sociales in Guatemala, November 11–13, 1992, pp. 4–7; and José Luis Piñeyro, "Presencia Política Militar Nacional en el Distrito Federal: Propuestas de Análisis," in *D.F. Gobierno y Sociedad Civil,* edited by Pablo González Casanova and Juan Manuel Ramírez Sáenz (Mexico, D.F.: Ediciones El Caballito, 1987), pp. 69–76.

9. Luis Alamillo Flores, "La Nación en la Segunda Guerra Mundial," in *Seis Años de Actividad Nacional,* edited by Manuel Avila Camacho (Mexico, D.F.: Secretaría de Gobernación, 1946), pp. 101–2.

10. Interview, January 1991. All individuals interviewed for this chapter requested anonymity.

11. Perhaps the most up-to-date summary of the army's civic-action activities can found in Secretaría de la Defensa Nacional, *Social Labour* (Mexico, D.F.: Taller Autográfico de la SDN, May 1993).

12. *Revista del Ejército,* May 1946, pp. 66–70.

13. Richard B. Craig, "La Campaña Permanente, Mexico's Antidrug Campaign," *Journal of Interamerican Studies and World Affairs,* Vol. 20, No. 2 (May 1978), pp. 107–8; and U.S. Department of State, *Foreign Relations of the United*

States 1947, Vol. XIII, *The American Republics* (Washington, D.C.: Government Printing Office, 1965), pp. 838–39.

14. Secretaría de la Defensa Nacional, *Memoria de la Secretaría de la Defensa Nacional Septiembre de 1949–Agosto de 1950* (Mexico, D.F.: Taller Autográfico, 1950), p. 116. Hereafter cited as *SDN Memorias* with appropriate years. Information also obtained from *SDN Memorias,* 1950–1951, p. 34, and 1958–1959, p. 30.

15. *Revista del Ejército,* July 1962, p. 15; and *SDN Memorias,* 1960–1961, p. 28, 1962–1964, p. 26, 1965–1966, p. 24, 1966–1967, pp. 33–34, and 1967–1968, p. 42.

16. Samuel I. del Villar, "The Illicit U.S.–Mexico Drug Market: Failure of Policy and an Alternative," in *Mexico and the United States: Managing the Relationship,* edited by Riordan Roett (Boulder, Colo.: Westview Press, 1988), pp. 196–201; and Craig, "La Campaña Permanente," pp. 109–12.

17. Francisco Ortiz Pinchetti, "La Operación Cóndor, Letanía de Horrores," *Proceso,* October 9, 1978; *Revista del Ejército y Fuerza Aerea Mexicanos,* February 1977, pp. 61–62; and "Campaña Contra Enervantes," *Revista del Ejército y Fuerza Aerea Mexicanos,* May 1981, pp. 18–20.

18. Craig, "La Campaña Permanente," pp. 116–18.

19. "Mexican President Vows War on Drugs," *Chicago Tribune,* October 5, 1989; and "Mexico Will Press Drug War, But Without Any U.S. Troops," *New York Times,* October 5, 1989.

20. Clark W. Reynolds and Stephen J. Wager, "Integración Económica de México y Estados Unidos. Implicaciones Para la Seguridad de Ambos Paises," in Aguayo Quezada and Bagley, eds., *En Busca,* pp. 223–26.

21. Interview, August 1989.

22. Interview, July 1991.

23. "Empleo y Actuación de los Cuerpos de Defensas Rurales," *Revista del Ejército y Fuerza Aerea Mexicanos,* February 1973, pp. 44–46; Ramiro G. Bautista Rosas, *El Ejército en el México Actual—Misión y Perspectiva* (Thesis for Licenciado en Derecho, Universidad Autónoma de México, 1976), p. 61; and Jorge Alberto Lozoya, *El Ejército Mexicano* (Mexico, D.F.: Jornadas 65, 1984), pp. 110–15.

24. Lorenzo Meyer, "Ejército y Cananeas del Futuro," *Excélsior,* September 6, 1989.

25. Interview, September 1992.

26. This is from a U.S. official close to the situation. Interview, October 1992.

27. Interviews, September 1992 and July 1993.

28. Herrera Lasso and González, "Balance y Perspectivas," pp. 402–3; and Daniel C. Levy, "Mexico: Sustained Civilian Rule Without Democracy," in *Politics in Developing Countries: Comparing Experiences with Democracy,* edited by Larry Diamond, Juan J. Linz, and Seymour Martin Lipset (Boulder, Colo.: Lynne Rienner, 1990), pp. 471–72.

29. Aguayo Quezada, "Los Usos, Abusos y Retos," pp. 120–22; and *Diario Oficial,* December 7, 1988, pp. 3–4.

30. George W. Grayson, *The North American Free Trade Agreement,* Headline Series No. 299, Summer 1992 (New York: Foreign Policy Association, 1993), p. 71.

31. The most recent and sensationalistic accusations have implicated the army

in the assassination of a Roman Catholic cardinal in the city of Guadalajara. Official Church sources had accused certain military officials of being involved with the drug traffickers who were responsible for the murder. The facts surrounding the incident have still not been officially disclosed. See Alberto Aguirre, Felipe Cobián, and Guillermo Correa, "Los Asesinos Forcejearon con el Cardenal y su Chofer antes de Acribillarlos," *Proceso,* May 31, 1993; and Rodrigo Vera, "Acusa el Clero al Ejército, Adultera Documentos y Se Divide ante las Marchas," *Proceso,* July 5, 1993.

5

State–Labor Relations in Mexico: Old Tendencies and New Trends

María Lorena Cook

Organized labor occupies a special place in any effort to characterize the changes and identify the challenges facing contemporary Mexico. Of the three sectors comprising the PRI, labor traditionally has been the most autonomous and consequently the most important politically. Although the labor movement is frequently portrayed as co-opted and subordinated to the state, historically the state-labor relationship has been more conflictive and has involved continuous negotiation over the terms of the relationship.[1]

Today one cannot talk about the changes affecting organized labor without talking about changes in the social bases of the regime, and thus about regime change. Organized labor has long been a central pillar of the post-revolutionary regime. The regime's departure from the principles of its revolutionary-nationalist past clearly undermines and threatens its historic yet "contradictory alliance" with labor.[2] At the same time, NAFTA, which was approved by the Canadian, U.S., and Mexican legislatures in 1993, will have important implications for labor. The final decade of this century is therefore likely to be a watershed in which the new terms for labor's role in the economy and political system will be defined and set.

This chapter discusses some of the most important recent trends and changes in state-labor relations and their future implications. First, it identifies changes in three major areas: (1) labor's role in the party and its participation in other institutional arenas, (2) the political and strategic composition and evolution of the labor movement, and (3) models of unionism likely to be strengthened by further restructuring and free trade. Finally, it analyzes the implications of these changes for the future of state-labor relations and regime change; in particular, how might a loosening of the links between organized labor and the regime affect the balance of forces pressuring for democratization?

THE "DEINSTITUTIONALIZATION" OF STATE-LABOR RELATIONS

Analysts have typically referred to the Mexican regime since the 1930s as corporatist, pointing to the sectoral composition of the official party and to the central role of the state in structuring, subsidizing, and mediating social groups. This label has been most frequently applied to state-labor relations, in which state regulation of union registration, strikes, and worker grievances has accompanied subsidies of unions and labor participation in tripartite agencies, wage-setting commissions, and the official party. This "inclusionary" corporatism provided labor with important bargaining leverage at the same time that it facilitated state control over labor and ensured political stability.[3]

An analysis of state-labor relations has to ask in what way the terms of this relationship have changed. In the 1970s and 1980s, observers referred frequently to a "crisis of corporatism" due to the emergence of unincorporated groups within the labor movement and among rural and urban popular sectors. An important element contributing to this situation was the economic crisis, particularly its adverse impact on the ability of official organizations to deliver economic and other resources to their members, which then undermined the capacity of these organizations to channel and control popular demands. Recently some analysts have begun to refer to the appearance of "neocorporatism,"[4] a label that suggests that state controls over social groups (and especially over labor organizations) have not disappeared but merely been repackaged. This term contrasts with the Salinas administration's preferred name for the emerging configuration of state-society relations in Mexico—"social liberalism"—a phrase that implies the autonomy of social groups. What these labels reflect is agreement that state-society and, particularly, state-labor relations are changing. Less clear is what the balance among "old" and "new" elements of the relationship is and what picture will finally emerge.

As of the mid-1990s, the following trends can be identified: (1) the maintenance of traditional state controls over labor and, in some cases, their strengthening; (2) the continued and perhaps growing crisis of representation within unions, reflected in the lack of internal democracy and continuing struggles over union representation; and (3) the depoliticization of the labor movement, reflected in the decline of labor's influence and participation in the political system (especially in the party).

Although it can be argued that state constraints on labor have always been strong and that relations between official union leaders and their members have been in crisis for some time, it is the third point that represents a relatively new development and increases the significance of the first two conditions. In the past, the largest and most important of Mexican labor organizations, the Confederation of Mexican Workers (CTM), typically agreed to contain wage demands and withhold protests over economic conditions in exchange for political concessions. Labor traditionally exchanged short-term economic sacrifice and self-control for future bargaining power by expanding its presence and influence in the political arena. The viability of this exchange has been permanently threatened by recent efforts to restructure the PRI in a way that diminishes the role of corporate sectors in favor of territorial representation. Labor has been asked to contain its wage demands, refrain from protest, and stand by while traditional sources of patronage are transferred out of its control. At the same time, it has been told not to expect an expanded future role in the party or the political system. Labor has been getting less and giving more, yet it has developed few strategic alternatives to maintaining an alliance with the state.

A number of recent developments and reforms point to labor's reduced role in the party. The "sacrifice" of labor politicians during the 1988 federal congressional and presidential elections was the clearest and earliest indication of the party's new orientation under the Salinas administration: Labor's PRI candidates could no longer expect automatic ascension to political office. (Since 1988, the CTM has received a declining number of federal congressional seats and has had a reduced presence in the National Political Council of the PRI.)[5] The sector's failure to mobilize the vote on behalf of the PRI presidential candidate in 1988 signaled to the government the exhaustion of labor's ability to lend political support and the significance of the gap between union leaders and members. Subsequent efforts to reform the party to capture a disaffected electorate further fostered the perception of organized labor as an obstacle to needed political reform. The reform of the PRI's statutes during the 1990 National Assembly, in which a resolution was adopted eliminating the requirement that party affiliation be through membership in mass organizations, was a blow to most official union leaders and further weakened the traditional role of unions in channeling participation in the party. Subsequent attempts to restructure and rename the constituent organizations of the PRI, however, reflected a representation of organized labor's interests and thus appeared to signify a compromise with labor on the eve of the politically sensitive presidential succession. In spite of this concession to labor, the reforms to the PRI under the Salinas administration did weaken labor's role relative to territorial representation and noncorporate interests.[6]

Other recent developments point to the decline of labor participation in those institutions in which labor has traditionally played a role, and even the reduced importance of the institutions themselves (e.g., the National Minimum Wage Commission and the Labor Conciliation and Arbitration

Boards). The work of the National Minimum Wage Commission, for example, was severely circumscribed by the succession of "pacts," begun under President de la Madrid and continued by Salinas, in which government, business, labor, and rural organizations signed on to agreements covering wage increases and price controls. The declining influence of the Wage Commission led CTM leader Fidel Velázquez to declare angrily that it should disappear because "*no sirve para nada*" (it's not worth anything).[7] Although these pacts covered a wider range of economic issues, labor played little role in shaping the content of such agreements. As Denise Dresser noted, "[The pacts] took away the power labor leaders had to negotiate wage increases, and placed it in the hands of the Executive, specifically, the economic cabinet."[8] Although one can argue that labor never had much leeway in determining minimum wage increases, especially during the years of economic crisis, the point is that the role of key tripartite institutions in which labor has traditionally participated has declined. In the wage area, at least, the ad hoc social pacts that have superseded some of these institutions serve to limit rather than expand labor's influence.

Official unions have traditionally used their control over important resources and services as a source of patronage and to sustain membership support. Reforms in 1992 in areas such as the workers' housing fund (*Instituto del Fondo Nacional de la Vivienda,* INFONAVIT) undermine union influence over such resources by removing INFONAVIT's control over the employers' housing contribution funds and depositing these monies instead in the hands of commercial banks, which then deal directly with individual workers. Other reforms similarly affect workers' pension funds.[9] Although such changes may directly benefit individual workers, they have important implications for official unions, whose legitimacy often resided in their ability to control and dole out nonwage benefits and concessions during times when they were unable to secure adequate wage increases.

A third tripartite institution in which labor has played a role is the Federal and Local Labor Conciliation and Arbitration Boards, which are responsible for determining the legality of strikes and for making decisions on collective and individual workers' grievances. Recent unofficial discussion of a future Federal Labor Law reform has included the proposal that these tripartite boards be eliminated due to their inefficiency and lack of autonomy from the executive branch.[10] Union leaders have strongly opposed any changes to the Federal Labor Law at a time when they perceive themselves and the economy to be weak. Former Labor Congress president Mario Suárez declared that he would defend the boards because they were "the only tribunal created by the Revolution for the defense of the workers."[11]

These developments point to the overall weakening of official unions and to significant changes in the corporatist dimensions of state-labor relations: restrictions on labor's role in the party, the increasing irrelevance of tripartite institutions involving labor participation, and the removal of important worker subsides from union control. Another important trend in recent years concerns the increasingly hostile (to labor) role of the state in labor conflicts and the state's active efforts to weaken and, in some cases, destroy unions that resist restructuring. These actions reflect a more systematic turn away from the state's traditional (albeit not always practiced) role as mediator between employers and workers (and even as protector of workers) toward one of collaboration with employers against unions. Efforts to restructure industries and exact higher productivity from the work force have at times included violence or direct government intervention in the unions, and the results have frequently violated existing collective bargaining agreements.[12] Labor boards have ruled against strikes in the most visible cases to discourage their use, and government interventions in the strongest and most traditional unions have served to warn "dinosaur" labor politicians against resistance to sectoral reforms.[13]

State tolerance or use of repression against unions is not new; nor is state control over labor court decisions, strikes, and union registration. It is important and somewhat ironic to note, however, that these traditional methods of authoritarian control are being implemented at a time when the government has called for a more modern, democratic, and autonomous labor movement to meet the challenges of a more modern, globally competitive Mexico.

The declining significance of institutional spaces for labor participation has occurred alongside another trend that emerged during the Salinas administration. Key labor organizations have become more dependent on the government than before, and in particular more dependent on the executive. In a context of often brutal restructuring that has severely weakened or transformed many unions, the guarantee of survival and a political future for some important unions came to depend primarily on whether leaders could secure a strong personal relationship with Salinas, not on whether they could mobilize their members or develop alliances within the labor movement. With important sources of bargaining leverage having been removed from unions over the course of the past decade, the few inducements offered to labor under Salinas appeared to be in the form of personal guarantees of survival and recognition from the president in exchange for the willingness of unions to moderate their political positions and make difficult changes, often risking the dissent of rank-and-file members.[14] The result has been state-labor relations that are both more personalized and more centralized *within* the state, in the office of the executive.

Mexican inclusionary corporatism has traditionally consisted of arenas for the institutional participation of labor and not only for state regulation and control. These arenas of institutional participation provided union leaders with the opportunity to strengthen their relationship with their members and gave official unions some independent source of bargaining leverage vis-à-vis the government. Labor's ability to move about in the political arena of the party was especially important in this regard. Although recent changes point to the erosion of these institutional arenas, it is not yet clear whether or what new institutional means for expressing labor's interests will emerge. It appears that labor is being "disincorporated," in the sense of its removal from those arenas and institutions that defined Mexican corporatism and that consisted of the formal, institutionalized representation of labor's collective/sectoral interests in the party and in tripartite agencies. In this sense, we can say that state–labor relations have become increasingly "deinstitutionalized" during the Salinas *sexenio*. It is important to emphasize, however, that this trend toward disincorporation or deinstitutionalization has been accompanied by the maintenance of political, economic, legal, and bureaucratic controls over labor by the state, by the increased relative importance of labor ties to the executive, and by a stronger exercise of presidential authority or *presidencialismo* in areas that concern labor.

STRATEGIC COMPOSITION AND EVOLUTION OF THE MEXICAN LABOR MOVEMENT

To understand what future trajectory state-labor relations may take, it is important to look not only at what the state has done to labor but at the evolution of political and strategic currents within the labor movement. When speaking of state-labor relations, analysts generally refer to the state's relations with "official" unions, the dominant organizations within the labor movement. However, state-labor relations are often affected by the appearance and actions of new groups that emerge, either in the form of dissident movements within unions, independent unions, or organizations competing within the Labor Congress for a privileged relationship with the state.

The current strategic and political composition of the labor movement may be better understood by contrasting it with the composition of the labor movement during the 1970s.[15] Table 5.1 divides union strategic currents into two categories with four subgroups. The two categories are autonomous and revolutionary-nationalist; the two subgroups under the autonomous category are economistic and political and under the revolutionary-nationalist are radical and corporatist. (A third category, which I have called conciliators, emerged in the late 1980s.)[16]

Labor organizations in the corporatist category included the CTM; national industrial unions such as the oil, mining, and railroad workers' unions and electrical workers in the SUTERM (*Sindicato Unico de Trabajadores Electricistas de la República Mexicana*); and the teachers, a major national public sector union. These were the "official" unions that

Table 5.1
Strategic Currents in Mexican Trade Unionism 1970–1990

	Autonomous		Revolutionary-Nationalist		Conciliators*	
	Economistic[1]	Political[2]	Radical[3]	Corporatist	Neocorporatist	New
Sector	modern industry, parastatals & transnationals	current w/in official unions; coalitions	older industry, parastatals & state-owned	national confederations, national industrial unions	corporatist unions	restructed parastatals/newly privatized services
Unions	auto, locals of mining & metal-working, telephone, UOI	CNTE (dissident) teachers), ANOCP, FNDSCAC, FAT/RMALC[4]	Democratic Tendency, SUTIN, railroad union (MSF), SME, university unions	CTM, oil, railroad, & mining unions, SUTERM, teachers	oil workers' union, musicians' union, FSTSE, teachers[5]	SME, telephone, airlines (FESEBES)
Tactics/ demands	strikes, breakaways, actions against incumbents/labor process, union democracy	mass mobilizs., labor-popular coalitions/ autonomy from party/state, union democracy	labor-popular coalitions/state intervention in economy, nationalization	bargaining w/ state, political-electoral influence & representation	no mobilizs., cooperation w/ govt., internal reorg. w/govt. intervention	no mobilizs., bargaining w/ employers to retain role for union

(continued)

Table 5.1 (continued)

| | Autonomous | | Revolutionary-Nationalist | | Conciliators* | |
	Economistic[1]	Political[2]	Radical[3]	Corporatist	Neocorporatist	New
Internal relations	newly democratic	mass-democratic	democratic	oligarchic, repression of internal dissent	oligarchic, but less entrenched than before	from democratic to "managed" democracy
Political Identif.	apolitical, autonomy from parties & govt.	autonomous	PCM/MAP/PSUM, *lombardismo*	PRI	PRI	individual choice but leadership ties to executive
Alliances	varies	other: *coordinadoras* & independent unions	broad alliances incl. independent unions & "progressive" sector of party/state	Labor Congress	none, or FESEBES (teachers)	FESEBES & teachers' union

*Category emerges after 1989.

[1]Category exists through 1970s until early 1980s.

[2]Category emerges in 1979–80.

[3]Category exists in 1970s and until early 1980s.

[4]Appears in this category in 1990.

[5]In terms of strategic outlook, the teachers' union could also fit in the "new conciliators" category.

have traditionally had privileged access to the state and played an important role in the PRI.

The radical revolutionary-nationalists included some of the more important labor movements of the 1970s and early 1980s, such as the mid-1970s Democratic Tendency of the electrical workers, the dissident movement among railroad workers in the early 1970s (*Movimiento Sindical Ferrocarrilero,* MSF), the nuclear energy workers in the SUTIN (*Sindicato Unico de Trabajadores de la Industria Nuclear*), and the electrical workers of the SME (*Sindicato Mexicano de Electricistas*). They also included many of the university unions that began to organize at this time. These movements were characterized by their commitment to revolutionary-nationalism (their support for state intervention in the economy and national control of key industries) and union democracy. They believed in broad alliances with other labor and popular groups and with more "progressive" sectors of the party and state, and they were generally allied with the communist party or the MAP (*Movimiento de Acción Popular*) current, both of which became dominant poles in the PSUM (*Unified Socialist Party of Mexico*).[17]

In the autonomous broad category, we find many of the other insurgent movements of the 1970s: automobile unions, telephone workers after 1976, some locals in mining and steel, and the UOI (Independent Workers' Unit), an independent labor federation that several of the auto unions became affiliated with. These were the movements involved in breakaways from official confederations or in the democratization of their unions or locals. In general, they were militant, concerned with struggles over wages and working conditions, and apolitical in the sense that they were unaffiliated with party currents and supported union autonomy from parties and the state. Another current within this general category emerged in the late 1970s and early 1980s and was represented by the dissident teachers' movement, the CNTE (National Coordinating Committee of Education Workers), and by short-lived popular and labor coalitions such as the ANOCP (*Asamblea Nacional Obrero Campesino Popular*) and the FNDSCAC (*Frente Nacional de Defensa al Salario y Contra la Austeridad y la Carestía*), in which the CNTE played a key role.[18] This political-autonomous current also supported the position of union autonomy from political parties and the state, but it was more concerned with broader political issues such as democracy in society and the effects of austerity on the popular sector, concerns which drove it to seek alliances with other popular organizations.

What does this "map" of strategic currents in the labor movement look like in the mid-1990s? First, two entire categories have disappeared: the radical revolutionary-nationalists and the autonomous-economistic category. All of the movements in the first category disappeared in the 1970s or early 1980s, with the exception of the SME. Most of the movements in the second category suffered decisive setbacks during the industrial restruc-

turing of the 1980s; only the telephone workers' union was able to survive
by shifting strategies. The disappearance of these currents was due to either
repression (the case of the Democratic Tendency in 1976 and the SUTIN
in 1983) or the closing or restructuring of plants in which these unions
were active (autos, mining, and steel).

In 1990, the telephone workers' union and the SME, along with four
other unions, formed the Federation of Goods and Services Unions (FES-
EBES), which has come to represent a new strategic current in Mexican
labor. Composed in part by unions in restructured services (telephones,
airlines, electricity generation), the FESEBES has tried to increase union
participation in workplace changes and in determining standards of productivity and quality. The unions in this group have traditionally been considered more democratic than those in the corporatist category, and they
are not formally affiliated with any party, although both the SME and the
telephone workers' unions have moved closer to the PRI than they were
before. One characteristic of this group was their close relationship with
and dependence on President Salinas, who gave the FESEBES his backing
and often used it to pressure the CTM. Although it was not formally a
member of the FESEBES, the teachers' union under its new leadership (the
traditionalist labor leader was removed in 1989) also fit into this new category, which I have called the "new" conciliators.

Other changes in the earlier categories include the transfer of some corporatist unions into a new "neocorporatist" grouping under Salinas (another subgroup in the "conciliator" category). In this neocorporatist group
are those official unions that were reorganized and whose leaders were
removed through government intervention. Thus, the oil workers' union,
whose leader was removed in 1989, fits into this category, as did initially
the teachers' union. Other organizations that received this treatment include the musicians' union and the FSTSE (Federation of State Employees
Unions). The results have been most dramatic in the case of the oil workers.
Once probably the most powerful union in the country, the new union
leadership did nothing to resist the extensive reforms that caused thousands
of layoffs, eliminated benefits and seniority, and radically altered the collective bargaining agreement. Similarly, the new leadership of the teachers'
union was unable to forestall the long-awaited decentralization of the education system, a measure successfully resisted by the former labor boss on
the grounds that it threatened to weaken the central authority and bargaining power of the national teachers' union.

Hence, the evolution of strategic currents in Mexican unionism in the
last twenty years has moved in the general direction of less union autonomy
from the state and a narrowing of the range of political/ideological perspectives within the labor movement. The "conciliator" category includes
labor organizations that may have a more equivocal relationship with the
ruling party but, I would argue, less autonomy with respect to the state.

The militancy and democratization struggles once found in the "autono-mous-economistic" category are largely gone, as are the radical revolution-ary-nationalists, a political/ideological position which has lost viability in this era of privatization and free trade. The autonomous-political current, represented largely by the CNTE, was also weakened during the 1980s; the popular fronts the CNTE spearheaded were short lived, and the CNTE itself settled into a precarious accommodation with the new union leader-ship after 1989, diluting its earlier interlocutory role. Moreover, no current within the labor movement (with the possible exception of the Authentic Labor Front)[19] has yet brought out a proposal for the direction national economic and social policy should take and what labor's role should be in national development, along the lines of the Democratic Tendency's "Dec-laration of Guadalajara" in 1975 or the congressional labor deputies' "Manifesto to the Nation" in 1978. The promise of the FESEBES, the group that seemed most capable of articulating an alternative for the labor movement, appeared to be fading toward the end of Salinas' term, as se-rious differences among member unions began to emerge and the presiden-tial succession forced the government to seek a rapprochement with the CTM at the new federation's expense. In fact, the perception by other labor groups that the FESEBES lacked autonomy vis-à-vis the goverment weak-ened its chances of becoming an effective alternative interlocutor for the labor movement.

Paradoxically, during the Salinas *sexenio* the autonomous-political cur-rent began to gain new visibility. Although the CNTE no longer played the prominent role that it did in the early 1980s and in 1989, another labor organization became increasingly visible both within Mexico and in the international arena. The Authentic Labor Front (FAT) is a small, inde-pendent organization which was formed in 1960 and was active during the 1960s and early 1970s. In the 1980s, it virtually disappeared from public view. In 1989–1990, however, it reemerged as one of the most vocal critics of NAFTA. The FAT was one of the key organizations behind the Mexican Free Trade Action Network, a coalition of approximately fifty labor, pop-ular, and citizens' groups that was created to propose alternative forms of North American economic integration and to criticize the NAFTA process. The FAT and the Network actively sought out allies among unions and citizens' groups in Canada and the United States and recognized the im-portance of the latter as an arena in which Mexican politics was increas-ingly likely to be played out. The organization built a reputation outside Mexico and used this leverage to gain access to the Mexican government and U.S. politicians. Although the FAT represented a relatively small num-ber of workers (approximately 50,000), it was able to exert a dispropor-tionate influence on the free trade debate; indeed, on the Mexican side it helped to create a debate where there might not otherwise have been one.

The Network brought together roughly the same coalition of labor and popular groups and Mexican nongovernmental organizations (NGOs) that have provided the dissenting voice in Mexican society during the last twelve years. The crucial difference was the change in international context wrought by NAFTA, including the expansion of cross-border contacts as well as the Mexican government's sensitivity to outside pressure and criticism as it waited for the treaty's approval. The debate that preceded NAFTA changed the political context in ways that permitted the mobilization of citizens' organizations, the use of cross-border allies, and the manipulation of international pressure to bear on the government. If, now that NAFTA has been approved, outside scrutiny of Mexico's domestic policies continues to increase, this current of labor and popular organizations may remain an important voice in the future.

RESTRUCTURING, FREE TRADE, AND MODELS OF UNIONISM

The 1980s were a decade of extensive change in Mexican industry. Due to the economic crisis and trade liberalization, numerous industrial plants were either permanently closed or restructured and/or privatized, affecting hundreds of thousands of workers. With the further opening of the economy indicated by the approval of NAFTA, industries have come under even stronger pressure to become more competitive, and many small domestic firms have been forced to close. Pressures on companies to become more efficient have translated directly into workplace changes, and these have frequently met with worker resistance. In some key instances, employers have responded to strikes by closing plants and firing workers, only to rehire them later with fewer benefits and greater flexibility built into the collective bargaining agreement. Indeed, labor flexibility has more often been imposed on workers than negotiated with unions.

Freer trade in the North American region is likely to deepen this restructuring of Mexican industry and produce further changes that will have important implications for unions. Although the Mexican experience is marked by a great deal of heterogeneity in industrial relations across industries and even within the same industry, certain models or styles of unionism have often been associated with particular kinds of industries. Furthermore, increased levels of trade and investment are likely to produce important changes in the structure of industry in the coming years, which in turn may determine which types of unionism will predominate.

One of the fastest growing manufacturing sectors during the 1980s was the *maquiladora* (in-bond assembly plants) sector along Mexico's northern border. At one time, work in these plants was mostly unskilled, turnover was high, and women made up a large percentage of the work force. *Maquilas* now present a more varied picture and include highly automated and high-technology production as well. However, unionization in this area remains weak relative to other manufacturing sectors; many plants are non-unionized.[20] Where unions do exist, they are typically affiliated with one of the official labor confederations that compete in the zone. Many unions operate under "protection contracts," in which the union signs an agreement with employers to represent workers in the plant without their knowledge and, in many cases, before the work force is even hired.[21] In these instances, workers are often unaware that a union exists until they try to organize a union themselves and find that they cannot because Mexican law only recognizes one union in any given plant.

In spite of the wide variety in levels of automation and in skills required in the *maquiladoras,* industrial relations in these plants tend to be of the most flexible kind, with employers unilaterally dictating wages and working conditions and the union, where it exists, often collaborating with management in hiring and controlling the work force.[22] On-site services and improvements such as health clinics, subsidized cafeterias, and free transportation to and from home are often the result of competition among *maquiladora* managers for workers, not the result of collective bargaining. NAFTA is likely to expand the number of assembly plants, although not all of these may locate on the border and the wide variety in levels of skill, technology, and automation may continue to be reflected in the new plants. However, the model of unionism or workplace relations—that of maximum labor flexibility with little or no union presence—may also expand.

The auto industry is another sector which stands to benefit from the free trade agreement. Most major auto makers have established plants in Mexico (e.g., Ford, GM, Chrysler, Nissan, Volkswagen, and Mercedes-Benz), many in the north. The older terminal auto plants established in the center of the country during the 1950s and 1960s generally had strong, militant unions with relatively high wages, generous benefits, and strong collective bargaining agreements. In the 1980s, several of these plants were closed and new plants established in the north with a new, younger work force, lower wages than those obtained by workers in the center, fewer benefits, and greater flexibility built into the contract. Some of the older established unions had been affiliated with independent federations such as the UOI, or had participated in the democratization movement among auto unions in the early 1970s. Even some CTM-affiliated unions experienced some degree of internal union democracy and militantly pursued gains for their members.[23] All of the newer plants, however, signed contracts with the CTM, in spite of strong resistance in some cases on the part of unions that remained in the older plants. The new plants incorporated so-called Japanese production techniques (quality circles, work teams, just-in-time inventories), although the exact forms these have taken vary widely.

One clear distinction between the northern auto plants and the older ones that remain in the center is that the northern plants, like the *maquilas,* were "born flexible," while in some of the central plants (such as Ford-

Cuautitlán and Volkswagen) flexible production techniques and labor flexibility were imposed on the workers and met with strong union resistance. The imposition of labor flexibility in the older plants often demanded dramatic and repressive measures by management that have undermined union democracy and collective bargaining. In the newer plants, management and the labor confederations have also tried to curb worker militancy, although strikes for higher wages have occurred in several auto plants. The combination of relatively high rates of productivity, high levels of worker participation in production decisions, and low wages may generate an increasing number of struggles over wages and representation, especially efforts to establish union autonomy from parent confederations. Thus, in spite of the fact that production in most auto plants has now been "made flexible," the industry is likely to be the site of strong labor conflict over such issues in the future.

Industrial relations in most sectors is moving toward greater flexibility. The degree of flexibility, however, and the way in which it is arrived at, varies. As stated earlier, *maquilas* and new plants tend to be "born flexible," while flexibility in other sectors must be imposed or negotiated. The situation of the telephone workers' union at TELMEX provides an example of negotiated flexibility with relatively strong union participation; newer auto plants tend to be somewhat closer to the *maquiladora* example.[24] In spite of the recent emphasis on productivity, quality, the need for a skilled and trained work force, and calls for a "strong, autonomous and participatory unionism,"[25] it is likely that the more "bilateral" flexibility and participatory model of unionism, such as is found in the telephone industry, will remain relatively circumscribed, while the more traditional, "unilateral," paternalistic, and occasionally repressive model of unionism will continue to be widespread among *maquiladoras* and small and medium-sized domestic firms. The reason for this is that the bilateral model requires relatively strong, established unions located in plants that cannot easily be shut down or transferred and in industries or sectors that are not likely to disappear with economic changes. The "unilateral" model of unionism, moreover, typically ensures low wages, low levels of militancy, and effective control over workers and thus serves the interests of many employers. Under this scenario, organizations such as the CTM—often depicted as outmoded—may continue to play an important role and could even expand their presence. Some of the more modern sectors, such as autos, may eventually evolve into a more bilateral and negotiated model of workplace relations because of their relatively strong bargaining power via their location in a strategic industry. Meanwhile, the typically docile "company union" (*sindicatos blancos*) common in the industrial region of Monterrey will likely continue unchallenged, and nonunion workplaces may become more common with the increased presence, in response to NAFTA, of U.S. companies and subsidiaries.

Traditionally, a wide gulf has existed between actual workplace practices and Mexican labor legislation. One of the central issues facing labor and employers in the near future is reform of the Federal Labor Law, generally considered one of the most progressive in Latin America. The most elaborate proposals for reform have come from the Mexican Employers' Confederation, COPARMEX. The sense of these proposals is in the general direction of increasing employer flexibility vis-à-vis workers and reducing the prerogatives of unions (for instance, employers would like to eliminate seniority, reduce the number of paid holidays, and reduce their obligations with regard to housing, profit sharing, and severance pay).[26] The Salinas government postponed the revision of the labor law in the face of strong labor opposition, and possibly also to avoid potential conflicts prior to the consideration of NAFTA in the U.S. Congress. Yet it is likely that changes will come soon. Increasingly, the reform of the Federal Labor Law is being seen in Mexico as not only long overdue, but as constituting little more than an adaptation to a long-standing reality, at least with respect to flexibility in the workplace. Nonetheless, the final shape of the law will have important consequences for the future of unions. Although enforcement of the law has remained a problem, as has its ambiguity, it has provided workers and unions with an important reference point and baseline for their struggles and demands. The recognition of labor flexibility in law as well as in fact will permanently alter the terms of the relationship between workers, employers, and the state in ways that will further undermine the traditional bases of union power.

STATE-LABOR RELATIONS AND REGIME CHANGE

There is no doubt that state-labor relations are in an important period of transition. As yet unclear is the nature of the redefinition of labor's relationship with a regime that has effectively abandoned its alliance with labor. One conclusion from the preceding discussion is that, in the current economic and political transition, state-labor relations have come to be characterized more by domination than by hegemony. The administrative and political controls exercised by the state to shape union behavior have not changed much in recent decades. What has changed is the number and nature of the concessions extended to labor, labor's political influence, and its sense of its role in Mexican national development.

In the past, the state's incorporation of labor through the party was widely seen to be responsible for the regime's ability to rule hegemonically. In other countries, such as Brazil, relations between labor and the regime were unmediated by a political party and characterized more by state domination, ultimately resulting in greater political instability than in the Mexican case and leaving labor relatively free to form alternate political ties.[27] We have to ask, then, whether recent changes in state-labor relations and the declining significance of the party and of labor's role in it may serve to undermine further the hegemonic basis of the Mexican regime's rule. The reduction of labor's role in the party and other institutional arenas signals labor's political and ideological "delinking" from the regime. This, in turn, leaves a labor movement that, while presently limited in its political and strategic options, is potentially free to shift its commitment and support to another party, were a viable political alternative to emerge. By removing labor from the political arena and undermining its political and ideological ties to the party, elites also make possible labor's political autonomy.

The likelihood that labor will shift its political allegiance to another party is, of course, tied to the possibility that electoral democracy can be established. Under Salinas, the government appeared intent on making economic performance, not electoral democracy, the basis on which the regime's legitimacy was renewed. Regardless of Mexico's economic performance in the coming years, however, democracy is likely to remain a central issue in the 1990s. Paradoxically, efforts to bolster the PRI's electoral appeal in the aftermath of the 1988 presidential elections have increasingly focused attention on the fairness of the electoral process. The new international visibility that Mexican politics has acquired because of NAFTA may also increase foreign and domestic pressures for democratization. Although organized labor's general weakness and declining political influence may prevent it from playing a leading role in any push for greater democratization, labor may also be increasingly unable—and, given a viable alternative, unwilling—to defend an authoritarian regime.

The Mexican government has tried to curtail labor's political influence; its vision of a future regime does not contemplate a central role for organized labor. Nonetheless, the government has had to grapple with a strong contradiction in its efforts to restructure its relations with labor. Although it recognizes the official labor sector to be an obstacle to economic and political reforms, it has found that, in the short term at least, it must nonetheless appeal to organized labor to ensure stability during a critically sensitive period in Mexican politics—the presidential succession. The CTM's support of the social pact, NAFTA, the productivity accords, and the PRI's presidential candidate are still worth much in a context of political and economic insecurity and flux. In the midst of significant changes in the party, the electorate, and the economy, the government may have found that its traditional ally remains its most stable ally and cannot yet be dispensed with, even in its weakened condition. For its part, the CTM's strategy has traditionally reflected this assessment of labor's political importance to the regime—it accounts in part for what remains of labor's bargaining power and for its (ever more feeble) gestures of regime support in the face of an onslaught of antilabor policies. As long as the Mexican regime is committed to the continuity of authoritarianism, its relationship with labor will continue to reflect these inconsistencies and contradictions.

NOTES

1. See Ian Roxborough's criticism of the "standard account" of state-labor relations, in his *Unions and Politics in Mexico: The Case of the Mexican Automobile Industry* (London: Cambridge University Press, 1984), chapter 1.

2. This phrase, which aptly describes the history of state-labor relations, is taken from Ruth Berins Collier's *The Contradictory Alliance: State–Labor Relations and Regime Change in Mexico* (Berkeley: University of California, International and Area Studies, 1992).

3. On inclusionary corporatism, see chapter 3 in Alfred Stepan, *The State and Society: Peru in Comparative Perspective* (Princeton: Princeton University Press, 1978).

4. See, for example, Enrique de la Garza Toledo, "Organized Labor and the Restructuring of Corporatism in Mexico," forthcoming in *The Politics of Economic Restructuring in Mexico,* edited by María Lorena Cook, Kevin J. Middlebrook, and Juan Molinar Horcasitas (La Jolla: Center for U.S.–Mexican Studies, University of California, San Diego); and Neil Harvey, "The Difficult Transition: Neoliberalism and Neocorporatism," in *Mexico: Dilemmas of Transition,* edited by Neil Harvey (London: University of London, Institute of Latin American Studies, and British Academic Press, 1993).

5. Max Ortega, "Oposición Cetemista a la Neoliberalización del PRI," *La Jornada Laboral,* July 30, 1992.

6. Ibid. More significantly, Salinas succeeded in initiating structural reforms in the PRI, where previous administrations had failed due largely to the opposition of organized labor.

7. *La Jornada,* November 4, 1992.

8. Denise Dresser, "Embellishment, Empowerment, or Euthanasia of the PRI? Neoliberalism and Party Reform in Mexico," in Cook et al., *The Politics of Economic Restructuring.*

9. For details, see Bureau of International Labor Affairs, U.S. Department of Labor, *Foreign Labor Trends: Mexico 1991–1992* (Washington, D.C.: U.S. Government Printing Office, 1992), pp. 15–16.

10. Andrea Becerril, "Hay Ya Anteproyecto Para Reformar la LFT," *La Jornada,* November 24, 1993.

11. "Rechazo Obrero a Toda Reforma a la Ley Federal del Trabajo: Fidel Velázquez," *La Jornada,* November 25, 1993.

12. One dramatic recent case was the Volkswagen strike in July–August 1992, during which the entire 14,200-member work force was fired and most of them later rehired, after gutting the collective bargaining agreement. See Talli Nauman, "VW Gets Its Way; Workers Get Grief," *El Financiero International,* August 31, 1992; "Mending the People's Car," *The Economist,* August 22, 1992; and José Othón Quiroz and Luis Méndez, "El Conflicto de Volkswagen: Crónica de una Muerte Inesperada," *El Cotidiano,* No. 51 (November–December 1992), pp. 81–91. On changes in the oil workers' union after government intervention there, see Rafael Loyola Díaz and Liliana Martínez Pérez, "The Labor Costs of Restructuring in Petróleos Mexicanos, 1989–1993," paper presented at the International Workshop on Regional Integration and Industrial Relations in North America, New York

State School of Industrial and Labor Relations, Cornell University, October 1–2, 1993.

13. The Salinas government used the army to arrest Joaquín Hernández Galicia ("La Quina") and other leaders of the oil workers' union in January 1989. In April 1989, the leaders of the national teachers' union were asked to step down in the midst of a massive strike. On the teachers' strike and its immediate aftermath, see María Lorena Cook, "Organizing Dissent: The Politics of Opposition in the Mexican Teachers' Union," Ph.D. dissertation, Department of Political Science, University of California, Berkeley, 1990.

14. This has particularly been the case with the FESEBES (Federation of Goods and Services Unions), which obtained its legal registry two years after it first formed, and with the Sindicato Mexicano de Electricistas (SME), a member of the FESEBES. In the latter case, a union official told me that the union's survival depended on "*la relación con el presidente*" (a relationship with the President), which required that it refrain from criticizing the regime and from allying with other independent unions and popular organizations, as it once did. Personal interview, June 29, 1992. On rank-and-file discontent with the leadership of the SME over its relationship with the Salinas government, see Pilar Vázquez, "¿Qué Onda con el Apoyo al PRI del SME y los Telefonistas?" in *Crónica del Nuevo México,* edited by Equipo Pueblo (Mexico, D.F.: Equipo Pueblo, 1989); and Salvador Corro and Guillermo Correa, "Los Lideres Electricistas, Acusados de Corruptos; Sánchez, Protegido, Alcaine Espera Caer," *Proceso,* June 12, 1989.

15. For a more detailed discussion and description of the various movements and strategic currents listed here, see Maria Lorena Cook, "Restructuring and Democracy in Mexico: Twenty Years of Trade Union Strategies (1970–1990)," paper presented at the International Congress of the Latin American Studies Association, Washington, D.C., April 1991. Also see Enrique de la Garza Toledo, "Independent Trade Unionism in Mexico: Past Developments and Future Perspectives," in *Unions, Workers, and the State in Mexico,* edited by Kevin J. Middlebrook (Center for U.S.–Mexican Studies, University of California, San Diego, 1991).

16. This classification is not intended to be exhaustive; only the most important union projects and strategies are mentioned, and only the clearest exponents of those strategies. The characterization of strategies also represents an effort to create a composite picture of unions in each category and should not be taken as an accurate reflection of all of the practices of each union mentioned.

17. On the origins of the PSUM, see Barry Carr, "The PSUM: The Unification Process on the Mexican Left, 1981–1985," in *Mexican Politics in Transition,* edited by Judith Gentleman (Boulder, Colo.: Westview, 1987); on its subsequent development into the PMS and later the PRD, see Barry Carr, "The Left and Its Potential Role in Political Change," in *Mexico's Alternative Political Futures,* edited by Wayne A. Cornelius, Judith Gentleman, and Peter H. Smith (La Jolla: Center for U.S.–Mexican Studies, University of California, San Diego, 1989).

18. On these coalitions, see Ana María Prieto, "Mexico's National Coordinadoras in a Context of Economic Crisis," in *The Mexican Left, the Popular Movements, and the Politics of Austerity,* edited by Barry Carr and Ricardo Anzaldúa Montoya (La Jolla: Center for U.S.–Mexican Studies, University of California, San Diego, 1986).

19. The FAT, through the broader Mexican Free Trade Action Network, has

been active in proposing *continental* alternatives to NAFTA in alliance with Canadian and U.S. organizations.

20. See Jorge Carrillo V., "Evolution of the Maquiladora Industry: Labor Relations in a New Context," in Middlebrook, ed., *Unions, Workers, and the State;* Edward J. Williams, *The Unionization of the Maquiladora Industry: The Tamaulipan Case in National Context* (San Diego: Institute for Regional Studies of the Californias, San Diego State University, 1992); and Cirila Quintero Ramírez, "Tendencias Sindicales en la Frontera Norte de México," *El Cotidiano,* No. 56 (July 1993), pp. 41–46.

21. Enrique de la Garza Toledo, "Industrial Democracy, Total Quality and Mexico's Changing Labor Relations," paper presented at the International Workshop on Regional Integration and Industrial Relations in North America, New York State School of Industrial and Labor Relations, Cornell University, October 1–2, 1993, p. 19.

22. See Alfredo Hualde, "La Industria Maquiladora de Exportación: Relaciones Laborales y Tradado de Libre Comercio," in *Las Relaciones Laborales y el Tratado de Libre Comercio,* edited by Graciela Bensusán Areous (Mexico, D.F.: FLACSO, Fundación Friedrich Ebert, UAM-Xochimilco, 1992); and de la Garza Toledo, "Industrial Democracy," pp. 18–20.

23. See Ian Roxborough, *Unions and Politics in Mexico;* also Jorge Carrillo V., ed., *La Nueva Era de la Industria Automotriz en México* (Tijuana: El Colegio de la Frontera Norte, 1990).

24. For a discussion of different models of labor flexibility and union participation, see Enrique de la Garza Toledo, *Reestructuración Productiva y Respuesta Sindical en México* (Mexico, D.F.: Instituto de Investigaciones Económicas, Universidad Nacional Autónoma Metropolitana, 1993), pp. 170–82.

25. Luis Donaldo Colosio, cited in Luis Méndez and José Othón Quiroz, "En Busca de Una Nueva Legislación Laboral," *El Cotidiano,* No. 50 (September–October 1992), p. 68.

26. See Graciela Bensusán Areous, "The Mexican Model for Labor Regulation and Competitive Strategies," paper presented at the International Workshop on Regional Integration and Industrial Relations in North America, Cornell University, October 1–2, 1993; and Méndez and Othón Quiroz, *En Busca,* pp. 62–72.

27. See Ruth Berins Collier, "Popular Sector Incorporation and Political Supremacy: Regime Evolution in Brazil and Mexico," in *Brazil and Mexico: Patterns in Late Development,* edited by Sylvia Ann Hewlet and Richard S. Weinert (Philadelphia: Institute for the Study of Human Issues, 1982), pp. 57–109.

6

Mexico's New Environmental Policy: An Assessment

Stephen P. Mumme

In June 1991, Carlos Salinas de Gortari accepted the first "Green Nobel Prize" from United Earth, dramatizing his administration's high-profile environmental initiatives. For an instant, world attention was drawn to Mexico's policy achievements rather than its failures in that arena. Even so, Mexico remains a metaphor for the environmental costs and policy dilemmas confronting rapidly industrializing countries in Latin America and the less industrialized world.

Since the mid-1980s, Mexico's environmental predicament has captured global attention as a leading example of the perils of rapid industrialization as well as the possibilities for policy reform. North American economic integration has also drawn attention to the Mexican case. Since 1990, North American environmentalists have focused on Mexico's environmental problems to an unprecedented degree, using the country as a test case for linking environmental regulation to trade. The resulting debate has raised serious questions concerning Mexico's regulatory capacity and its ability to cope with the environmental effects of rapid economic growth.

This chapter reviews the Salinas administration's contribution to Mexican environmental policy reform and evaluates its promise for improved environmental management in the near term. Such an appraisal is important in view of the projected environmental pressures arising from the surge of economic growth expected to follow in the wake of NAFTA. Environmentalists in Mexico and the United States are skeptical of Mexico's capacity to manage this new growth without accelerating the pace of ecological decline associated with Mexican industrialization over the past forty years. An appreciation of the strengths and weaknesses of Salinas' much-heralded policies is thus essential in anticipating the problems and possibilities that will shape Mexican environmental management into the next century.

ENVIRONMENT AND DEVELOPMENT IN MEXICO

If, in the 1980s, *crisis* was the most common adjective used to describe the Mexican economy, much the same could be said of its environmental predicament. Forty years of rapid industrialization, which thrust Mexico into a leading position among the Latin American economies, had taken a devastating toll on its natural resources and the health of its citizens. Its ecological crisis was seen in the net reduction of its forests at a rate exceeding a million acres annually (second only to Brazil in Latin America), the reduction of the Lacandon forest zone by 70 percent since 1950, and the disappearance of thousands of species of fauna and flora in a nation with one of the world's highest levels of biodiversity. The threat from environmental pollution was evident in the severe degradation of its two most celebrated natural lakes, Lake Chapala and Lake Patzcuaro; the contamination of over 60 percent of its rivers; severe oil spills along the Mexican Gulf coast, damaging national fisheries and aquatic life; inadequate sanitation and sewerage facilities in more than half of Mexico's municipalities, both large and small; the virtual absence of hazardous waste disposal facilities throughout the nation; and, perhaps most notoriously, the venomous air pollution blanketing the world's largest urban area, Mexico City, and one of the highest rates of pulmonary disease on the globe. It is hardly an exaggeration to say that the deterioration of Mexico's environment has been comprehensive and on a magnitude with few rivals in Latin America and the industrializing world.[1]

Mexico's environmental predicament, similar to that of other advanced industrializing countries in Latin America, is rooted in an economic development strategy favoring rapid industrialization over rural development.[2] That policy, pursued by successive administrations since World War II, has imposed a high price on society. Neglect of rural areas has displaced rural populations and fed migration to urban centers, which grew at rates in excess of 6 percent annually from 1960 to the present. That same neglect contributed to the erosion of soils and the depletion of forests, and it contributed to declining productivity and wealth in the rural subsistence economy. Nor have the ecological consequences of Mexico's development policy spared the urban masses presumed to benefit from those policies. The urban underclass, already burdened with inadequate employment, poor working conditions, inadequate health and welfare services, and other problems afflicting Latin America's slum dwellers, is even more vulnerable to the health risks associated with pollution.[3]

Over the past two decades, such conditions have gradually become recognized as policy problems. Although still reluctant to acknowledge the environmental costs of Mexico's development strategy, political leaders have become sensitive to international environmental concerns as well as the political risks of neglecting popular demands for environmental improvement.

Mexico's Environmental Policy Framework: Structure and Development

It is important to situate Mexico's experience with environmental policy in the context of its unique one-party-dominant presidentialist political system. By any standard, the Mexican political system is one of the world's most enduring single-party-dominant systems. The PRI has monopolized the electoral and policy arenas for over sixty years, conferring enormous policy authority on Mexican executives during their six-year nonrenewable term of office and structuring interest representation hierarchically, along quasi-corporatist lines. Although policy factions inside and outside government are frequently consulted by officials, and some—the entrepreneurial sector, in particular—may exercise considerable influence on government decisions, most policy development resembles the "inside access" pattern of elite-dominated policy formation described by comparative policy theorists.[4]

Mexican environmental policy has been forged in this context. Mexico's first environmental law, adopted in 1971 by the administration of Luis Echeverría, was generated almost entirely in-house at the upper levels of Mexico's Ministry of Health and foreign policy bureaucracy, with little input or participation by organized interest groups or private citizens. Implementing legislation on air and water pollution remained largely unenforced throughout Echeverría's six-year term as president.

José López-Portillo, Echeverría's successor, did little to remedy this state of affairs. Toward the end of his *sexenio,* rising public concern with air quality in Mexico City, articulated by several professional organizations and the media, provoked a modest federal expenditure on an air quality monitoring network and incipient attention to the study of vehicular emissions in the Federal District. Some measure of the relative unimportance of environmental concerns, however, is seen in the utter omission of any reference to environmental preservation in national planning documents and presidential speeches.

The de la Madrid administration, inheriting the economic crisis associated with the collapse of the peso in 1982, was, rather ironically under the circumstances, the first to put environmental reform on the presidential agenda. Amending the earlier law, de la Madrid created a new cabinet-level ministry, the secretariat of urban development and ecology (SEDUE). His administration simultaneously undertook a year-long campaign to promote environmental concern, encouraged the formation of environmental interest groups, and elevated public and official attention to environmental values, incorporating "ecology" as a policy category in government planning documents. Unfortunately, the severe climate of austerity restricted environmental policy to symbolic and educational activities. The emergence of a number of small but vocal environmental advocacy groups during these years did, however, significantly increase media attention as well as criticism of the government's lack of responsiveness to environmental matters.

Criticism of SEDUE's ineffectiveness and the failure of Mexican environmental law led to another round of legal reform in March 1988. This law, currently in force, improved on the past in several respects. At the administrative level, it enhanced SEDUE's authority, investing it with greater coordinating power, strengthening its hand in enforcement of environmental regulations, and clarifying the authority of related agencies with environmental mandates. It specifies, for example, a division of labor between SEDUE and the Federal District government in enforcing environmental regulations within the Federal District. The law further requires environmental impact assessments for all federal public works; potentially polluting industries; mining, tourist development, and sanitary facilities; and new construction in the private sector. The law mandates the elaboration of specific technical standards (*normas técnicas*) for monitoring compliance with environmental laws. It further provides for the development of state and local laws to reinforce and supplement federal regulations, and it amplifies the space for civic participation in environmental enforcement.

Adopted less than five months before the 1988 presidential election, the new law supplied the statutory foundation for policy reform under the Salinas administration. Indeed, it was crafted by several of Salinas' closest advisers, including Manuel Camacho Solís, head of SEDUE in 1987–1988 under the de la Madrid administration. In a series of well-publicized speeches during his campaign, Salinas signaled his awareness of the salience of environmental concern in Mexican politics and pledged to restructure policy upon assuming office. He stressed the need to improve substantive regulation, prioritize environmental remediation, and move beyond the rhetoric in programs.

After assuming office, the Salinas administration took a number of highly visible policy actions, earning plaudits from foreign observers while generating controversy among environmentalists at home and abroad. Salinas' reforms were set in the context of his initiative to secure NAFTA with the United States and Canada, debate on which focused attention on Mexico's environmental policy performance. It is important, then, to review his initiatives before turning to an evaluation of their long-term significance.

THE SALINAS ADMINISTRATION'S POLICY REFORMS

Salinas' environmental reforms may be reviewed in two steps: (1) by describing policy innovations undertaken during his tenure, and (2) by evaluating their impact on basic patterns of policy formulation and implementation. The discussion that follows emphasizes both formal policy change and government accountability. In practice, of course, these are interdependent variables. Thus, some discussion of the politics associated with Salinas' reforms will be incorporated in the analysis of their policy impacts.

Policy Reforms

Salinas' reforms include legal and administrative measures aimed at specifying and enhancing compliance with regulatory norms, the elaboration and prioritization of several high-profile programs, and a number of specific, although essentially ad hoc, enforcement actions aimed at affirming the government's environmental commitment. Chronologically, these reforms proceeded in two phases: the first, from 1988 to 1990, the second, from 1990 through 1994.

The first phase, from December 1, 1988, through the end of December 1990, is defined by an emphasis on administrative continuity and cautious policy development within the context of budgetary austerity. Departing from past administrations, Salinas chose to retain several of de la Madrid's most senior advisers for environmental affairs. In particular, Manuel Camacho Solís became head of the Federal District (Department of the Federal District, or DDF) with policy authority for the development and implementation of the government's highest priority environmental policy program—the new vehicular emissions/air quality program for Mexico City. At SEDUE, where Patricio Chirinos, a close Salinas associate, took the helm, Sergio Reyes Luján and René Altamirano were retained in command of the Environmental Department. Given the norm of wholesale personnel turnover from one administration to the next in Mexico's patronage-driven bureaucracy, these changes signaled an emphasis on continuity and professional competence in environmental administration.

The Salinas administration, with the 1988 environmental law in pocket, also elected to arm the law with the technical standards and regulatory norms essential to effective implementation. Until 1988, only two such regulatory laws (*reglamentos*) were in force in the area of environmental law, one setting standards and specifying compliance in air quality, the other dealing with water quality. Since the summer of 1988, a battery of new *reglamentos* and *normas técnicas* have been issued by SEDUE, DDF, and other agencies pertaining to environmental enforcement. SEDUE officials indicated a desire to produce several hundred such ordinances by the end of the Salinas *sexenio*. By any measure, this is an impressive improvement on the past and provides the necessary statutory foundation for administrative action.

In terms of new programs, the Salinas government was selective, prioritizing goals and avoiding blanket rhetorical commitments typical of previous administrations. Its top priority was regulating Mexico City's pernicious air quality, a program initiated by Salinas' predecessor. Among the new Federal District programs, announced just two weeks after Salinas took office, were a new municipal traffic system, mandatory vehicular emissions testing, the introduction of lead-free gasoline (labeled *magna sin*), and a water conservation program.[5] Salinas also gave increased attention to the Federal District's greenspace, sanitation and garbage collection, and reforestation needs, building on de la Madrid's precedent.

As for implementation, the government assigned responsibility for industrial pollution within the Federal District to SEDUE, while DDF received the mandate to address other problems—vehicular pollution, garbage, greenbelts, and so forth. In October 1990, seeking even greater interagency coordination, these programs were incorporated into a single initiative, the *Programa Integral Contra la Contaminación Atmosférica de la Zona Metropolitana de la Ciudad de México*, capitalized at $4.6 billion and financed heavily by multilateral bank, U.S., and Japanese credits.[6]

Beyond the Federal District, the administration initiated several programs under the rubric of a new national *Programa Nacional de Conservación Ecológica y Protección al Ambiente*, set out formally in January 1989.[7] Prominent among these were new laws regulating water quality and forest management; a focus on certain high-visibility protected zones, such as the Lacandon forest; and a basinwide clean-up of Mexico's notoriously polluted Lerma-Chapala and Coatzacoalcos River basins—both of which serve and receive the effluent from numerous urban-industrialized regions. Among a variety of high-visibility actions undertaken in 1988–1990 were a three-month ban on the extraction of forest products in the Lacandon,[8] the mobilization of the Mexican army in a national campaign of reforestation,[9] a ban on development of new water systems in the Federal District,[10] a moratorium on the harvest of marine turtles,[11] the announcement of a multiagency campaign to improve water quality in the Lerma-Chapala river basin,[12] and the initiation of negotiations for Mexican entry into the Convention on International Trade in Endangered Species of Wild Fauna and Flora (CITES).

The second phase of Salinas' reforms responded to NAFTA-related controversies and extended roughly from January 1991 to December 1994. The NAFTA initiative was Salinas' topmost economic priority, the engine to which all other domestic programs were harnessed. Announcement of the Free Trade initiative in October 1990, and its expansion to include Canada in January 1991, provoked a storm of controversy among North American environmentalists. The furor was unanticipated by senior policy officials in both the United States and Mexico, who were accustomed to considering trade issues independently of social issues.

The environmentalists' critique of NAFTA was wide ranging, focusing on the trade distortions and health risks associated with lower environmental standards in Mexico and the potentially adverse impact of accelerated economic growth in the U.S.–Mexican border region and Mexico.[13] Environmental groups initially attempted to block renewal of the Bush administration's "Fast Track" authority from Congress to negotiate NAFTA unfettered by congressional interference. The June 1, 1991, deadline for Fast Track renewal added urgency to the issue.

Seeking to deflect criticism, the Salinas administration undertook a number of extraordinary policy measures in the spring of 1991. First, it accelerated the pace of industrial inspections and plant closures associated with the violation of air quality standards. The bulk of the regulatory effort centered on Mexico City, although the new intensity of enforcement was evident in other major industrial cities, from Puebla and Guadalajara to Monterrey. The capstone of this drive was closure of the aging March 18 petroleum refinery, one of the largest sources of industrial air pollution in Mexico City. The refinery had already been designated for closure, although not on such an accelerated timetable.

Second, in collaboration with the Bush administration, the Salinas team expedited work on an October 1990 agreement to generate a comprehensive plan addressing environmental problems along the U.S.–Mexican border. In May 1991, the two governments agreed to produce a draft Integrated Border Environmental Plan (IBEP) for discussion and refinement with the participation of the binational border community and accelerate its implementation.

Third, Salinas announced a decision to enter the CITES agreement, and he agreed to shelve temporarily Mexico's protest, submitted to GATT, of a U.S. embargo of Mexican tuna.[14] This embargo sanctioned Mexico for using driftnets in the harvest of migratory fish—mainly tuna—a violation of the U.S. Marine Mammal Protection Act.

Fourth, Salinas announced a significant augmentation of SEDUE's corps of environmental inspectors in the interior and along the U.S.–Mexican border, increasing the pool from 85 nationwide to 250.[15] This buildup of SEDUE's inspection capacity was accompanied by the announcement of additional *normas técnicas,* regulatory laws, and new state-level environmental statutes.

Finally, in January and February, the Salinas administration dispatched a series of high-profile officials to Washington, D.C., to promote Mexico's environmental image and highlight its accomplishments. Manuel Camacho Solís, Patricio Chirinos, and Sergio Reyes Luján, among others, pitched Mexico's environmental efforts to the U.S. Congress, American trade associations, and environmental organizations. In April, Salinas made a whirlwind coast-to-coast visit to the United States to promote NAFTA and lobby for Fast Track approval. These measures effectively blunted criticism of Mexico's environmental performance, and in May Congress approved the Fast Track initiative in separate House and Senate floor votes.

Fast Track approval, however, marked the beginning of intensive U.S.

debate on NAFTA. The Salinas administration, while resisting environmentalists' proposals for incorporating "green language" in the draft, remained keenly aware of the issue's salience for the U.S. public. The debate was joined at two levels: (1) over the particulars of the draft IBEP; and (2) on the draft NAFTA text and parallel, but related, initiatives for improving trilateral environmental management in the context of a NAFTA accord. These controversies kept Mexico's performance under close international scrutiny.

By far the most significant initiative undertaken by the Salinas administration, however, was its decision to abolish SEDUE and merge its functions into a new superministry, the secretariat of social development (SEDESOL). Created on June 4, 1992, the new ministry combined the administrative functions of urban affairs, ecology, the National Solidarity Program (PRONASOL), and the Institute for Indigenous Affairs (INI) into a single organization, under the leadership of Donaldo Colosio, a close associate of Salinas and former head of the PRONASOL. The environmental functions of SEDUE were divided and allocated to two semiautonomous agencies, the National Institute for Ecology (INE) and the Federal Attorney General for Environmental Protection (PFMA), whose directors were to be appointed by the president.[16] In this new arrangement, INE was, among other functions, given full responsibility for the development of environmental regulations and technical norms and the development of compliance agreements with state agencies and the private sector; primary responsibility for administering protected areas not specifically mandated to other federal agencies; and primary responsibility for the monitoring of environmental conditions nationwide. PFMA, in turn, was to concentrate exclusively on enforcement; monitoring the compliance of potential polluters; receiving and investigating complaints of noncompliance with environmental regulations; prosecuting violators with the assistance of the Mexican Justice Department; and functioning as the general mechanism for public participation in policy formulation and implementation.

This administrative change, which caught Mexico's environmental community by surprise, was justified as a requirement for improving administrative coordination, strengthening enforcement, integrating and strengthening policy oversight of social programs, and infusing new resources into the social-environmental sector.[17] It has not yet occasioned a change in the basic environmental law—the 1988 statute—although it will inevitably require at least nominal changes in the basic code.

These, in brief, were Salinas' principal initiatives. In terms of the sheer number and variety of programs, financial commitments, and official rhetoric, he clearly surpassed his predecessors. Unquestionably, the intensity and timing of these measures were stimulated by the NAFTA initiative. But to gain a better perspective on their significance, one must take a more analytical and focused look at them.

THE POLICY SIGNIFICANCE OF SALINAS' REFORMS: IMPLEMENTATION AND FORMULATION

In considering the policy significance of these reforms, I will depart from conventional practice and deal with policy implementation before policy formulation. This is because Salinas' principal contributions lie in the former.

Policy Implementation

Policy implementation in Mexico's presidentialist system is highly centralized, dominated by the federal bureaus that control the lion's share of the national budget, and subject to presidential oversight. In addition, it exhibits certain features which prevail across substantive policy areas: First, much Mexican policy is liable to the charge of "formalism"—that is, statutory gestures tend to substitute for material commitments. Second, implementation is disjunctive and discontinuous, if only due to the disruptive effects of the sexenial cycle and the extraordinary shuffling of personnel from one administration to the next. Third, implementation has been historically dominated by *políticos* rather than *técnicos,* and even here many of the latter lack specialized skills necessary to the effective conduct of their office due to the political demands of a patronage-dominant system. Fourth, implementation tends to be ad hoc and nonprogrammatic, despite the use of quasi-indicative planning instruments, due to economic scarcity, lack of budgetary accountability (including the relative ease of shifting funds across institutional accounts), and the semiautonomous character of many cabinet-level agencies short of direct presidential intervention and oversight.

Each of these characteristics is evident in the development of environmental policy, one of the youngest substantive fields on the Mexican policy agenda. Until recently, environmental policy was highly formalistic in nature, with little presidential commitment to the area. This changed under de la Madrid, who, as seen earlier, incorporated environmental issues into planning documents and elevated ecology to a cabinet-level concern. Even so, economic conditions precluded serious investment in this area.

On the second point, it is certainly true that environmental policy has been plagued by sexenialism. In the 1982 sexenial transition, for example, almost none of the qualified specialists in the old subsecretariat of environmental improvement were invited into the newly formed ecology division of SEDUE, squandering precious talent and institutional experience.

As for the politicization of implementation, environmental policy is such a new domain that politicization was virtually unavoidable during the de la Madrid administration due to the lack of technically trained environmental engineers, biologists, and policy specialists. Even when such specialists were available, political goals routinely overrode technical expertise in implementation decisions.

Finally, the ad hoc, nonprogrammatic nature of policy implementation is evident in the fractionalization of agency mandates; lack of prioritization of environmental objectives; limited authority of central coordinating institutions, such as SEDUE and the National Ecology Commission under de la Madrid; lack of follow-through in announced projects; reliance on short-term public campaigns; general paucity of fiscal resources allocated to enforcement; and uncertainty concerning government fiscal commitments.

In addition, environmental policy in the 1980s was characterized by a voluntarist, less punitive approach to regulatory compliance. Government officials were outspoken in rejecting punitive means of achieving compliance with regulations, preferring instead a strategy of *concertación* (state–society cooperation), which is in practice a blend of exhortation and negotiation with actual or potential polluters.[18] Until late in the de la Madrid administration, few polluters were seriously penalized. The government preferred signing *convenios* (written pledges of compliance) with parastate and private sector enterprises to achieve its regulatory aims. Frequently honored in the breach, such agreements exemplified the preference for persuasion over coercion.

Taken as a package, Salinas' regulatory reforms through 1992 did not fundamentally alter the character of environmental policy implementation. In several respects, however, they did significantly improve on the past. Among his most important contributions was the specification of standards for giving force to the 1988 environmental law—the battery of regulations and *normas técnicas* mentioned earlier. Although the articulation of such standards by no means ensures better enforcement, it is necessary, even if not sufficient, to that purpose. It has thus laid the foundation for a less formalist policy.

Muddying the waters, however, Salinas also vigorously pursued the development of state laws and municipal ordinances. To date, over twenty states have adopted ecology laws, and it is likely that nearly all of Mexico's thirty-one states will have such legislation by the time Salinas leaves office.[19] These measures, undertaken as part of a general policy of administrative decentralization and devolution of powers to the states,[20] are highly problematical. Although state powers are to be consistent with the 1988 environmental law, state ecology laws create ambiguities and potential conflicts with federal legislation which may hamper enforcement. The more fundamental problem here, however, is that states have little real autonomy from central authorities and relatively little independent budgetary authority. Thus far, environmental policy decentralization has not been accompanied by similarly enhanced budget authority for the implementation of state functions.[21] Under these circumstances, state laws may have actually impeded enforcement of federal law by blurring lines of administrative responsibility.[22]

As seen earlier, Salinas also took a swipe at sexenialism, retaining several senior environmental administrators from the de la Madrid administration and placing a greater emphasis on the development of a skilled corps of *técnicos* in the environmental ministry. Early indicators suggest that he also retained the bulk of SEDUE's environmental staff in merging its functions into the new superministry, SEDESOL.[23] Moreover, he increased SEDUE's staff and committed his administration to increasing the numbers of technically qualified personnel in environmental administration.[24] Here, however, the results remain to be seen. The staff buildup since 1991 has been in haphazard fashion, and it is by no means clear that these new personnel have adequate technical training for their assignments. Training takes considerable lead time, and these efforts have yet to mature.[25] Thus, they have not yet had a significant impact on SEDUE's (now INE's) technical capacities. Moreover, the only real test of the extent to which sexenialist tendencies have diminished will be the decisions of Salinas' successor in the administrative transition of 1994–1996.

It is certainly true that Salinas brought a more programmatic approach to environmental policy, although much remained ad hoc and responsive to immediate political pressures. The administration limited its formal commitments in the environmental field, focusing investment on a few high-priority programs. Here, Mexico City air quality, the IBEP, forest preservation, and river basin clean-up stood out. Salinas also energetically pursued foreign assistance and credits to fund key programs: $4.6 billion earmarked for Mexico City pollution abatement comes largely from a package of external credits, and Mexico's commitment of $466 million to implementing the IBEP is also substantially predicated on external credits. He likewise solicited technical assistance from the United States and a number of European countries.

Many of Salinas' actions, however, including some of the most dramatic measures, resembled the ad hoc approach of the past. Plant inspections and sanctions, for example, increased sharply in 1991 in response to the scrutiny directed at Mexico in the NAFTA debate context,[26] but appeared to subside in 1992.[27] Few permanent closures resulted; the celebrated demobilization of the March 18 refinery remained an anomaly.[28]

Salinas likewise maintained and intensified the voluntarist approach to achieving compliance with environmental standards. Numerous *convenios* continued to be signed with commercial and industrial establishments. These agreements committed the signees to meet government pollution standards, specified timetables for installation of antipollution equipment, and stipulated other implementation objectives. To a considerable extent, economic austerity and the threat of unemployment associated with fines and closures accounted for this nonpunitive approach. Budgetary resources have increased since 1989, and Salinas pledged 1 percent of the national budget to environmental protection. Even so, in 1992, national environmental protection received only $66.8 million.[29]

Along these same lines, the Salinas administration has been enamored of privatization and market-based policy instruments. Although few market-based incentives are presently in place, user fees, pollution permits, licenses, and other means of privatizing the costs and burdens of environmental preservation are being considered. New laws on agrarian reform and fisheries already adopted, and forestry and water management legislation under consideration, all incorporate such approaches to resource management.[30] Revision of sanitation policy for the Federal District and other municipalities is also underway, which would privatize some sanitation functions (e.g., municipal garbage collection) and assess user fees. Such policies, while incipient, are consistent with Salinas' strategy of economic liberalization.

The recent restructuring of environmental administration associated with the creation of SEDESOL may indeed strengthen the programmatic character and further rationalize the administration of policy. Much remains to be seen, however. In principle, consolidating SEDUE's powers in two functionally distinct, semiautonomous agencies has merit, but the administrative change in itself is not sufficient to overcome the structural deficiencies in policy.

Two general problems with the new change are immediately apparent. First, environmental functions have been folded into a new and very powerful agency while reducing the formal visibility associated with these functions. Ecology is no longer a cabinet-level function. This may diminish its political visibility. Within SEDESOL, ecology functions have received greater fiscal support but still account for only 1.8 percent of the agency's programmed expenditures for 1993.[31] If budgets are at least a partial indicator of the influence and priority attached to subsidiary parts of an organization, ecology is presently a minor priority within the total structure of SEDESOL's commitments. To compensate, the heads of the ecology bureaus must have some degree of access to the president; otherwise they are likely to be subordinated to the much superior functional imperatives of social and urban development.

Second, although the reform is intended to rationalize the regulatory arena and enhance enforcement, the division of labor between the two agencies, as well as other interagency divisions of labor, remains ambiguous. This is magnified by a lack of articulation in the 1988 environmental law. For example, DDF presumably retains its jurisdiction over ecology programs in the Federal District (established in the 1988 law), but this remains unclear in the constitutive authority for the new environmental agencies. Implementation of agency functions is contingent on shared authority with various other cabinet departments, yet the division of labor has still not been specified. In the case of enforcement, for instance, it is unclear what the division of labor will be between the attorney general for environmental protection and the justice department.[32] The division of some functions also appears contradictory and confusing. At present, the Ecology Institute is the mandated authority for the administration of certain protected areas; yet the PFMA is responsible for investigating potential infractions of the environmental law. As another example, the Ecology Institute is given the authority for developing laws, norms, and standards regulating environmental protection, but PFMA is the agency responsible for channeling citizen participation in environmental policy formulation and implementation. Obviously, these potential contradictions and ambiguities must be reconciled if the two agencies are to synchronize their functions properly and exercise meaningful policy authority in this sphere.[33]

Finally, as I have noted elsewhere, Salinas' environmental policy reforms have been very political. Because this aspect of his approach directly affects the process of policy formulation, it is useful to treat it in that context.

Policy Formulation

Policy formulation in Mexican politics tends to center on the "output" side of the political process, which is another way of saying that representative assemblies play a diminished role in deciding policy. Analysts tend to describe Mexico as a state corporatist system in which interest articulation and aggregation are limited and directed in ways which shore up state authority. In this context, autonomous interest groups and private citizens must frequently resort to a petitionary or bargaining approach with government officials in order to place issues on the agenda. Much policy is simply initiated inside the government, relegating interest groups to a reactive and supportive role.

Environmental policy fits this pattern. Environmentalist organizations have few effective channels through which to pursue their policy goals. Representation is dominated by the government party, of which many citizens remain suspicious and cynical. Although some activists have elected to work within the PRI, most eschew formal association. Opposition parties remain a minority and at best offer the potential for playing a symbolic role in interest articulation through party fora, platforms, and occasional speeches in Congress. On the administrative side, environmentalists are often consulted. But since government officials enjoy considerable discretion regarding who they invite, environmental leaders have been cautious in participating in government-dominated consultative fora.

Nor does the justice system currently offer an alternative avenue for interest group influence. Environmental groups have virtually ignored use of the courts to enforce the law. To date, not a single case has been successfully brought by an environmental advocacy organization against the government or the private sector. This is due to several factors: First, Mexico's system of judge-made law lends itself to considerable delay, greatly increasing the costs of legal action by plaintiffs. Injunctive relief can be readily obtained by defendants in the form of the *amparo,* a broad-based stay of action against government enforcement that may be granted by courts at the request of the regulatee. Second, until recently, a lack of technical norms and regulatory standards made it virtually impossible to sustain a claim. Indeed, the law was far more serviceable to defend the interests of polluters than to punish them. This was particularly true when the government was the potential defendant, given the broad discretion of federal justices in the absence of precise standards. Finally, environmental groups are small and resource poor. They generally lack the money to pursue legal action.

Such structural barriers can be seen in the pattern of policy initiative over the past two decades. Since 1971, environmental initiatives have come mainly from within government bureaus, with modest support from a limited number of professional organizations and educators. In 1980, very few environmental organizations existed, and those that did were elite-dominated conservationist groups, such as Ducks Unlimited, the Nature Conservancy, and PRONATURA, with limited functional interests. These groups were content to work behind the scenes to influence senior officials and loathe to insert themselves into a broader and more politically volatile debate on sustainable development and pollution prevention. In 1982–1983, de la Madrid broke from this pattern by encouraging the formation of broad-based, pollution-oriented advocacy groups, providing them with at least a limited voice in policy making. Under the 1983 policy regime associated with the creation of SEDUE, environmental organizations were legitimized and ceded new channels for petition and protest at SEDUE and DDF. Groups such as the new Mexican Ecology Movement, the *Grupo de Cien* (Group of One Hundred), the *Alianza Ecologista* (Ecologists' Alliance), and the *Partido Verde* (Green Party) were invited to participate in government fora, given access to the government-dominated press, and provided with formal channels for expressing their concerns.

The result was a significant increase in reportage of environmental issues and an embarrassing tide of criticism directed at government policy failures. Environmentalists contributed to the stream of criticism associated with human-made and natural disasters in Mexico City in 1984 and 1985, delayed the initiation of Mexico's first and only nuclear reactor at Laguna Verde, and contributed to SEDUE's image as the most troubled cabinet ministry during the de la Madrid administration. By 1988, public sensitivity to environmental problems in Mexico City was reflected in polls which identified urban pollution as either the second or third highest priority, exceeded only by economic recovery and personal security.[34] In sum, by 1988 the environment had become a significant political preoccupation in the nation's largest urban areas, tarnishing the government's image.

Salinas thus assumed office at a time of unprecedented environmental concern. Instead of offering environmental groups a greater institutional voice in policy making, however, the administration opted to restrict their influence. Shortly after taking office, it made overtures to leaders of a number of fledgling groups, several of whom joined the government. This was a classic co-optative device designed to legitimize the government's actions. Various organizations also complained of intimidation and selective exclusion from policy fora, and there is circumstantial evidence that this indeed occurred.

Advocacy groups are also concerned about government responsiveness to citizen complaints under the 1988 environmental law. That statute provides that ordinary citizens may file a formal protest with SEDUE (now *Procuraduría Federal de Protección al Ambiente* [PFPA], SEDESOL's Ecology Institute), which then has fifteen days to inform the violator and thirty days to investigate and produce a formal response indicating the action to be taken. Advocates have been reluctant to employ the procedure, complaining of delays and failure to apply all but symbolic sanction to violators.[35]

The government's decision to change the structure of environmental administration—the 1992 SEDESOL initiative—temporarily worsened the situation by clouding the procedures for environmental groups.[36] For months, the two new agencies were not fully functional, and environmental organizations were in the dark concerning the implementation of the new procedures for soliciting public input.

Under these circumstances, the preferred action-generating strategy of advocacy groups has been to dramatize problems in the media or other public settings, hoping to embarrass the government into taking administrative action. The media have thus become a favorite mechanism for communication. Foreign media are preferred to domestic, since foreign media (particularly U.S. media, due to the economic linkages between the two countries) shape the opinions of elite decision makers with influence on Mexican economic affairs. Such media-oriented strategies have been particularly evident since the NAFTA debate intensified.

In sum, the Salinas administration's contributions to improved policy formulation have been limited to (1) the development of regulatory norms and standards which may shore up the long-term potential for using the courts to enforce environmental standards, and (2) the assignment to SEDESOL of responsibility for implementing the law. These changes are of minimal importance and are not likely to have much effect on policy formation during what is left of the Salinas *sexenio*. Indeed, the evidence thus far suggests a heightened politicization of interest articulation and a greater government effort to manage the expression and influence of environmental interests within the policy system.

THE FUTURE OF MEXICAN ENVIRONMENTAL POLICY:
INTO THE NEXT ADMINISTRATION

Salinas' most enduring contributions to Mexican environmental management lie in the specification of norms and standards prerequisite to effective application of the environmental law. Although such changes are not sufficient, they are necessary, and in themselves they constitute an important and positive step toward building regulatory capacity.

Beyond this, however, the administration's legacy is less certain. It is very likely that several of the president's highest priority remediation projects will survive into the next administration, particularly those aimed at regulating air quality in Mexico City. This is due to the political salience of the issue in the metropolitan area and the substantial investments already committed to controlling vehicular emissions, providing cleaner energy sources for industry and auto transport, managing solid waste disposal, and related programs. Salinas has banked considerable prestige on such programs and funded them with foreign credits, thus building an external accountability function into their implementation. It will be very difficult for his successor to back away from them.

In other areas, however, the picture is clouded. Salinas' long-term strategy for environmental improvement is linked directly to economic assumptions that correlate economic growth with environmental improvement. Apart from the fact that the validity of such assumptions is contested, his reforms have not directly tackled the structural impediments in environmental administration that restrict their functioning. Mexico's capacity for enforcement remains limited. Budgetary commitments to environmental regulatory agencies through 1992, while larger than in the past, remained scanty and cannot be expected to improve automatically under SEDESOL or into the next *sexenio*. Mexico suffers a severe deficit of technically trained personnel, which will take the better part of a decade to reverse even with a serious commitment to educating environmental professionals. Even then, it is by no means clear that the sexenialism of the past will not extract a toll on regulatory capacity as the requirements of political patronage prevail over expertise.

Apart from the specification of enforcement standards, which is valuable and likely to endure, Salinas' administrative reforms and regulatory approach have not fundamentally challenged the institutional character of environmental management. True, he focused on a narrower set of priorities and adopted a more programmatic approach. And he significantly increased the number of enforcement actions in response to free trade concerns. But with the exception of a few high-visibility projects, it remains uncertain whether these priorities will prevail in the next administration. The new administrative arrangement at SEDESOL retains a number of the jurisdictional and functional ambiguities that dogged SEDUE in the past, and it has not sufficiently jelled for us to be confident of its potential for overcoming those weaknesses. In the absence of enhanced fiscal authority, the decentralization of authority to Mexican states has further blurred jurisdictional lines and functional responsibilities. Moreover, policy under Salinas remained essentially noncoercive, with a preference for privatization and market-based instruments. All this should temper expectations of more strenuous law enforcement in the future.

Furthermore, many of the structural deficiencies associated with public administration are in the political sphere. Salinas has accomplished least with respect to amplifying public participation and influence on policy formation and implementation. Few channels yet exist for citizens and advocacy groups to participate in the crafting of environmental policy or to hold officials accountable for environmental management. Mexican environmentalists are faced with the difficult choice of joining the government and cooperating directly with policy makers, or pursuing a more critical role as watchdogs, resorting to government-managed and foreign media and opposition parties to insert their concerns on the policy agenda. Of these, ironically, the foreign media appears to be the most successful avenue to influence. The problems faced by environmental organizations are, of course, the same problems confronting other interest groups and civic activists in the political system and raise the broader, more systemic, issues associated with democratization and the transition from one-party political dominance.

Conclusion of the 1993 environmental protocol to NAFTA offers some additional opportunities for Mexican environmentalists. The accord establishes a new trinational Commission on Environmental Cooperation (CEC) to oversee national enforcement of domestic environmental laws consistent with NAFTA expectations. It provides a mechanism that gives environmental groups standing to denounce lax enforcement and bring violations to trinational dispute resolution panels for judgment and specification of remedies. The CEC may apply sanctions to national parties when a persistent pattern of violation is found. Additional agreements provide for a new Border Finance Facility associated with the North American Development Bank (NADBANK) initiative and a Border Environment Cooperation Commission (BECC) to oversee NADBANK's proposals and projects for environmental improvement along the U.S.–Mexico border. These institutions create new channels for exerting public pressure and compelling member governments to improve enforcement. Their full impact, however, will not be felt until the next Mexican administration takes office.

In sum, Salinas made an essential and lasting contribution to environmental management through regulatory law and undertook several high-profile projects in vital areas. But he is now passing the torch to another administration. Environmental protection is a secondary priority to economic recovery and likely to remain so. Much depends on the extent to which President Zedillo is committed to his predecessor's reforms. Given the new regulatory context of free trade, even more will depend on emerging alliances between environmentalists in the trilateral (United States, Mexico, Canada) milieu and their ability to hold governments accountable in that regulatory arena. What is certain is that Mexico's capacity for managing its environmental predicament is about to be seriously tested and that many of the enduring structural weaknesses associated with past management remain in place.

EDITOR'S POSTSCRIPT

Recently, the economic crisis that struck in December 1994 has called into question Mexico's ability to fulfill its commitments under NAFTA's environmental protocol. The federal budget has been cut nearly 10 percent, with the result that several important border clean-up projects have been postponed. Of special concern to U.S. environmentalists are sewage-treatment projects in Tijuana and Ciudad Juárez. In both cities, hundreds of U.S.–owned assembly plants have contributed to severe environmental degradation and a population explosion fueled by Mexican migrants searching for jobs. Tijuana's aging sewage system is so overwhelmed that raw sewage sometimes flows into the streets and is carried to the Pacific Ocean where it makes its way northward to San Diego's beaches.

Similar concerns have been raised in El Paso and Ciudad Juárez, where construction on sewage-treatment projects had just begun. In addition, a project to install gas-fired furnaces in brick-making factories along the border has been put on hold, which means that those plants will continue to burn old tires as fuel—a major source of pollution. According to the Arizona-based Border Ecology Project, moreover, the North American Development Bank, established under NAFTA to fund the border clean-up, may be in trouble because Mexico cannot provide its share of the institution's funding.

Whether financing (presumably foreign) can be found to enable Mexico to keep its environmental commitments remains to be seen. Meanwhile, however, environmental groups are pushing ahead with the first test of the mechanisms established under the NAFTA side agreement. A petition has been filed with the North American Commission on Environmental Cooperation, asking for an investigation of one of the largest bird kills ever reported on the continent—the death of some 40,000 waterfowl that landed on the Silva Reservoir in central Mexico in December 1994. The Mexican government's investigation had concluded that unidentified persons had dumped pesticides into the reservoir; the environmentalists suspect that local industries have been discharging chemicals into rivers feeding it.

—Donald E. Schulz

NOTES

1. For statistics cited, see "77% de las Cuencas en Nivel Crítico," *Excélsior,* July 10, 1990; *The News,* July 9, 1989; Angus Wright, *The Death of Ramón Gonzáles* (Austin: University of Texas Press, 1990), p. 95; *Excélsior,* July 7, 1988; World Resources Institute, *World Resources 1990–91* (Oxford: Oxford University Press, 1990), p. 193.

2. Roger Hansen, *The Politics of Mexican Development* (Baltimore, Md.: The Johns Hopkins University Press, 1971); Raymond Vernon, *The Dilemma of Mexico's Development* (Cambridge, Mass.: Harvard University Press, 1963).

3. See David Barkin, *Distorted Development* (Boulder, Colo.: Westview Press, 1990), pp. 41–56.

4. Stephen P. Mumme, C. Richard Bath, and Valerie J. Assetto, "Political Development and Environmental Policy in Mexico," *Latin American Research Review,* Vol. 23 (1988), pp. 9–11.

5. "Anuncia Camacho Solís Acciones Concretas Ante la Contaminación," *Excélsior,* December 15, 1988.

6. U.S. Department of State, "Update of Mexico's Anti-Pollution and Conservation Efforts: Staying the Course," unclassified memorandum to U.S. Department of State, American Embassy, Mexico City, April 9, 1991; Embassy of Mexico, *Mexico Environmental Issues: Fact Sheets* (Washington, D.C.: Office for Press and Public Affairs, Embassy of Mexico, Washington, D.C., 1992), p. 29.

7. "Rompamos el Ciclo que Hace del Progreso Vía de Infición: CSG," *Excélsior,* January 20, 1989.

8. "Decreto CSG Veda Forestal de 3 Meses en la Lacandonia," *Excélsior,* January 14, 1989.

9. "Solicitan que el Ejército Resguarde los Recursos Forestales del Estado de México," *Uno Más Uno,* March 11, 1989; "Ni Simulación Ni Oferta Irresponsable: CSG," *Excélsior,* June 6, 1989.

10. "No Se Harán Mas Obras Para Traer Agua: DDF," *Uno Más Uno,* April 4, 1989.

11. "Salinas Orders End to Mexico's Turtle Industry," *Arizona Daily Star,* May 30, 1990; "México Reguarda el Ambiente Marino," *Excélsior,* May 30, 1990.

12. "La Naturaleza Se Rebela," *Uno Más Uno,* April 28, 1991; "Las Cuencas Mas Contaminadas: Lerma-Santiago, Panuco, Balsas y San Juan," *Excélsior,* May 7, 1991.

13. See Stephen P. Mumme, "Environmentalists, NAFTA, and North American Environmental Management," *Journal of Environment and Development,* Vol. 1 (1993).

14. "No Presionara México al GATT por el Embargo Atunero: Von Bertrab," *Excélsior,* November 5, 1991.

15. Sergio Reyes Luján. Remarks by SEDUE's undersecretary for ecology at a congressional briefing on the North American Free Trade Agreement, Cannon House Office Building, Washington, D.C., March 21, 1991; U.S. General Accounting Office (GAO), *U.S.–Mexico Trade: Assessment of Mexico's Environmental Controls for New Companies,* GAO/GGD-92-113, August 1992, p. 18.

16. Secretaría de Desarrollo Social, Reglamento Interior, *Diario Oficial* (Mexico City: Gobierno de México, June 4, 1992), pp. 70–71.

17. See comments by Luis Donaldo Colosio in "Firmeza Ante Retos Ecológicos: Colosio," *Uno Más Uno,* May 30, 1992.

18. See Salinas' views on this point in "No Solucionara la Infición con Medidas Coercitivas," *Excélsior,* February 18, 1988.

19. See SEDUE, *Gaceta Ecológica,* Vols. 1–5 (1988–1992). GAO interviews with SEDUE officials in 1992 revealed that SEDUE planned to eventually decentralize all environmental protection responsibilities to the states. If so, this plan is not likely to be implemented under Salinas in view of the SEDESOL initiative, which still assumes a centralized approach to policy management. See GAO, *U.S.–Mexico Trade,* p. 21.

20. For comment, see Edward M. Ranger, Jr., "Environmental Regulation and Enforcement in Mexico," in *Maquiladora Industry Annual Review* (Mexico, D.F.: Seguros de México, S.A., 1991).

21. According to the GAO, the World Bank's recent loan package of $80 million for Mexican environmental protection includes a project to fund the new state-level environmental agencies. See GAO, *U.S.–Mexico Trade,* p. 21.

22. A more optimistic appraisal is provided by David Wilk, "The Complementarity between Environmental Plans, Regulations and Lessons from Ciudad Juárez, Chihuahua," paper presented at the XVII International Congress of the Latin American Studies Association, September 24–27, 1992. Wilk agrees that local government regulatory capacity is limited, but he argues that environmental mobilization at the local level can supplement federal regulatory capacity in policy implementation.

23. Sergio Reyes Luján, for example, directs SEDESOL's Ecology Institute.

24. SEDUE's staff increased from 647 to 1,134 personnel between 1989 and 1992. See GAO, *U.S.–Mexico Trade,* p. 18.

25. To compensate for the lack of qualified inspectors, the administration has recruited university personnel to help with inspections in the Mexico City metropolitan area. See "Especialistas de UAM Hará la Verificación Industrial," *Uno Más Uno,* August 8, 1992.

26. GAO, *U.S.–Mexico Trade,* p. 19.

27. Evidence here, admittedly, is sketchy, based on actions reported in the Mexican press. A report issued by SEDESOL for the first six months of 1992 indicated a total of 843 inspections for the period, leading to 183 partial closures and 10 complete closures (not permanent). If this is accurate, the rate of inspections and closures in 1992 is roughly half that of 1991. See "Cierre Partial de 183 Empresas y Total de Otras Diez por parte de la SEDESOL," *Uno Más Uno,* August 1, 1992.

28. Only two permanent closures were reported in the GAO investigation of Mexican environmental enforcement between 1989 and 1992. See GAO, *U.S.–Mexico Trade,* p. 19. On the other hand, INE Director Sergio Reyes Luján is on record claiming 100 permanent closures since Salinas assumed office. He also claims a total of 8,756 inspections, with 909 partial closures and 418 total closures, both for temporary intervals. Reyes Luján asserts that one of four inspections results in closure of some form. See "Inspecciona el Instituto de Ecología Casi 9 Mil Industrias," *La Jornada,* September 20, 1992. See also Embassy of Mexico, *Mexico Environmental Issues: Fact Sheets,* 1992, p. 18.

29. GAO, *U.S.–Mexico Trade,* p. 20; *Excélsior,* November 2, 1992.

30. "Se Promulga la Ley Agraria y la Ley Orgánica de los Tribunales Agrarios," *Comercio Exterior,* March 1992, p. 230; "Nueva Ley de Pesca," ibid., July 1992, p. 622; E. Miguel Szekely, M. Angelica Sánchez P., and Francisco Abardia M., "The Free Trade Agreement and Constitutional Agrarian Reform, Possible Implications for Forest Exploitation," paper presented at the Latin American Studies Association, September 24–27, 1992.

31. "Presupuesto de Egresos de la Federación para 1993," *El Mercado de Valores,* No. 23 (December 1, 1992), p. 23.

32. In a recent case in which a number of toxic waste handlers operating along Mexico's border with the United States were shut down by SEDESOL, the Mexican Justice Department (Procuraduría General de la República—PGR) reported it had not received a formal complaint from SEDESOL against the offending companies. The PGR spokesman indicated that PFMA enjoyed a separate mandate, but that PGR and PFMA were to keep each other mutually informed of actions in the environmental sphere. What this means in practice is unclear. See "La PGR No Ha Cedibido Denuncia Sobre Contrabando de Desechos Tóxicos en BC," *Uno Más Uno,* August 8, 1992.

33. *Diario Oficial,* June 4, 1992.

34. "Contaminación y Crimen Lo Que Mas Preocupa," *Excélsior,* January 24, 1988. For a more recent assessment, see Luis López Hermosa, "La Contaminación No Conoce Fronteras," *Uno Más Uno,* June 1, 1992 (*Este País,* p. 10).

35. Author's interviews. The new PFPA director, Sergio Onate Laborde, admitted that his agency as yet lacked the means to investigate citizen complaints. See "Grupos No Gubermentales Han Hecho de Ecología su Causa," *Uno Más Uno,* July 7, 1992.

36. Advocacy groups' criticisms of the reform are found in Raúl Monge, "Se Impugnan 29 Grupos Ecologistas que un Simple Comisión Sustituya a la SEDUE," *Proceso,* No. 810 (May 11, 1992), p. 18.

7

Free Trade with Mexico and U.S. National Security

Al I. Pérez

On August 12, 1992, President George Bush announced that the United States, Canada, and Mexico had completed negotiation of NAFTA. The pact provided for the phasing out of trade barriers and the elimination of investment restrictions in North America, leading to the creation of a huge open market with over 350 million people and over $6 trillion in annual output. This chapter places the agreement (which was ratified by the U.S. Congress in November 1993 after a prolonged and fierce political struggle) within the context of U.S. national security and explores some of the economic and political implications for the United States and Mexico.

THE ECONOMIC CHALLENGE

The end of the cold war and the breakup of the U.S.S.R. are having a profound impact on U.S. foreign and security policy. For nearly five decades, U.S. policies were anchored in containing and countering the Soviet threat. Our concern for the threat shaped our political, economic, and foreign aid policies around the world. U.S. leaders and the average American generally understood the threat and developed an enduring consensus on how to deal with it. With its economic power and military strength, the United States became the undisputed leader of the free world.

The United States retains its economic and military might, but the bipolarity that defined world politics for so long has ended. We are seeking a new vision to help define our new role in the world. There is no national consensus on how we should approach the next century, but there is an emerging view that the United States must learn to live in a multipolar world, where international decision making is more equally shared with other industrial giants, and that continued U.S. global power will depend largely on our ability to respond to fierce economic competition from a Germany-led European Community (EC) and a Japan-led Asia. As stated by Lester Thurow, "In 1992 there is one military superpower, the United States standing alone, and three economic superpowers, the United States, Japan, and Europe, centered on Germany, jousting for economic supremacy. Without a pause, the contest has shifted from being a military contest to being an economic contest."[1]

Trade and National Security

Post–World War II U.S. foreign policies consistently supported economic growth based on free markets and expanding trade. This was driven by, among other things, our national security interests. Free trade would generate prosperity. Prosperous nations would be immunized against the communist virus and would join the United States in confronting the Soviet threat. Our policies succeeded brilliantly. Democratic European and Asian countries developed world-class, export-oriented economies and became key allies against a slumping Soviet empire.

While our allies became export powers, our own export performance lagged. U.S. economic growth was instead driven by internal demand. Although in 1991 the United States regained its status as the world's largest exporter, and since 1989 it has had record overseas sales, these impressive gains only accounted for about 10 percent of U.S. GDP. Comparable figures for Japan and Germany are 13.5 percent and 28 percent. In the words of one analyst, the United States became the "world's biggest export underachiever."[2] One explanation is that our economy is so huge that U.S. businesses can prosper by satisfying domestic demand. Another is that foreign governments have been much more willing to support export promotion than has our own government.

A New Direction

U.S. policy makers are keenly aware of the economic and trade challenge the United States faces from the European Community and Asia. The 1991 White House National Security Strategy explicitly noted that "while the U.S. trade deficit has continued to decline, trade imbalances with Japan and many other countries remain substantial. Reducing these imbalances remains a priority."[3] In announcing NAFTA in August 1992, the White House declared that "the president's trade strategy, which is a key part of his overall economic growth plan, is designed to create new markets for American products and provide new opportunities for American companies and workers."[4] While campaigning for the presidency, Bill Clinton repeatedly stressed the need to be more competitive in the global economy, and since assuming office his administration has continued to push that theme. In the words of Vice-President Al Gore: "Our belief in sustainable development through economic reform, trade and democracy is rooted in the inescapable realities of the modern world. We have arrived at a consensus about the right way to grow. Lower trade barriers. Ensure that industries are competitive. Compete in international markets."[5] In short, "America's economic health is the country's number one national security interest."[6]

There was also another cloud on the horizon driving U.S. trade concerns. As C. Fred Bergsten observed, "If the Uruguay Round of the General Agreement on Tariffs and Trade (GATT) were to fail, . . . European–U.S. trade conflict would join existing Japanese–U.S. tensions to threaten a two-front war that would elevate the economic priority even more rapidly."[7]

Looking for Trading Partners

As the global economic and trade competition stiffened, the United States took steps to safeguard export markets in the hemisphere. In the late 1970s, the Carter administration proposed the idea of a North American energy accord. In the early 1980s, President Reagan surfaced the concept of North American free trade cooperation. In both instances, the Mexicans demurred.

In 1989, the United States and Canada entered into a free trade agreement, which the Bush administration viewed as the first step toward an eventual North American regional trade bloc. In June 1990, President Bush announced the Enterprise for the Americas Initiative (EAI), stating that "to expand trade, I propose that we begin the process of creating a hemisphere-wide free trade zone."[8] Even before this announcement, however, the administration had been reviewing a request for free trade talks from an unlikely source—Mexico.

In February 1990, Mexican President Carlos Salinas arrived in Switzerland for a gathering of the World Economic Forum. Salinas was to headline the meeting and deliver a major address extolling Mexico's dramatic economic reforms—privatization of state industries, reduced inflation and government spending, GATT membership, the Brady Plan on debt, and more liberal treatment of foreign investment. He hoped to lure European investors to help finance his new economic program. Salinas returned home empty handed. European investment capital, he was told, was already earmarked to help Eastern Europe's development.

Shortly thereafter, Salinas called President Bush and in a stunning political act requested free trade talks. The administration moved quickly and on June 10, 1990, Presidents Bush and Salinas met in Washington, D.C., and issued a communiqué stating their conviction that "free trade between Mexico and the United States can be a powerful engine for economic development, creating new jobs and opening new markets."[9] Soon after, Mexican and U.S. trade experts (joined later by their Canadian counterparts) launched marathon negotiation sessions, which concluded with the August 1992 announcement that the United States, Mexico, and Canada had concluded a North American free trade accord.

President Bush's reaction to Salinas' appeal was consistent with the support he had expressed for free trade with Mexico during the 1988 presidential campaign and his hemispheric free trade goal set forth in the EAI. For Salinas this was a dramatic departure from generations of Mexican foreign policy. Mexico had traditionally taken pains to project independence from U.S. foreign policies and was wary of perceived U.S. hegemonic designs, and a strong leftist component within the government and the PRI had long been hostile toward the United States. As a leading Mexican opposition leader noted, "Mexico's entire history has been an effort to increase our economic and political independence from the superpower we have as our neighbor. Now we are turning our back on everything."[10]

IMPLICATIONS FOR THE UNITED STATES

The Bush administration argued that a free trade pact would promote the national interest by increasing U.S. exports and creating jobs, ending (eventually) Mexican illegal immigration, and promoting stability in Mexico. The Clinton administration concurred, although it called for supplementary agreements to increase protection for U.S. workers and strengthen environmental requirements. It would be useful, then, to approach an assessment of NAFTA's implications for the United States by looking at these three elements. Since Mexican stability is of major concern for U.S. foreign and domestic policy, the main thrust of this analysis will focus on how NAFTA could impact on Mexico's political structure.

Table 7.1 sets forth some key economic and social indicators for the United States and Mexico. The most striking thing is the enormous difference in GDP between the two countries. In 1992, U.S. economic output was roughly eighteen times that of Mexico. The latter's per capita GDP was between one-sixth and one-seventh that of the United States—$3,600 compared to $23,400.[11] Equally striking was the gap in hourly wages; a Mexican worker earned about 12 percent of his or her U.S. counterpart. (The comparison will be even more one-sided today, in the wake of the recent devaluation of the peso.) Clearly, Mexico offers a vast pool of cheap labor. Moreover, its young population (about half will be under age twenty-five by the year 2000) and comparatively high population growth rate suggest that Mexico will have surplus labor for years to come.

Recent trade figures indicate that the two economies are increasingly connected. Due to lower trade barriers and other economic changes implemented under the de la Madrid and Salinas governments, Mexico has become a major U.S. trade partner. Between 1986 and 1992, U.S. exports to

Table 7.1
Social/Economic Indicators

	United States	Mexico
Population (1994)	260,713,585	92,202,199
Population Growth Rate (1994)	0.99	1.94
Percent Population Under 25 Year (est. for year 2000)	33.9	48.7
Gross Domestic Product (1992)	$5,951 Billion	$328 Billion
Hourly Wages (1992)	$14.83	$1.85

Sources: "Mexico" and "United States," *The World Fact Book, 1993* (Washington, D.C.: Central Intelligence Agency, 1993), pp. 256, 405; ibid., *1994*, pp. 260, 416.

Mexico soared from $12 billion to $44 billion, making it our third largest customer after Canada and Japan.[12] Mexico overtook Japan as the second largest market for our manufactured exports. In 1991, the United States recorded a substantial trade surplus with Mexico for the first time in ten years. Despite sharp differences in wealth between Mexico and EC countries, on a per capita basis Mexicans bought more from the United States annually than did EC citizens—$295 compared to $263.[13] About seventy cents of each Mexican dollar was spent on U.S. goods and services. As of 1992, U.S. jobs supported by exports to Mexico had doubled to 600,000.[14]

Significantly, only about 5 percent of U.S. exports went to Mexico, and about 5 percent of U.S. imports came from Mexico. In contrast, about 70 percent of Mexico's exports were sent to the United States, and about the same percent of its imports came from the United States.[15] [Editors' note: All figures are prior to the beginning of NAFTA's implementation in 1994.] Essentially, the Mexican economy had become almost totally dependent on U.S. economic activity.

Economic Impact of Free Trade

What will NAFTA do? Economists agree that it will stimulate trade with Mexico by reducing, and in many cases eliminating, tariff barriers on U.S. exports. Approximately 65 percent of U.S. industrial and agricultural exports to Mexico will be eligible for duty-free treatment either immediately or within the first five years. Studies done by the U.S. International Trade Commission found that NAFTA would increase U.S. real GDP up to 0.5 percent a year once fully implemented. The Institute for International Economics has projected that by 1995, over 1 million jobs will be supported by U.S. exports to Mexico under NAFTA.[16]

NAFTA will also increase U.S. global competitiveness by providing U.S. industry with a source of low-wage labor. Japan's ability to remain globally competitive is a result of its ability to find low-wage factory labor in other Asian countries. NAFTA will provide low-wage Mexican labor to help lower production costs, permitting U.S. corporations to retain a competitive edge and, in some instances, making it possible for them to survive. As M. Delal Baer noted, "NAFTA will enhance U.S. competitiveness vis-à-vis Europe and Asia through the economies of scale and specialization in production with continental rationalization."[17]

NAFTA opponents, especially U.S. organized labor, claim that free trade with Mexico will cost U.S. jobs because businesses will move to Mexico, and workers in certain sectors will be unable to compete with Mexico's cheaper labor.[18] Most analysts agree. They caution, however, that the cost of labor is only one factor businesses consider in deciding whether to relocate outside the United States. Other factors include the level of education of the work force, the capacity of the infrastructure, the distance from consumers, and long-term political stability. Compared to the United States, Mexico is disadvantaged in all these areas. In an interview with *Fortune* magazine, President Salinas made the telling point that in macroeconomic terms the "United States is losing jobs not to countries with lower wages but ones with higher wages."[19] What he was pointing out is that large chunks of U.S. industries and corresponding jobs (i.e., automotive and consumer electronics) have been lost not to underdeveloped countries in Africa and Latin America, but to the more advanced countries such as Japan and Germany.

Moreover, while organized labor has tended to emphasize the number of U.S. workers that will be displaced by cheaper Mexican labor, it has failed to give proper weight to the number of U.S. jobs that will be created by NAFTA. More importantly, the jobs gained will be high-wage/high-skill, while those lost will be low-wage/low-skill.

A point usually lost in the political dialogue is that even without NAFTA, U.S. corporations have been shifting production abroad (in the case of Mexico, through the *maquiladora* program wherein U.S.–produced parts are sent to Mexican border areas for assembly and then reexported to the United States as finished goods). This trend will continue with or without NAFTA, but NAFTA could be an inducement for U.S. corporations to move to nearby Mexico rather than to countries much farther away. In addition, NAFTA would place the *maquiladora* program within the larger free trade context and help open Mexican markets for our exports. As Rudiger Dornbusch has concluded, "The choice is not so much to keep jobs here or lose them to Mexico. Competition from low-wage countries has been going on for more than a decade. The right question to ask about free trade with Mexico is whether we should prefer that, when jobs do go abroad, they go south rather than Asia."[20]

Finally, NAFTA's economic and trade impact has to be placed in a macroeconomic context. It is doubtful that most Americans really grasp the enormity of the U.S. GDP and what it takes to affect U.S. economic activity significantly. The Mexican economy is too small and insufficiently diversified to substantially influence the U.S. economy. For example, in a study using five computational general equilibrium models to identify the short-term gains and costs of NAFTA, the authors concluded that, while increasing living standards in all three countries, an agreement with Mexico would *not* be a big source of overall gains (or losses) in the United States and Canada.[21]

Immigration

Closely linked to U.S.–Mexican economic activity is the flow of undocumented Mexican workers to the United States. Immigration from Mexico has a long and troubled history. Although NAFTA does not provide for the free flow of labor in North America, it was inevitable that the illegal immigration issue would be linked to the trade pact. U.S. trade representative Carla Hills, for example, told the Senate Finance Committee that NAFTA would improve living conditions in Mexico and ease "pressures for illegal immigration. The lesson is clear. If opportunities do not go to the people, people will go to the opportunities."[22]

For Mexico, movement of its workers to the United States has long been a socioeconomic and political escape valve. These workers also have been an important source of revenue for the families they leave behind. In the United States, however, they have been a source of controversy—they are breaking the law, they are too many, and they are over here. Yet with few exceptions, nobody really sees Mexican workers as a threat to the national security. Political and social sentiment for or against them generally reflects U.S. economic conditions and, to some degree, racial stereotypes. The fact that the United States is getting able-bodied workers for which it paid nothing to rear and nurture is lost in the debate. Will NAFTA really have a major impact on this immigration? The answer is no in the short term, and not clear in the long term. As Table 7.1 shows, almost half of the Mexican population is under age twenty-five, and over 50 percent will be between fifteen and forty-nine years of age by the year 2000.[23] The Mexican birthrate is almost twice that of the United States. The U.S. population is graying, and some economists postulate that we will need to import workers in the years ahead. The wage differential is large and likely to remain so for years to come. Finally, the U.S. economy will continue to generate jobs in low-skill service industries that low-skill immigrants can perform.

The wage differential is crucial since, even if Mexicans find work in their country, the more energetic and talented will continue to migrate to the

United States as long as this disparity exists. Looking at the long-term effect of free trade on Mexico's wage levels, Peter Morici concluded that

although free trade will eventually narrow the wage gap between semiskilled workers in the United States and Mexico, it will not do so quickly. . . . In 1990, the wage of the average Mexican industrial worker was 12 per cent of his U.S. counterpart. Even if Mexican real wage growth were to exceed performance by an unlikely 7 percentage points a year, Mexican wages would only reach 25 per cent of U.S. levels after 10 years and 50 percent in about 20 years.[24]

As a way of comparison, Morici went on to note that due to a large labor surplus, wage levels in four East Asian newly industrializing countries increased only from 12 percent of U.S. levels in 1980 to 25 percent in 1990.

U.S. Border Patrol figures show that the number of people caught entering the United States illegally from Mexico decreased from around 1.6 million in 1986 to about 800,000 in 1989, but spiked to 1.1 million in 1990.[25] The decrease in illegal immigration was probably due to the 1986 federal law making illegal the hiring of undocumented workers. The volume picked up again in 1990, however, and analysts have concluded that the effect of the employer sanctions legislation was only temporary. Clearly, there were push-and-pull factors operating beyond the control of either the United States and Mexico—in particular, the shift in the United States from a manufacturing to a service economy, which created a demand for low-skilled workers; the aging of the U.S. population; and the growth of the Mexican population. Furthermore, as Rodman D. Griffin has noted, "the case can be made that so long as wages are 10 times higher in the United States than in Mexico, mass immigrations will continue, regardless of U.S. immigration policy or Mexican economic policy."[26]

Domestic Political Implications for Mexico

With a population of about 100 million, a 2,000-mile common border, and over 50 billion barrels of proven oil reserves,[27] Mexico's political stability is crucial to U.S. interests. Political unrest in Mexico would create enormous problems for the United States.

Most people in the United States have taken Mexico's stability for granted and overlooked that Mexico has a closed political system and that a single party—the PRI—has been in power for most of this century. In recent years, Mexico has implemented a major privatization program, mended relations with the Catholic Church, and changed the *ejido* cooperative system to allow land users to buy and sell their plots. However, the political structure has been characterized as authoritarianism, a "perfect dictatorship," a "Tammany Hall–style political system," a "thuggish one-party regime," an "extreme form of presidential government," and other similar designations. A more charitable assessment is that Mexico has a qualified democracy: "The country's political system is dominated by one party, but there is a significant—and increasing—degree of pluralism."[28] The consensus, however, is that Mexico still lacks real democracy.

Democracy has been defined as a system in which parties lose elections in political competition organized by rules: "Democracy is the act of subjecting all interests to competition, of institutionalizing uncertainty. The decisive step toward democracy is the devolution of power from a group of people to a set of rules."[29] Since its founding in 1929, the ruling PRI has won nearly every national election by a landslide. Furthermore, although Mexico has a constitution and an electoral code, there is persuasive evidence that the PRI leadership has repeatedly ignored the rules and manipulated the electoral system to win elections.

One of the basic tenets of U.S. foreign policy is the support of democracy. For years, the United States has sought to nudge Mexico in that direction, but it has not pursued this goal aggressively because (1) U.S. relations with Mexico were determined by the U.S. communist containment strategy, and as long as Mexico remained noncommunist it met U.S. overall strategic interests; (2) Mexico's authoritarian regime maintained stability on the southern flank of the United States, assuring substantial social order and providing a buffer from Central America's recurring conflicts; and (3) Mexico was an important player in Latin America, requiring the United States to temper its criticism in order to secure Mexico's cooperation for key U.S. foreign and security policies in the region.

The U.S. government has contended that NAFTA would make Mexico a "more stable neighbor," but it has not expressly claimed that NAFTA will democratize Mexico. The Bush and Clinton administrations argued that Mexican political stability would best be assured by the long-term economic growth NAFTA would provide.[30] If this stability was based on one-party, authoritarian rule, so be it. (In all fairness, after the outbreak of violence in Chiapas in January 1994, the Clinton administration began pressing the Mexican government more vigorously to ensure that the general elections in August would be reasonably honest and credible.)[31]

There are some, however, who believe that NAFTA will help democratize Mexico.[32] How realistic is this expectation? Will political liberalization (and presumably stability) follow from the liberal economic policies NAFTA will require of Mexico? The answer is that economic liberalization does not automatically lead to political liberalization. Peter H. Smith, for example, contends that the agreement can lead to four possible scenarios: NAFTA will contribute to democratization; NAFTA will contribute to the consolidation of authoritarianism; NAFTA will have no meaningful impact on democratization; or NAFTA will contribute to the debilitation of the state. To exemplify, Smith points to countries such as Taiwan and Singapore, which have open economies but closed political systems. On the other hand, he recognizes that Mexico might go the route of countries such as Chile, where a closed political structure (in this case a military government) created a liberal economic system, which led to the restoration of democracy. The changes would be sequential—first economic and then political. Smith concludes that

free trade and economic liberalization could loosen the social moorings of the present political system in Mexico and, thus, create objective conditions for a far-reaching political transition. However, whether and how this opportunity is used entails the exercise of political will, skill and management at the uppermost levels of power—especially the presidency. Given a realignment of social forces, it would be just as conceivable for Mexico's leaders to resort to repression and install some new form of authoritarianism as it would be for them to embark on a quest for authentic democracy.[33]

Adam Przeworski is more compelling in concluding that authoritarian regimes such as Mexico's have only two real options when faced with pressures for change: Incorporate some new groups and repress everyone else, returning to the authoritarian stasis; or "open the political agenda to the problem of institutions, that is of democracy." Przeworski found that although many authoritarian regimes have sought to stay in power by implementing political liberalization in small doses, they have all failed because "liberalizations are either reversed, leading to grim periods euphemistically termed normalization, or continue to democratization."[34] This is because managed political liberalization is impossible when the regime also seeks to perpetuate itself in power. The regime inexorably moves toward democracy or regresses to authoritarianism.

Under this theory, the PRI cannot undertake real political reforms without losing control. It is this fear of losing control of both the process and its power that has prevented the PRI from fully accepting the democratic principles of "institutionalized uncertainty" and of devolving power to a "set of rules." Until a concatenation of pressures (to be discussed shortly) in the first half of 1994 forced President Salinas to change direction, it was clear that he had decided to thwart further democratic liberalization and reassert the PRI's hegemony.

A key development was the 1988 presidential election. In that contest, Salinas won barely 50 percent of the vote and only after the tabulation was flagrantly manipulated. Subsequently, he engineered changes to the electoral code that strengthened the PRI's power at the expense of opposition parties and orchestrated a national strategy to co-opt key members of the opposition.[35] As one study concluded,

It soon became apparent that Salinas' commitment to political liberalization had limits. Despite his post-election promises (to end the virtual one-party system, encourage a competitive political system, and ensure both transparent elections and respect for the vote), the political leadership concentrated its efforts on restoring its political authority. . . . The regime's broader political agenda focused upon reviving its own waning authority and involved a strategy of co-opting various elements, such as the political Right-wing, the business community and the intelligentsia (domestic and international).[36]

This is consistent with one of the outcomes predicted by Przeworski's theoretical construct—an incipient political liberalization is reversed and followed by a hardening of the authoritarian regime through repression and/or co-optation.

Przeworski's theory also provides one explanation of why President Salinas sought free trade with the United States. Przeworski contends that authoritarian regimes use fear or economic payoff (i.e., "exchange of material prosperity for passive acquiescence" of potential competitors)[37] to maintain power. In the case of Mexico, he concluded that the pre-1982 PRI regime relied on economic payoff to maintain control. After 1982, the PRI's control was based on fear. A regime's control through fear generates a lot of resentments, whereas regimes based on economic payoff are susceptible primarily to economic crisis, the kind Mexico experienced in the mid-1980s. Thus, Salinas' 1990 decision to ask for free trade with the United States can be seen as a shift in strategy from control through fear to control through economic payoff, with NAFTA being the vehicle. That is, it was at least in part an attempt by Salinas and the PRI to maintain power by reverting to economic payoff to secure the acquiescence of disgruntled groups hurt by the mid-1980s economic downturn.[38] And, in fact, the 1991 midterm elections showed a major swing toward the government.

President Salinas made no apologies for Mexico's political system. In a 1990 interview, he said somewhat disingenuously, "I keep hearing that in Mexico one party has held power for years, but when I think of how one party has ruled long in countries like Japan and Italy, I pay less attention to the criticism."[39] Salinas further spelled out his views after the opposition called for international supervision of elections following controversial elections in the state of Mexico: "Our democracy is sovereign. Certainly, yours [the opposition's] is the universal ideal of self-government by means of representation based on a universal secret ballot. But one does not imitate nor subordinate oneself to foreign criteria. Discussion on our democracy knows no bounds and has only one decisive judge: the Mexican people."[40]

Foreign Policy Implications

The United States is unlikely to press Mexico hard to implement fundamental political reforms. It has not in the past, and it refused to include political issues in the NAFTA negotiations. The U.S. government has said little publicly of PRI manipulations of the electoral and political process. Of more apparent importance to Washington is assuring Mexico's political stability and securing its cooperation in foreign affairs. As former U.S. Ambassador John Negroponte said in a confidential report to the State Department, "From a foreign policy perspective, an FTA would institutionalize acceptance of a North American orientation to Mexico's foreign policy."[41]

In fact, NAFTA can help the PRI maintain control by generating economic benefits, which can be used to keep contentious groups passive and acquiescing with the authoritarian regime. If NAFTA fails to generate economic benefits, the PRI, to remain in power, will be forced to carry out further repression.

There is no doubt that NAFTA would increase the United States' economic, political, and cultural penetration of Mexico, which might create the environment for U.S.–style democratic practices and institutions, but it is not clear what impact this would have on Mexico's national political process. Sidney Weintraub provides an optimistic view, noting that expanded economic, cultural, and organizational ties are already having some impact on the political system: "Democracy is entrenched in the United States, whereas it is qualified in Mexico; it is no accident that Mexico's northern border is the region most infected by the yearning for effective suffrage."[42] Miguel Angel Centeno and Sylvia Maxfield found that a new dominant group (techno-bureaucrats) has already arisen within the Mexican political elite, a group that has gained power at the expense of the ruling PRI and traditional politicians.[43] Many of these new players have been educated in the United States and have experienced U.S. democracy.

This is all well and good. However, according to Przeworski, as much as the masses might "yearn" for political change, they will be unsuccessful unless a liberal element within the ruling elite decides to become reformers and go along with the change. Such liberals have appeared periodically in Mexico, but in the past they have always been discredited, paid off, or eliminated.

In the long term, NAFTA's most profound impact could be in redefining U.S. relations with Latin America. The goal of the Enterprise for the Americas Initiative to create a Western Hemisphere free trade zone sparked great hope in Latin America. The free trade pact with Mexico is a powerful message that the United States wants to make the EAI work. This will have enormous implications for U.S. foreign and security policy. NAFTA, and indications that the United States intends to enter into free trade talks with Chile, are strong inducements for other Latin countries to orient their economic and trade policies toward the United States. This would provide U.S. exporters with a key advantage as they battle for markets. This should not be underestimated, since the United States now exports more to Latin America than to Japan.

The United States has stressed that free trade with Latin America is an attempt to liberalize global trade rather than create an exclusionary regional trade bloc. Certainly, both the United States and Latin America would benefit from a liberal global trading system. Whether or not regional trade blocs form, however, is not solely in U.S. hands—witness the creation of the European Community. NAFTA, and by extension a potential hemispheric free trade zone, could be a tool to promote freer global trade. As Robert Pastor has noted, for the United States "the regionalist option remains a potent reminder to Europe that it will pay a price for protectionism."[44]

CONCLUSION

The pursuit of economic growth through trade is in the U.S. national interest. Mexico has become a major export market for the United States. NAFTA will stimulate further exports from both countries. However, U.S. economic activity is so huge that in the near term NAFTA's impact on the U.S. economy will be statistically marginal. NAFTA will cost U.S. jobs, particularly in labor-intensive industries, but these losses will be offset by NAFTA-created jobs in higher-wage sectors.

In the long term, NAFTA has the potential for combining U.S. and Canadian capital and technology and Mexican resources and labor into a powerful global force that will keep the United States competitive in global markets:

The integration of the North American economies would fundamentally alter the composition of resources and market opportunities available to U.S. businesses. It would instigate a major movement of labor and capital from activities emphasizing ordinary factory labor . . . to more technology-intensive pursuits. Free trade thus has the potential to be of enormous mutual benefit to the United States and Mexico in the long term.[45]

The major differences in social and economic levels between the United States and Mexico mean that undocumented immigration from Mexico to the United States will continue. NAFTA is unlikely to influence this trend in a major way in the medium term. To cautious observers, there is even doubt that NAFTA will have much of a long-term impact. In fact, it can be argued that by the time NAFTA does have an effect, the free trade pact will have been amended to provide for the free flow of transnational labor, eliminating the necessity of Mexican illegal immigration.

Although NAFTA requires Mexico to implement economic reforms more consistent with free markets and will probably result in new economic and social power centers, this will not per se lead to reform of Mexico's authoritarian regime. Furthermore, the PRI and the Mexican government cannot manage a political liberalization process if the end sought is to remain in power. President Salinas and the PRI did not want to lose power. Thus, the political liberalization of the late 1980s was neutralized and a political strategy implemented to assure that the PRI's hegemony continued. NAFTA may, in fact, contribute to this outcome.

The United States has refused to leverage NAFTA to secure a more democratic Mexico, and it is unlikely to press for effective democratization in the years ahead, even though the communist threat has been eliminated and Central America is enjoying relative peace. Washington still values the PRI-based political stability, and there is misplaced expectation that NAFTA will somehow generate a democratic transition.

NAFTA's more important contribution will be to redefine U.S. relations with Latin America. It is likely to anchor an eventual hemispherewide free trade zone and orient the trade policies of Latin nations toward the United States. This will provide the United States with important trade and political advantages as it battles for export markets with global competitors such as Japan and the EC. NAFTA may or may not be the ideal trade agreement, but it is a clear recognition that our economic future and prosperity are inextricably linked to international economic competition and trade.

EDITOR'S POSTSCRIPT

The dramatic events of 1994 require some amendment of the preceding analysis. The spiral of violence in Mexico, including the rebellion in Chiapas, the assassination of Luis Donaldo Colosio, and various other killings and kidnappings, shocked Mexican political leaders. At the same time, the beginning of NAFTA's implementation and the approach of the August elections focused even more international—especially U.S.—attention on Mexico and linked politics and economics even more tightly than had been the case prior to the U.S. congressional approval of the trade agreement. This concatenation of pressures convinced President Salinas of the need to place renewed emphasis on democratization, which had been consigned to the back burner, in order to ensure that the elections were reasonably fair and credible.

These developments were discussed in detail in chapter 1, and we need not recount them here. The point is that although this democratic resurgence—a flurry of reforms and relatively clean elections—represented a significant step forward, it did not mean that the process was complete or the gains irreversible. The circumstances of the 1994 campaign were, after all, fairly unique. The confluence of a variety of pressures made it difficult for Salinas and Zedillo to resist democratization in the short run. But whether the new president would continue to push the issue once those pressures eased was anybody's guess.

In short, the struggle for democracy will continue. Within the PRI, the "dinosaurs" still have a strong foothold. They can be counted on to try to protect their power and privileges by obstructing political reform by all means possible, both fair and foul. During the campaign, Zedillo was forced to embrace the "dinosaurs" for the sake of party unity in order to assure victory. The question now is whether—or to what degree—he will be willing and able to free himself from their grasp so that reform can be continued, or even accelerated.

The problem is that democratization poses very real dangers for the PRI, its leaders, and many of their constituents. The potential loss of political dominance and all of the opportunities and spoils that go with it is nothing to sneeze at. Moreover, democratization carries risks for Zedillo as well. If he pushes too hard, he risks the same fate as Colosio and Ruiz Massieu. Beyond this, the erosion of *presidencialismo* would weaken his ability to carry out his programs—including further democratization, should he choose to pursue that course. Then too, there is the fear of losing control, the fear that democratization might lead to political instability.

Thus, there is a temptation to limit, halt, or even reverse the reform process. By the same token, it is by no means clear that current and future U.S. administrations will be all that interested in continuing to push for democratization. Certainly, Al Pérez's analysis of U.S. behavior prior to 1994 is not encouraging.

None of this, of course, necessarily means that democracy is about to be frustrated. However, that possibility is strong enough to temper any inclinations toward unbridaled optimism. Perhaps the best that can be said is that democratization will be a long, drawn-out process; moreover, it will not be unilinear. There will be setbacks as well as victories. It is hoped that there will be more of the latter than the former.

—Donald E. Schulz

NOTES

1. Lester Thurow, *Head to Head: The Coming Economic Battle Among Japan, Europe and America* (New York: William Morrow and Company, Inc., 1992), p. 14.

2. William H. Nordruft, quoted in Stuart Auerbach, "The U.S. as Exporter: Superpower or Subpar?," *Washington Post*, September 20, 1992; "North America: USA," *World Outlook 1992: Forecasts Of Political and Economic Trends For 1992 in Over 165 Countries* (London: The Economist Intelligence Unit, 1992), p. 26.

3. The White House, "Relating Means to Ends: An Economic Agenda for the 1990s," *National Security Strategy of the United States* (Washington, D.C.: GPO, August 1991), p. 20.

4. The White House, Office of the Press Secretary, *Fact Sheet on the North American Free Trade Agreement* (Washington, D.C.: GPO, August 12, 1992), p. 1.

5. "Toward a Western Hemisphere Community of Democracies," address to Mexican, American, and Latin American Chambers of Commerce, Mexico City, December 1, 1993.

6. In the words of Lawrence Eagleburger, U.S. Department of State, "Department 'Gets Down to Business' By Assisting U.S. Firms, Promoting American Exports," *Dispatch*, Vol. 2, No. 17 (Washington, D.C.: U.S. Department of State, April 29, 1991), p. 306.

7. "The Primacy of Economics," *Foreign Policy*, No. 87 (Summer 1992), p. 3.

8. "Remarks Announcing the Enterprise for the Americas Initiative," *Weekly Compilation of Presidential Documents*, Vol. 26, No. 26 (July 2, 1990), p. 1010.

9. "Mexico–United States Joint Statement on Negotiation of a Free Trade Agreement of June 11, 1990," *Weekly Compilation of Presidential Documents*, Vol. 28, No. 20 (May 18, 1992), p. 28.

10. Judith Gentleman and Voytek Zubek, "International Integration and Democratic Development: The Cases of Poland and Mexico," *Journal of Interamerican Studies and World Affairs*, Vol. 34, No. 1 (Spring 1992), p. 73.

11. "Mexico" and "United States," *The World Fact Book, 1993* (Washington, D.C.: Central Intelligence Agency, 1993), pp. 256, 405.

12. Peter Morici, "Free Trade With Mexico," *Foreign Policy*, No. 87 (Summer 1992), p. 89.

13. Robert Fisher, "The North American Free Trade Agreement: A U.S. Perspective," *SAIS Review*, Vol. 12, No. 1 (Winter–Spring 1992), p. 46.

14. Office of the U.S. Trade Representative, "Overview," *The North American Free Trade Agreement* (Washington, D.C.: Office of the U.S. Trade Representative, August 1992), p. 1.

15. Nora Lustig, "The North American Free Trade Agreement: A Mexican Perspective," *SAIS Review*, Vol. 12, No. 1 (Winter–Spring 1992), p. 61.

16. The White House, *Fact Sheet*, p. 2; Office of the U.S. Trade Representative, "U.S. Jobs and Adjustment," *The North American Free Trade Agreement* (Washington, D.C.: Office of the U.S. Trade Representative, August 1992).

17. "North American Free Trade," *Foreign Affairs*, Vol. 70, No. 4 (Fall 1991), p. 140.

18. The AFL–CIO strongly opposed NAFTA, claiming that 500,000 American jobs would be lost because low-wage Mexican labor would lure U.S. companies. Baer argues that "these claims probably overstate the likely impact of a free trade agreement, given the large differences in labor productivity and the fact that Mexico's economy is one-twenty-fifth the size of America's." Ibid., p. 143.

19. Ani Hadjian, "Salinas Speaks Out on Free Trade," *Fortune*, December 28, 1992, p. 47.

20. Quoted in Rodman D. Griffin, "Mexico's Emergence: Would a Free-Trade Pact Be Good for the United States?" *Congressional Research Quarterly*, Vol. 1, No. 11 (July 19, 1991), p. 501.

21. Leonard Waverman, "Mini-Symposium: Modelling North American Free Trade, Editorial Introduction," *The World Economy*, Vol. 15, No. 1 (January 1992), p. 9.

22. "Statement by U.S. Trade Representative Carla Hills to the Senate Finance Committee, September 8, 1992," in *Foreign Policy Bulletin*, Vol. 3, No. 3 (November–December 1992), p. 24.

23. Saúl Trejo Reyes, "Labor Market Interdependence Between Mexico and the United States," in *The Dynamics of North American Free Trade and Investment: Canada, Mexico and the United States,* edited by Clark W. Reynolds, Leonard Waverman, and Gerardo Bueno (Stanford, Calif.: Stanford University Press, 1991), p. 251.

24. "Free Trade with Mexico," p. 97.

25. Cited in Griffin, "Mexico's Emergence," p. 499. Since illegal immigration is inherently surreptitious, the precise volume of this flow is impossible to measure. These figures are helpful in providing an indication of the volume of undocumented immigration based on the number of people apprehended. It should also be noted, however, that not all of those are of Mexican origin.

26. Ibid.

27. "Latin America/IPE Atlas: Mexico," *International Petroleum Encyclopedia 1992,* Vol. 25 (Tulsa: PennWell Publishing Company, 1992), p. 124.

28. Griffin, "Mexico's Emergence," p. 502.

29. Adam Przeworski, *Democracy and the Market: Political Reforms in Eastern Europe and Latin America* (New York: Cambridge University Press, 1991), p. 14.

30. It is significant that the United States refused to leverage NAFTA to seek political liberalization in Mexico. Gentleman and Zubek, for example, in noting the increasingly restrictive nature of the PRI's political posture in 1990–1991, concluded that "to the Mexican leaders . . . it was clear that the United States was determined to ignore the . . . hardening of the Salinas governing stance and its reluctance to pursue a more liberal political process. The U.S. administration was perceived as (a) willing to overlook the disturbing political drift and (b) intent on pursuing its desire to proceed with integration." They went on to quote assistant secretary of state for interamerican affairs Bernard Aronson as saying that the negotiating agenda for NAFTA did not address political issues: "It's already been decided; commerce and investment, nothing more." See Gentleman and Zubek, "International Integration," p. 81. This is consistent with views expressed to this author by other State Department officials, who stressed that "NAFTA was a trade pact, and did not include a political agenda."

31. Tim Golden, "Christopher Presses Mexico to Insure Its Election Is Fair," *New York Times,* May 10, 1994.

32. Baer, for example, contends that "a free-trade agreement may help reinforce decentralized economic decision-making, erode the dirigiste tendency of an authoritarian state and decouple the economy from exclusive party control." Where Baer goes awry, however, is in her assertion that "liberalized politics tend to accompany liberal economics." See "North American Free Trade," p. 136.

33. "The Political Impact of Free Trade on Mexico," *Journal of Interamerican Studies and World Affairs,* Vol. 34, No. 1 (Spring 1992), pp. 19–20.

34. *Democracy and the Market,* p. 60.

35. See Andrew Reding, "The Crumbling of the 'Perfect Dictatorship': Mexico's Democratic Challenge," *World Policy Journal,* Vol. 8, No. 2 (Spring 1991), pp. 258–61. See also Stephen D. Morris, "Political Reformism in Mexico: Salinas at the Brink," *Journal of Interamerican Studies and World Affairs,* Vol. 34, No. 1 (Spring 1992), pp. 27–57.

36. Gentleman and Zubek, "International Integration," pp. 79, 80.

37. Przeworski, *Democracy and the Market,* p. 59.

38. Other forces also motivated Salinas to seek free trade: a 40 percent unemployment rate, Western Europe's decision to focus its resources on Eastern Europe to the detriment of Latin America, and the need to modernize the Mexican economy before it got left irrevocably behind. What was clear to Mexico's political elites, however, was that these reforms were essential to maintain the PRI's legitimacy and power.

39. Tim Padgett, "Reform at Two Different Rhythms," *Newsweek,* December 3, 1990, p. 39. Salinas also claimed that the lack of political pluralism in Mexico is "due to the weakness of the opposition." As has been noted, however, there is persuasive evidence that Salinas and the PRI have deliberately undermined the opposition.

40. Quoted in Jorge Chabat's "Mexico's Foreign Policy in 1990: Electoral Sovereignty and Integration with the United States," *Journal of Interamerican Studies and World Affairs,* Vol. 33, No. 4 (Winter 1991), pp. 13–14.

41. As quoted in Smith, "The Political Impact," p. 17.

42. Sidney Weintraub, *A Marriage of Convenience: Relations Between Mexico and the United States* (New York: Oxford University Press, 1990), p. 155.

43. Miguel Angel Centeno and Sylvia Maxfield, "The Marriage of Finance and Order: Changes in the Mexican Political Elite," *Journal of Latin American Studies,* Vol. 24, Pt. 1 (February 1992), p. 84.

44. "The Latin American Option," *Foreign Policy,* No. 88 (Fall 1992), p. 123.

45. Morici, "Free Trade," p. 96.

8

NAFTA and Beyond: The United States–Mexican Borderlands in Transition

Edward J. Williams

Significant change promises to characterize the U.S.–Mexican Borderlands as the region approaches the 21st century. As the bilateral relationship between Mexico and the United States assumed increasing importance in recent years, the Borderlands also commanded growing attention. Both governments rediscovered their border regions; they found a variety of virtues and vices hardly known and barely understood in Washington and Mexico City. The blessings and curses of economic growth have transformed the area, and the trend will continue into the next century.

As the centerpiece of a series of forces propelling economic change, NAFTA portends significant consequences for the U.S.–Mexican Borderlands. Many implications are positive, but the negative ramifications also weigh heavily. The clearest of the several advantages involves measurable, continuing economic gains. The social implications of NAFTA-propelled economic change tend to be more diffuse, but they should bring positive advances in social standing and prestige, especially for Mexican and Mexican-American populations. NAFTA also exemplifies the region's evolving political muscle. It spells a major victory for the southwestern United States and the North of Mexico and reflects shifting demographic bases of political power in both nations. Finally, the treaty implies incremental gains for participatory democracy in Mexico and for national security in the United States. Both have specific meaning for the binational Borderlands.

On the other hand, the negative effects of the economic growth concomitant to NAFTA and other influences are equally significant. They combine with ongoing rapid population expansion and poverty to promise overload on the area's insufficient physical and human infrastructure. In truth, the infrastructure is already stressed in the mid-1990s from several decades of booming population growth and economic development. Increased growth also portends even more environmental degradation of the area's air and water, which are already suffering from some of the most serious environmental problems in Mexico and the United States. Beyond ecological defilement, perils to public health threaten residents on both sides of the line as the effects of growth, poverty, ignorance, and relative political impotence take their toll.

ECONOMIC AND SOCIOPOLITICAL PROGRESS

Economic Progress

Analysts have devoted considerable attention to the economic significance of NAFTA. The emphases and forecasts vary, but substantial agreement exists on the major thrust. With isolated exceptions in a few economic sectors, the treaty presages economic growth on both sides.

The exceptions in the U.S. Borderlands are mostly in labor-intensive industry. Some fret about a negative impact on retail business, but the predictions vary. On the Mexican side, previously protected higher-tech industries are suffering, but they amount to precious little in the immediate border region, where the overwhelming percentage of economic activity centers on the *maquiladora* industry, retail sales, and services. Many of those services are provided across the line to wealthier U.S. clients and consumers.

The economic projections vary, but all wax optimistic. The U.S. trade representative in 1991 calculated sharp growth in the binational Borderlands economy ranging between 5 and 15 percent annually even without NAFTA. Texas brags about increasing its exports to Mexico by at least U.S. $1.8 billion over a ten-year period. Arizona stands to gain somewhere between 2,000 and 5,000 new jobs created by increased trade with Mexico.

In sum, the overall economic picture is bright. Most U.S. and Mexican Borderlanders will become richer (or less poverty stricken) as free trade works its economic influence in the region. Several specific conditions support the larger claim that the Borderlands will benefit economically. Businesses in areas like transportation, communications, and services are geographically well placed to reap the advantages of burgeoning trade. Border metropoli like El Paso/Juárez, Los Dos Laredos, and Ambos Nogales are already flourishing centers of international trade, and their experience and circumstances are nurturing even more interchange as a result of expanding bilateral trade encouraged by NAFTA.

By experience, culture, and linguistic abilities, Borderlanders also have an edge on competitors in other regions of their respective countries. Mexican businesspeople and merchants have been doing successful business with their counterparts in the United States for decades. On both sides of the boundary, many Mexicans and *gringos* are bilingual and possess understanding of and sensitivity to the other's society and culture.

Comparatively speaking, American high-tech industries are gaining more from free trade than most other sectors of the U.S. economy. The Southwest Borderlands house relatively more high-tech industries than other regions, adding to their comparative advantage as the distribution of economic gains from NAFTA crystallize. Moreover, increased prosperity in both countries spills over more wealth onto the Borderlands than to other areas, defining another increment of economic advantage for the region. As the trade agreement spurs economic growth in both nations, the economic spillover in the Borderlands increases significantly. Almost all border cities now depend heavily on reciprocal transborder shoppers for their economic sustenance, and the border states host large numbers of tourists from the other country. In the Arizona/Sonora border state economic equation, for example, 96 percent of all Mexicans who visit Arizona emanate from Sonora.[1] NAFTA suggests more numerous and richer shoppers and tourists and, in the process, an additional contribution to the Borderlands economy. Again, the economic gains for the Borderlands will be higher than for other regions of Mexico and the United States.

Finally, increased investment is flocking to the Borderlands on both sides of the line. As Mexican industry moves north and U.S. industry moves south to locate nearer potential new markets, the Borderlands are prospering in the short run from an upturn in construction and will gain in the longer run from additional industries and businesses. In sum, free trade implies significant economic benefit to Mexico's northern frontier as well as to the U.S. Southwest Borderlands.

Sociopolitical Progress

Sociopolitical progress for Borderlanders intrinsic to NAFTA tends to be more diffuse and long range than the economic gains. Sociopolitical change evolves slowly, and it often defies exact measurement. Nonetheless, the consequences of free trade are defined clearly enough to invite relatively confident prediction. Moreover, they are certainly important enough to demand description and analysis.

The sociopolitical significance of NAFTA encompasses all Borderlanders, but it is particularly important for Mexicans and Mexican Americans living in the area. A major premise of NAFTA entails increased prestige and acceptance of Mexicans and Mexican Americans in both countries. As the economic implications of the agreement take hold, they work to dignify Mexicans and Mexican Americans from a sociocultural perspective and increasingly empower them in the U.S. (and Mexican) political contexts. From a U.S. perspective, NAFTA signals that Mexico is important; it bestows a certain dignity on the country and, by extrapolation, on Mexican

Americans living in the U.S. Borderlands. After having disdained Mexico, *Mexicanos,* and Mexican Americans for more than a century, Anglo-Americans now embrace them as business partners. Indeed, no higher prestige or respect exists in the traditional white Anglo-Saxon Protestant mind than that attached to a business partner.

In the United States, Mexican Americans now boast salable skills and expertise. They know Mexico, possess an understanding of the culture and traditions, and speak Spanish. Many Mexican Americans have family and friends in Mexico; they have established a wide range of valuable contacts over the years. The upshot is that Mexican Americans now are recruited to America's corporate boardrooms, the corridors of its political power, and the halls of its most prestigious academic institutions. Mexican Americans have increasingly become important people in the United States.

Moreover, the Mexican government is also courting Mexican Americans. A series of initiatives, beginning as early as the 1970s, has sponsored meetings between Mexican officials (including the president) and Mexican-American elites. The Mexican government offers a scholarship program for Mexican-American students to study in Mexican universities. Early in his administration, President Carlos Salinas established the *Programa para las Comunidades Mexicanos en el Exterior* (Program for Mexican Communities Abroad). President Ernesto Zedillo has continued the program, which is housed in the Ministry of Foreign Relations. The program cultivates affinity between *Mexicanos* and Mexican Americans through initiatives like educational, cultural, and sporting exchanges and events. As of 1993, the Mexican government earmarked U.S. $20 million to promote joint ventures in Mexico between U.S. Hispanics and Mexican nationals in conjunction with NAFTA. In the same spirit, President Salinas had, by the early 1990s, awarded Mexico's Order of the Aztec Eagle to several Mexican Americans. The 1993 honors went to Gloria Molina and Raúl Yzaguirre, a Los Angeles County supervisor and a president of the National Council of La Raza, respectively.

Just as they are wooed in the United States, Mexican-American academics, businesspeople, cultural leaders, and politicos are also honored and courted in Mexico. As the implications of NAFTA have defined a new bilateral relationship between the neighboring countries, Mexican decision makers are moving to redefine their relationships with Mexican Americans.

For most of the same reasons, Mexicans are also more esteemed in the United States than in times past. Anglo-American businesspeople seek out their Mexican counterparts to launch joint ventures. U.S. politicos brag about their familiarity with Mexico and their knowledge of the Spanish language, and they show off their Hispanic in-laws. Universities seek Mexican students to grace their graduate programs and Mexican professors to receive fellowships and visiting teaching positions.

The sociopolitical implications of increasing prestige are profound and comprehensive. In the sociocultural context, for example, the education of Spanish-speaking children in the United States is facilitated by the growing prestige of the Spanish language. As the Spanish language gains esteem, so do those who speak it. Educators long ago confirmed the common-sense conclusion that children who possess a sense of their importance and dignity achieve at a higher level than those who feel themselves despised. As the millions of Hispanic children now in American schools begin to gain a diffuse sense of the growing prestige of their mother tongue, the logic of the process suggests that their increasing confidence will yield higher academic achievement. The socioeconomic calculation implies that they are bound to become more productive, sophisticated, and wealthier American citizens.

It appears equally obvious that sociocultural empowerment transfers to the political realm, signaling increased political influence for Mexican Americans in the U.S. Borderlands and beyond. In truth, NAFTA forms only one part of a larger and longer process nurturing a series of recent Mexican-American political successes designed to increase Mexican Americans' political punch. Inspired by the aggressiveness and success of Afro-Americans and the 1965 *huelga* (strike) of César Chávez, elements of the Mexican-American community became radicalized in the late 1960s. Organized as the *Raza Unida* Party, militant Chicanos gained their first significant political victory in 1970 in the Texas Borderlands' Crystal City.

Evolving from their own efforts through organizations like the Southwest Voter Education Project and aided by Washington's assistance through the Voting Rights Act, originally legislated in 1965, the numbers of Mexican-American office-holders has grown by leaps and bounds from the early 1970s through the early 1990s. The numbers are impressive: President Clinton appointed two Mexican Americans to his cabinet, Henry Cisneros as Secretary of Housing and Urban Development and Frederico Peña as Secretary of Transportation. Mexican Americans from border states in the federal House of Representatives increased from four to ten from 1973 to 1994. Elected Hispanic city officials also grew dramatically during the 1973–1993 period, registering an increase of 120 percent in Arizona, 60 percent in California, 55 percent in New Mexico, and 172 percent in Texas. Changes in elected county officials also reflected measurable increases: Arizona, 17 percent; California, 56 percent; New Mexico, 13 percent; and Texas, 58 percent. Mexican Americans also registered significant gains in state elected officials and on school boards and in special districts during the same period.[2]

To conclude, NAFTA's significance for the Mexican-American community in the U.S. Borderlands grows ever more important as it suggests movement toward sociopolitical change. NAFTA implies more individual efficacy among Mexican Americans, and it should lead to growing social mobilization, political participation, and power.

But the political import of NAFTA in the United States transcends Mexican Americans. The treaty may well mark the first major foreign policy victory of the American West (and Southwest). Following population realignments that have located the majority of voters and representatives in states west of the Mississippi, the decision to move toward North American free trade reflects a shift in the distribution of national political power. Political power now resides in the West. In turn, NAFTA signals a watershed from a foreign policy dominated by eastern and midwestern interests fastened on Europe and the Far East to an emerging foreign policy coalition composed of westerners, who see Mexico and Latin America as the logical focus of U.S. attention.

Somewhat the same process is reflected in the increasing prominence of the North in Mexico's political life. Recent presidents and presidential candidates of the PRI illustrate this point. President Salinas was born in the Federal District, but he was fond of calling attention to his *norteño* roots in Nuevo León. Luis Donaldo Colosio, the original PRI presidential candidate for the 1994 elections, hailed from Sonora. Although born in the Federal District, President Zedillo spent his formative years in Mexicali, Baja California.

The economic reforms embraced by the central government and the PRI teach the same lesson. Those neoliberal strategies have been preached by *norteños* for fifty years. Indeed, both the economic and political components of the de la Madrid, Salinas, and Zedillo programs reflect clearly traditional *norteño* thought.

The growing prominence of the National Action Party in Mexico's border states evolves from the same forces and has the same meaning. In the 1990s, PANista governors rule in both Baja California and Chihuahua, two important border states. The PAN also controls the state legislature in Baja California Sur. In tandem with other demographic and economic changes, NAFTA heralds the influence of PANista policy preferences for closer ties with the United States. NAFTA both propels and reflects new designs in the equation of Mexican political power. In embryonic form, the axis of power is shifting from the east–west Vera Cruz–Mexico City alignment to a Mexico City–Border States center of gravity.

Indeed, NAFTA symbolizes a move from a conceptualization of a world defined by an east-west axis to one organized north to south. For example, recent U.S. legislation calls for the identification, assessment, improvement, and development of existing and emerging trade corridors and transportation subsystems that facilitate commercial interaction among the United States, Canada, and Mexico.[3] The so-called Canamex Corridor is projected to connect cities like Vancouver, Edmonton, and Calgary in Canada's west with Guadalajara and Mexico City, and U.S. and Mexican cities en route like Denver, Salt Lake, Phoenix, Chihuahua, Cuidad Juárez, and Hermosillo. The initiative clearly departs from the historical emphasis on east-west movement in the United States.

The 1994 merger of the Burlington Northern and Santa Fe railroads follows the same path. The motivation for the merger flowed from the perceived economic advantage of confecting a rail system that connected Mexico and Canada.[4] What President Bush called the Enterprise for the Americas Initiative (or something like it spawned by the Clinton administration) forms the next stage of the unfolding of the new strategy as the U.S. foreign policy focus proceeds from Canada to South America.

The political significance of NAFTA extends to Mexico in still another way. The economic growth promised by the treaty may foster political change. Increasing economic prosperity implies support for the encouraging political developments afoot in Mexico. The country has been inching toward more authentic political participation for at least the last fifteen years. Although progress remains imperfect, presidents Salinas and Zedillo continued to push for more legitimate representation and increasingly honest elections. Economic development nurtures democratic government; it provides resources for educating the citizenry and offers a foundation of economic security that facilitates independent political participation. Again, the implications for the Northern Borderlands appear to be especially manifest. However imperfect the practice of participatory democracy may be in Mexico, it is more advanced in the Borderlands than elsewhere. NAFTA promises to nudge political reform a step further there.

Finally, Mexico's economic and political well-being serves the security interests of the United States. The United States enjoys more security with an economically viable and politically stable neighbor, especially when that neighbor shares a 2,000-mile border. Mexico's peaceful equilibrium is particularly important for Borderlanders. Widespread social dislocation leading to political instability in central or southern Mexico would spell massive migration to the northern Mexican border region and imply profound refugee problems in the U.S. Borderlands. As NAFTA-fostered economic growth cushions political change in Mexico, it accrues to the well-being of both sides.

In sum, NAFTA spells a continuum of changes for Borderlanders in Mexico and the United States. On the positive side, economic prosperity combines with social redemption and expanding political influence. But economic growth also carries negative implications, which may compromise the well-being and threaten the health and environment of those on both sides.

INFRASTRUCTURAL DEFICIENCIES, ENVIRONMENTAL DEGRADATION, AND THREATS TO PUBLIC HEALTH

Context

Even before the vices and virtues of NAFTA began to influence the Borderlands, the latter had serious problems dating as far back as the mid-

1970s. Today, the physical and human infrastructure suffers from underdevelopment and/or disrepair, environmental degradation blights the region, and threats to public health jeopardize the well-being of the population. Several factors have contributed to the situation: rapid population growth; poverty, ignorance, and the relatively low level of political articulation that flow from them; and governmental programs in Washington, Mexico City, and the various state capitals that reflect little interest in and less understanding of the area.

The 1990 U.S. Census showed the four border states as growing more swiftly than almost all others. All four ranked within the top twelve in rate of population growth: Arizona, 3; California, 5; Texas, 7; and New Mexico 12. The census calculated that the four states had more than 51 million of the nation's 246 million inhabitants. Population increases even more rapidly in the Mexican Borderlands, especially in the burgeoning border cities, where growth is nothing short of spectacular. Tijuana may well be the most rapidly growing large city in the world, increasing at a rate of more than 8 percent annually. Eight million seems a reasonable estimation for the population of Mexico's border cities, almost one-tenth of Mexico's total. Ciudad Juárez, Tijuana, and probably Mexicali exceed a million inhabitants; Nuevo Laredo, Reynosa, and Matamoros each hover at the 500,000 mark. The Sonoran cities of Nogales and San Luis de Río Colorado on the Arizona border count 250,000 apiece. Even relative backwaters like Agua Prieta, Sonora approach 100,000.

NAFTA will entice even more Mexican migrants to the Northern Borderlands. Both push-and-pull factors play into the picture. As discussed earlier, NAFTA means economic growth, which will pull relatively poor *Mexicanos* to the region in search of jobs. As for the push component of the equation, reforms of Mexican rural landholding patterns initiated under Salinas will combine with increased flow of cheaper U.S. agricultural products into Mexico to push poor *campesinos* from the land. One estimate has it that as many as 15 million peasants may be dislocated as the Mexican modernization program evolves.[5] Many of the dispossessed will find their way north to the binational Borderlands.

Poverty is another factor. Most Americans living in the Borderlands are poorer than their compatriots. San Diegans are the only exception. From San Diego looking east, border peoples suffer from increasing poverty. Texas border dwellers rank among the most poverty stricken in the country. Of the 313 metropolitan areas in the United States, Texas border communities occupy four of the last five places in per capita income. The McAllen-Edinburg metro area is the poorest in the country, followed by Laredo and Brownsville-Harlingen. El Paso ranks fifth in per capita poverty.

Compared to their compatriots, Mexican border dwellers are relatively wealthy, but of course Mexicans are quite poor in comparative terms—

about ten times poorer than U.S. citizens on a per capita basis. Therefore, Mexican Borderlanders are even poorer than their U.S. brethren. Moreover, during the 1980s Mexico suffered its most serious economic downturn since the Revolution and could ill afford to address the area's environmental problems. (Huge sums of money were being spent to service the foreign debt.) And, of course, the quality of life in the border cities went from bad to worse.

But that is not the end of the story. A third component of this sorry tale is political ineffectiveness and governmental nonresponsiveness in both countries. It comes as no surprise that poor people are usually ignorant (i.e., uneducated and unsophisticated) and that poor, ignorant people do not mobilize politically to petition for or demand responses from political decision makers. To complete the scenario, governments in both Mexico and the United States have always been uninformed about the northwestern and southwestern borders, respectively. Indeed, more than uninformed, Washington and Mexico City have been in varying degrees and at differing times mistrustful and disdainful of their respective Borderlands.

Problems

All of this leaves the Borderlands bristling with problems that may well become even more serious in the next century with the onset of NAFTA-generated economic growth. The continuum extends from infrastructural deficiencies through environmental degradation to threats to public health. A few illustrations will make the point.

A 1991 General Accounting Office (GAO) study[6] provides perspective on the scarcity of official human resources in the U.S. Borderlands. The "principal finding" holds that "an insufficient number of Customs and Immigration inspectors is the primary obstacle to the efficient operation of southwest border crossings." Admitting that the estimated additional needs lack precision, the study noted that in 1990 the two agencies needed 2,500 inspectors at the border, 700 more than authorized. If border traffic increased 100 percent beyond the 1990 level—probable by 1995—Customs and the Immigration and Naturalization Service (INS) would need 5,000 officers working the border, 3,200 or 300 percent more than were on duty in 1990.

Negative economic and environmental consequences flow from the lack of personnel at the border crossings. The free flow of people and merchandise is impeded, diminishing the very raison d'être of a trade agreement designed to increase the flow of goods and services. Perhaps less obviously, insufficient personnel at the line means that crossing lanes go unattended, contributing to long lines of idling vehicles spewing their pollution into the Borderlands' air. [Editors' note: The number of Border Patrol agents has been sharply increased in recent years. There are now over 5,000, and the Clinton administration has just proposed legislation to add 1,500 more.]

The situation on the Mexican side is just as deplorable, although for somewhat different reasons. Mexico lacks a cadre of trained personnel. Testifying to the problem in 1992, the Director of Mexico's National Institute of Ecology defined "the principal obstacle" in confronting environmental challenges in the 1990s as "the insufficiency of personnel at all levels." He noted, for example, that Mexico had only eighty-three environmental engineers in the entire country.[7]

Along with the first study, a companion GAO report looks at another aspect of the U.S. problem by analyzing physical infrastructure in the Borderlands.[8] In the early 1990s, the Texas State Department of Highways and Public Transportation estimated that $600 million of infrastructural improvements was needed to address *existing* congestion along the border. Arizona, New Mexico, and California demand additions and improvements in physical infrastructure totaling $90, $157, and $133 million, respectively. That is, everywhere in the Borderlands more personnel, improved highways, better crossings, and additional bridges are needed. All those demands exist in areas that rank among the poorest in the United States.

A critical report out of the city manager's office in Nogales, Arizona, captures still another aspect of the depressing scenario. In the first instance, the report complains that in 1990 the Arizona State Economic Commission estimated a population of 17,439 for Nogales, more than 25 percent below the 22,000 calculated by Nogales' officials. That is only half the problem. The Arizona officials failed to understand that Nogales includes a "service population" of an additional 20,000 to 30,000. Nogales, Arizona, of course, forms part of the urban center of Ambos Nogales (Both Nogaleses). Nogales, Sonora contributes to the urban agglomeration an estimated population of 250,000. The report gets to the essence of the conundrum of many U.S. border cities: "We are forced to try to provide infrastructure and community services for a city of at least 20,000 residents with a service population of at least twice that number on a budget determined by the State for 17,000."[9]

Infrastructural deficiencies weigh even more heavily in Mexico. Insufficient housing ranks as the border cities' number one problem. (A serious housing shortage also exists on the U.S. side.) In the Mexican Borderlands, the deficit from Tijuana to Matamoros may be as high as 500,000 units. Extrapolating from this figure offers a sense of the profundity of the problem. Assuming six persons per housing unit, about 3 million (or nearly 40 percent) of Mexicans living in the Borderlands are ill housed. In truth, that estimate may be rather low.

Beyond housing, inadequate transportation probably numbers as the second most frequently issued complaint of Mexico's border city dwellers. But housing and transportation tell only part of the story. Potable water is in short supply everywhere, streets are in poor condition and usually not lighted, sewage systems are inadequate, drainage systems are not well designed or are absent, and border crime increases as a result of the normal process of urbanization compounded by the impact of drug trafficking, a major scourge of every border city on either side of the boundary.

A local elite interviewed in the late 1980s seized the essence of the problem when he declared that "Mexicali is a mess." Although Mexicali does not appear as "messy" as some border cities, it reflects the predicament of the Mexican borderlands. A study sponsored by the local business association complained that the city's "urban infrastructure is saturated" and predicted little chance of resolving its problems for the foreseeable future.[10]

Like Mexicali, every other Mexican border city suffers from the saturation of its urban infrastructure. Conditions in the U.S. cities tend to be better but remain below par. The upshot is that insufficient infrastructure spawns environmental degradation, which, in turn, gives birth to a public health crisis that approaches catastrophic proportions. Several examples are as follows: (1) The comfort, well-being, and health of more than 3 million people in the San Diego/Tijuana border metropolis are threatened by open sewage flowing through the rivers of that area. The problem has been festering for 50 years. (2) In Ambos Nogales, hazardous and toxic wastes that flow into the sewage system and washes contribute to a rate of hepatitis far above the national averages. (3) In Douglas/Agua Prieta, respiratory problems are caused and aggravated by a severe dust upheaval that affects the communities almost every day as the *maquiladoras* complete each day's work. (4) The border metropolis of El Paso/Juárez suffers extremely degraded air and is almost totally dependent on ground water, which is being depleted at alarming rates and is threatened by pollution. (5) In Los Dos Laredos, industrial wastes, sewage, and herbicide, pesticide, fungicide, and rodenticide runoff from both sides of the Río Grande have led to a high level of pollution. The Río Grande is the foulest river in the United States.

The 1992 break in the sewage disposal pipe system in San Diego provided sufficient illustration that Americans contribute to the mess. The San Diego system spewed 180 million gallons of semitreated sewage a day into the ocean. San Diego does not disinfect its effluent to kill bacteria, which means that the sewage spilling into shallow coastal waters was laden with disease-causing pathogens and viruses.[11] This was an environmental disaster.

That is only one in a series of problems afflicting the Borderlands. These problems reflect the residue of years of environmental neglect. They are profoundly serious—far beyond the minor inconveniences that sometimes rivet the attention of elitist environmentalists. Moreover, the 21st century promises more of the same.

Threats to public health in the binational Borderlands form the final curse in the progression of deleterious cause and effect that begins with insufficient infrastructure and progresses to environmental degradation. In 1990, the American Medical Association endorsed a report by its Council on Scientific Affairs, which concluded that the major factors affecting environmental health in the border area are water and air pollution. The Council's report also charged that "the border area is a virtual cesspool and breeding ground for infectious diseases."[12] The situation has not improved since then. Indeed, it has gotten worse.

Insufficient Response

In the mid-1990s, some help is apparently on the way. In 1992, Presidents Bush and Salinas announced a clean-up fund for the Borderlands to be phased in over several years.[13] In the context of finalizing NAFTA, the United States and Mexico established the North American Development Bank (NADBANK). The NADBANK promises to fund projects approved by the Border Environment Cooperation Commission (BECC), another binational institution designed to respond to the problems of the region. Borderlanders welcome the initiative, but analysis suggests that the resources destined for the area may be too little, too late.

Looking first to the "too little" part of the equation, it is abundantly clear that the monies programmed for the Borderlands fall far short of what is needed to build the necessary infrastructure and reverse the region's environmental degradation. The initial Salinas–Bush pledge projected $700 million. At that time, the Environmental Protection Agency (EPA) estimated that an outlay of $3 billion was needed to respond to the problems of wastewater disposal alone. The $700 million pledged by Bush and Salinas for 1992–1995 supposedly covered the entire terrain—air, surface water, ground water, and hazardous and toxic wastes. That is, it amounted to about 23 percent of the cost of just one problem in a complex scenario. When participants returned to the drawing board with the promise of the NADBANK for early 1995, the relative numbers continued to be asymmetric. On the outlay side, a proposal for an environment and health commission estimated a need for $6 billion. Presumably adding other projects and infrastructure to the package, Commerce Secretary Ronald Brown in 1993 calculated a need for $15 to $20 billion over ten years. About the same time, the Sierra Club proposed a figure of $20 billion.[14]

On the income side, the figures tend to vary about as much, but all of the numbers are smaller than those just noted. The highest came from the Clinton administration in 1993—$8 billion. One critique charged "double counting" and "a vague reference to the private sector" as a contributor of $4 billion. A "Fact Sheet" on the NADBANK out of the Treasury Department posits a more modest "$2 billion or more in loans and guarantees, with an upper limit of $3 billion." Some simple calculations put the data in relief. The $8 billion figure comes to 40 percent of the $20 billion estimated outlay; $3 billion is 15 percent. The income is too little to meet the demands.[15]

To compound the agony, the help may well arrive too late. Some of the environmental distress afflicting the Borderlands has been festering and/or expanding for fifty years or more. As NAFTA fosters expanded economic growth, it also carries an increased threat of even more degradation. As more *Mexicanos* migrate north in search of prosperity and more Americans flock to the Southwest in search of jobs and/or the sun, the area's fragile ecology is threatened by overload. Like Alice in Wonderland, Borderlanders will have to run much more rapidly just to stay in place.

CONCLUSION

The coming century will be a mixed bag. NAFTA promises bittersweet results. The sweet part involves economic and sociopolitical progress bound to accrue to the border populations. NAFTA means more wealth. Business initiatives in the region are well placed to take advantage of economic opportunities in the train of the trade pact, and new economic enterprises are bound to move to the area in search of comparative advantage. Increased wealth is a blessing, but it seems particularly important in the poverty-stricken binational Borderlands. NAFTA is a positive contribution to a poor region.

The treaty also promises to prod sociopolitical change among Mexican-American minorities in the United States and to confirm the political power of America's West and Mexico's North. Economic progress means increased prestige and dignity for Mexicans and Mexican Americans in a social sense, and it will augment their political power. Mexican Americans can trade on their familiarity with Mexico to enhance their prestige and influence. *Mexicanos* gain in acceptance as their economy integrates with the United States and as they become business partners with U.S. counterparts. In the same process, economic progress and social recognition transfers to political leverage. In tandem with other influences, NAFTA nudges Mexican-American power another step forward as more Mexican Americans assume office at the local, state, and national levels of government. Beyond this, NAFTA also manifests the political import of the West in the United States and the North in Mexico. Such progress can only be heralded by Borderlanders on both sides of the boundary. They have suffered too long the slings and arrows of social disdain and political discrimination.

In a rather different, less immediate nuance, NAFTA's promotion of Mexican prosperity provides a context for political reform. Moreover, the pact has implications for the security of those who inhabit the Borderlands. A wealthier and more democratic Mexico is also more stable, diminishing the possibility of social and political upheaval.

Indeed, even from the perspective of recognizable problems, the situation has redeeming qualities. The dialectic of the serendipitous process suggests three hidden blessings. The first is recognition from Washington and Mexico City. The second is financial assistance. Although there is not nearly enough of the latter, what there is reflects movement in the right direction and appears to follow from the new discovery of millions of citizens living in the Borderlands. Finally, economic growth should generate more financial resources, facilitating state and local programs to renew the region's infrastructure and resist its environmental degradation.

But none of these positive contributions can diminish the negative influences that NAFTA threatens in the Borderlands. The newly evolving economic initiatives promise to overload an already insufficient human and physical infrastructure, compounding environmental problems that are an intrinsic byproduct of economic growth. Threats to public health complete the inevitable process of cause and effect that progresses from infrastructural overload to environmental degradation. It will demand a gargantuan effort from the United States and Mexico to avoid those deleterious consequences. That effort is not likely to materialize.

NOTES

1. Randall G. Hopkins, *The Economic Impact of Mexican Visitors to Mexico* (Tucson, Ariz.: College of Business Administration, 1992), p. 23.

2. See John A. García, "The Voting Rights Act and Hispanic Political Representation in the Southwest," *Publius,* Vol. 16, No. 4 (Fall 1986), esp. Tables 2, 3, 4, 5, 6; and National Association of Latino Elected Officials (NALEO), *1993 National Roster of Hispanic Elected Officials* (Los Angeles: NALEO, 1993), Tables 2 and 6.

3. See *Assessment of Border Crossings and Transportation Corridors for North American Trade* (Washington, D.C.: Federal Highway Administration, U.S. Department of Transportation, n.d.).

4. "Burlington Northern, Santa Fe Reach Deal on Railroad Merger," *Arizona Daily Star* (Tucson), July 1, 1994.

5. For the estimate, see "Rural Alert," *Latin American Weekly Report,* July 21, 1994.

6. United States General Accounting Office (USGAO), *U.S.–Mexico Trade: Survey of U.S. Border Infrastructure Needs* (Washington, D.C.: USGAO, November 1991), especially pp. 2–3.

7. "Los Especialistas en Ambiente Son Escasos," *El Informador* (Guadalajara), July 28, 1992.

8. USGAO, *U.S.–Mexico Trade: Concerns About the Adequacy of Border Infrastructure* (Washington, D.C.: USGAO, May, 1991).

9. Earl W. Sires, "The Impact of Population Growth on Community Services: Nogales, Arizona," paper presented at a Binational Conference on Border Health, Industry, and the Environment, Rio Rico, Arizona, 1990, p. 4.

10. Author's interview, Mexicali, July 1988. The study is CANACINTRA, *Análisis de Mano de Obra en Mexicali* (Mexicali: CANACINTRA, 1988).

11. "No Stopping Sewage Flow," *San Diego Union*, February 5, 1992.

12. Committee on Scientific Affairs, "A Permanent U.S.–Mexican Border Environmental Health Commission," *JAMA*, June 2, 1990, pp. 3319, 3320.

13. Christopher Connell, "U.S.–Mexico OK $700 Million Border Cleanup," *Arizona Daily Star* (Tucson), February 26, 1992.

14. On the several estimates, see Dolia Estévez, "White House Explores Options in Making Free-Trade Investments," *El Financiero Internacional* (Los Angeles), July 19–25, 1993; Dick Kamp, Letter to Leon Panetta, July 29, 1994, Bisbee, Arizona; and Pan American Health Organization/World Health Organization, "Proposal for the Establishment of a Preinvestment Facility in Health and the Environment on the U.S.–Mexican Border" (Phoenix, Ariz.: May 1994), p. 1.

15. The critique is "NAFTA's Border Funding Promises: Separating Hype from Help," *Borderlines*, Vol. 1, No. 4 (December 1993), pp. 1ff. The NADBANK figure is from "Fact Sheet on the U.S./Mexican Agreement" (Washington, D.C.: U.S. Department of the Treasury, n.d.), p. 2.

9

Mexican Modernization's Consequences for Mexican Undocumented Labor Migration

Jesús Tamayo

Amid the 1993 debate on NAFTA, advocates struck a responsive cord by arguing that the agreement would reduce undocumented Mexican migration to the United States. About the same time, California's Governor Pete Wilson played the same theme and set in motion a campaign to extract additional funding from the federal government to compensate states for monies spent to educate, incarcerate, and offer medical and social services to undocumented migrants.

In Mexico, the government of Carlos Salinas energetically pushed a series of reforms designed to modernize the economy. The measures achieved some successes in several sectors, but none reduced the number of undocumented Mexican workers moving to the United States in search of work. To the contrary, the reforms probably added additional push factors, increasing the number of *indocumentados* (undocumented migrants) crossing the border.

Reflecting those and other factors, a new wave of antimigration sentiment swept the U.S. political scene. In response, growing discord crept into U.S.–Mexican relations, jeopardizing the relatively good feelings that had characterized the bilateral relationship since the mid-1980s.

This chapter describes and analyzes Mexican undocumented migration, emphasizing the causal influences of Mexican modernization and the U.S. response to the growing number of Mexican workers. After providing a historical and conceptual context, coping strategies are set out and various scenarios analyzed. The treatment is as close to objective as any social science analysis gets, but it also frequently reflects a Mexican perspective on the issue. That perspective differs from many conventional U.S. foci and should add an increment of understanding to the multiple dimensions of the issue.

THE CONTEXT

After the Mexican–American War (1846–1848), the Mexican and Mexican-American presence in the U.S. Southwest diminished significantly, but before too long it experienced a resurgence. In the last third of the nineteenth century, Mexican workers returned to provide labor for the construction of railroads and the emerging mining and agricultural initiatives of the time.

In the first decades of the 20th century, flight from the violence of the Mexican Revolution catalyzed another movement of *Mexicanos* to the United States. At the same time, Mexican labor increasingly weaved into the warp and woof of the U.S. economy, particularly the agricultural sector of the Southwest. From that time on, permanent Mexican settlement became an important part of the migration of Mexican labor to the United States.

By the 1940s, the Bracero Program signaled another critical dimension of movement of Mexican labor. In the context of a binational treaty designed to replace U.S. farmworkers gone to fight in World War II, Mexican workers moved legally to the United States to work in agriculture and other sectors. Some Mexican nationals even joined the U.S. military and served in the war. The Bracero Program ended in 1964, but institutionalized demand for Mexican labor continued and, indeed, increased as time went on. A difference in the post-1964 period, however, was that almost all Mexican workers contributing to the U.S. economy worked without documentation. They were illegal. In spite of the ebbs and tides of migration, the schizophrenic reaction of the United States to the Mexican undocumented worker and labor flow persists and the stock of workers settled north of the border continues to grow. In the mid-1990s, the Mexican presence is significant and clearly on the increase.[1] In 1990, one of every four inhabitants of Texas was a Latino, almost all of Mexican heritage. According to U.S. demographers, Latinos composed 38 percent of California's population in 1995. Between 2000 and 2005, the percentage will grow to about 45 percent, with the Anglos in the minority, at about 40 percent.[2]

The significance of this undocumented labor for Mexico and the United States tends to differ with varying perspectives. For the Mexican worker, employment opportunities in the United States offer jobs at a relatively good wage. Unemployment and underemployment in Mexico are always high, and wages remain low. Indeed, in recent years the situation has been worse than ever, with fewer jobs at less pay. For their part, U.S. employers have benefitted from a hard-working labor force that is both reliable and formally unorganized.

Governmental perceptions of undocumented workers form another important dimension. When the issue surfaced in the 1970s, the U.S. government appeared to be preoccupied with getting a count of Mexican *indocumentados* and spent a fair amount of effort and money in the process. Fortunately, that sterile initiative no longer dominates the agenda. By the mid-1990s, both governments tended to be better informed and more realistic. The Mexican government is fully cognizant of the economic value of the remittances sent back by the workers. Although it jealously guards its own boundary line, its official position is that Mexican migration follows economic laws beyond the dictates of political sovereignty. Moreover, it increasingly emphasizes the need for the United States to be fastidious in respecting the human rights of Mexican workers.

From the U.S. side, flexibility and adaptability (or cynicism?) has guided policy implementation. For example, the boundary line is opened or closed depending on the needs of the regional labor force. In another strategy, the United States has used the issue of undocumented migration to soften the Mexican government on other bilateral issues.

From the mid-1980s through the early 1990s, it appeared that the U.S. and Mexican governments had arrived at a migratory status quo. A tacit agreement seemed to have emerged that promised stability to a situation that benefitted many people and groups on both sides of the border. The scenario included a series of reciprocal benefits. U.S. employers gained good workers, and Mexican workers found good employment. Large numbers of young Mexicans left their homeland, where they might have grown frustrated and rebellious. The Mexican government received foreign exchange from remittances.

As part of the implicit bargain, the Mexican government played down the infringement of human rights of Mexican *indocumentados* as isolated events caused by local aberrations. In turn, the U.S. government turned a deaf ear to groups pressuring for a more active policy against undocumented migration.

By the mid-1990s, the scenario had changed markedly. Antimigration sentiments skyrocketed in the United States. The Mexican government inched toward a more aggressive critique on human rights issues. A number of factors on both sides help explain the change, but the basic principle is relatively straightforward. In Mexico, some components of the economic modernization policy contribute to the push of undocumented workers to the United States. In the latter, attitudinal changes on the desirability of this migration were wrought by the persistent sluggishness of the U.S. economy, compounded by the agony of restructuring and downsizing. The NAFTA debate catalyzed the hypothesis of Mexican migration as a cause of U.S. economic problems.

Whatever the weights of these and other factors, the principle is simple.

Sometime around 1993, the Mexican migration rate superseded the rate of assimilation or social acceptability in the United States.

INTERNATIONAL AND BINATIONAL INFLUENCES

Three influences inform the present state of Mexican undocumented migration to the United States: (1) an evolution toward global economic integration that both influences and reflects moves toward hemispheric economic cooperation, (2) the more concrete exemplification of that trend in NAFTA and Mexican governmental efforts to evolve ever closer articulation with the U.S. economy, and (3) an uncertain economy in the United States that leads to apprehension on the part of American policy makers and concern from the public.

The emergence of a global economy derives from both economic and political changes. Technological advances in manufacturing have encouraged increasing economies of scale, and the rise of the multinational corporation has mirrored and fostered the move to economic organizations with worldwide production and distribution facilities. Current modes of production have outgrown the traditional nation-state. The rise of economic liberalism in the late 1970s also contributed to the establishment of the global economy. Many governments and international organizations became imbued with the ideology of free trade, thereby giving free reign to the multinationals.

Extrapolating from some of these factors, the Mexican–U.S. relationship has been greatly influenced by economic regionalism. Even before the ratification of NAFTA, the two nations had initiated a series of measures that, in retrospect, seemed to have inexorably led to growing levels of integration.

Reversing long-held economic and political positions, the Mexican government has moved rapidly to embrace a market economy and free trade. The hesitant initiatives of President Miguel de la Madrid Hurtado (1982–1988) began the process. President Salinas extended and intensified those measures in agreeing to the idea of NAFTA, while privatizing government-owned industries and cutting back some subsidies on the domestic front.

At the same time, de la Madrid and Salinas had to sell the new theory and practice to the increasingly impoverished middle sectors. Beyond the resurrection of economic liberalism, the post-1982 Mexican regimes had to prepare the country for a historic reconciliation with the United States. Government publicists held out the promise of future economic benefits, as they encouraged Mexicans to set aside their traditional fear of U.S. investment in the local economy. In one fell swoop, the government undid the state's patrimony and reconciled with the United States—both in the name of modernization.

Another part of the explanation centers on the U.S. economy, which has been experiencing significant difficulties since at least the mid-1980s. Mexicans, above all, appreciate the strength of their neighbor's economy, but they also recognize some of its weaknesses. The United States, for instance, is clearly challenged by the competitiveness of the European and Japanese economies. Even with Japan in relative recession, the dollar slipped below 100 yen in mid-1994 for the first time since the end of World War II. The U.S. trade balance remains endemically in a negative state. Unemployment and factory closures continue at a disturbingly high rate.

Some Mexicans fear that these difficulties will strengthen protectionism, decreasing the openness of the American economy, jeopardizing NAFTA, and threatening the Mexican economy. The ongoing attempt of the U.S. steel industry to box out Mexican imports is only one of several examples cited by critics.[3]

Nor do basic structural modifications in global production appear to be doing much to change the direction of the relative decline of the U.S. economy. Responding to global competition, particularly from the Pacific Rim, some American entrepreneurs have relocated their labor-intensive activities on "export platforms" in developing countries. The Mexican Border Industrialization Program (or *maquiladora* industry) is a case in point. Wage levels are low enough in those nations to more than compensate for any additional transportation costs incurred in the geographic relocation of plants.

Theoretically, this redeployment looked to export to other countries semiobsolete processes, encouraging the U.S. economy to specialize in high-tech activities. The scenario depicted a situation in which everyone would win and the world economy would be better off. But if those gains are being achieved, they are painfully slow. Furthermore, as the NAFTA debate so vividly exemplified, U.S. workers are ill inclined to sacrifice their present employment on the altar of a distant and uncertain future, no matter how radiant it may be in the minds of international economists or statespeople.

The implications of the psychology of protectionism in the United States are certain to apply to the flow of Mexican workers. As belt tightening progresses and impacts on the flow of U.S. imports, so will it spill over into the area of migration. If the popular will or the strategies of political leaders close out Mexican steel from entering the United States, the same process will soon lead to an attempt to close the border to undocumented workers.

SOME PROBLEMS WITH MEXICAN MODERNIZATION

The modernization program in Mexico may reap measurable benefits in the long run, but it is fraught with problems for the short and medium terms. Mexican industry has enjoyed government protection since the late 1930s. As protective tariffs fall and import licenses are no longer applicable, industry will be cast to the fortunes of international competition. It is no exaggeration to suggest that Mexican industry will either modernize or expire. The reconversion of traditional industry is unavoidable. The problem is that it must weather the economic storms of the transition before it can reap the benefits of reconversion.

By the early 1990s, it had become clear that the Mexican economy was still in trouble.[4] A 1993 study by a private consulting firm[5] found that only 17.5 million Mexicans sustained the national economy, with about 9 million unemployed or underemployed, about half in each category. From 1990 through 1992, the percentage of Mexico's productive plant capacity that lay idle had increased. In 1994, the government was admitting to even "greater unemployment due to the reorganization of companies, as well as the disappearance of others."[6]

Economic growth in 1993 registered a disappointing 0.5 percent, dramatically below the predictions of 3 percent and well below the rate of population growth. Thus, Mexico suffered negative growth per capita. In 1993, industries that produced footwear, textiles, and automobiles were all down from the previous year. Investment was off from 1992. By the end of the year, the price of Mexican oil on the international market had dropped to about $11 a barrel, roughly $2 below the price budgeted by the Treasury. Moreover, the petroleum situation looked no better for 1994 or 1995 and beyond.[7]

The nation's trade balance also continued to be negative. Most troubling, sizable increases in capital flight occurred. In 1992 and 1993, the trade deficit hovered around $20 billion; 1994 promised some improvement, but still a shortfall of some $16 billion. Tied to political turmoil and the overvaluation of the peso, these indicators encouraged a rash of capital flight in 1994, reportedly totaling $11 billion by midyear.[8]

These figures have everything to do with undocumented migration. Although the relationship is imperfect, the volume of migration is inversely proportionate to the strength of the Mexican economy. When the economy is vibrant, employment grows and wages tend to improve, reducing the incentive to leave. Conversely, a faltering economy pushes some of the unemployed and underemployed to the United States.

Political factors also form part of the equation influencing economic growth and migratory propensities. The country's political situation turned precarious in 1994, and the transition to the Zedillo administration remained uncertain. Events in the first half of 1994 struck fear in Mexico. The year began with the Zapatista rebellion in Chiapas. Not long after, an assassin gunned down the PRIista candidate, Luis Donaldo Colosio. A rash of kidnappings shook the confidence of the monied elite and catalyzed Salinas into establishing an ominous National Public Security Office.

Finally, the 1992 revision of Article 27 of the Constitution impacts directly on undocumented migration. The change revoked the noncommercial status of the *ejido,* permitting the peasant *ejiditarios* to sell their lands.

Highlighted by the Zapatistas as one cause of their uprising, the measure evokes passion throughout the Republic. Exact figures are difficult to determine, but at least 2 to 2.5 million peasants are expected to leave the land as they sell their holdings. Those millions will migrate to urban areas, and some will move to the United States.

This analysis may be a bit too pessimistic to be taken *in toto,* but the major premise stands. The modernization begun in the mid-1980s by President de la Madrid and embraced with a vengeance by President Salinas contributes to the flow of undocumented migration. As the supporters of NAFTA argued, in the long run modernization may help reduce the flow. But by then, we (and they) will all be dead.

Furthermore, strategies evolving in both Mexico and the United States indicate that others have arrived at the same conclusion. Undocumented migrants are going north in greater numbers in the mid-1990s than at any time since the early 1980s, the worst years of the recession. Moreover, in 1993 the planners at the federal government's *Secretaría de Desarrollo Social* (Secretariat of Social Development, SEDESOL) announced a proposal to anticipate significantly increased migration to Mexico's medium-sized cities. The SEDESOL planners focused on those peasants likely to leave the land in the wake of implementation of Article 27 revision. They did not, of course, note that many of those people would be moving to the United States rather than to Mexican cities, but their analysis of the migratory implications of this one dimension of the modernization program lends credence to the argument presented here.

The modernization program's contribution to infrastructural improvement combines with the growing overall sophistication of transportation and communication to add another element to those forces stimulating migration. Even the poorest Mexican village boasts a display of television antennas, attesting to the masses' familiarity with TV's romanticized version of the United States. Moreover, the Salinas administration has crossed the country with a vastly improved system of four-lane highways. The average Mexican knows more about the United States than in the past, and it is easier to travel there. Hence, there is a temptation to join the *indocumentados* wending their way north.

In a perverse way, the survival strategies developed by the urban poor in Mexico City and elsewhere also offer testimony to the dislocation wrought by modernization. Marginalized populations have flocked to the informal sector as street vendors; they have multiplied wage earners by sending wives and children into the formal and informal labor force; and some, sadly enough, have taken to vice and crime in an attempt to sustain themselves. Many are driven to those extremes to avoid the necessity of migration, but every clawing effort is an indication of the forces pushing Mexico's marginalized peoples to the United States.

Finally, many U.S. academic specialists and policy makers have concluded that modernization means increased pressures for migration. The decision to include this chapter in a volume on contemporary Mexican developments offers a measure of proof that scholars are aware that the issue is a salient feature of present-day Mexican reality.

In sum, there is abundant evidence that on the Mexican side of the boundary, many recognize the implications of modernization for undocumented migration. The poor scrape to keep the family in Mexico, the policy makers propose remedies and plan responses, the politicos fan public apprehension, and dislocated Mexicans move north.

THE CONTEMPORARY SETTING

Current prospects offer little promise of a resolution to the issue of undocumented workers. Trends in both Mexico and the United States offer no easy answer. Indeed, every indication points to more complications driving the two sides farther apart rather than closer to a negotiated settlement.

In the first instance, the erosion of U.S. competitiveness in the international market is not about to be reversed in the foreseeable future. Although the completion of the Uruguay Round of GATT offered some advantages to the United States, analysts in Mexico, the United States, and elsewhere have been lukewarm in their evaluation of those gains. All agree that the United States is not winning the trade war with Japan and Europe, and a solid majority would argue that it is still on the short end of the conflict. Thus, the future augurs more of the same. The United States promises to be engaged in frequent skirmishes with Europe and Japan over tariffs, quotas, intellectual property rights, health and safety standards, and dozens of other issues that confound the free interchange of goods and services between nations.

The same scenario will pertain within NAFTA and its Latin American extrapolations expected within the next decade or so. In Mexico, it is commonly thought that the trade agreement will be complicated by U.S. charges concerning putative Mexican transgressions of health and environmental restrictions, safety standards, dumping, export surges, and other real and imagined problems. Of course, the supposed threat of undocumented migration will wind its way through much of that debate.

As for Mexico, its role in NAFTA and its position on the agreement's expansion to other American countries remains uncertain. Even more germane to this analysis, the government's position on the role of Mexican undocumented (or documented) labor in the free trade zone continues to be ill defined. Some argue convincingly that the logic of a free trade area should include the free movement of labor as well as goods and services. If *gringo* widgets can enter freely into Mexico, then Mexican workers ought to enter freely into the United States. Others counsel that Mexico should do all it can to keep its workers at home to contribute to the national productive effort. Still others recognize the political realities on both sides of the border that prevent Mexico from energetically pressing either alternative. The Mexican government appears to have settled on an ambivalent policy in a vain attempt to please the several sides, while maintaining its political options.

Although all these considerations spell problems in the bilateral relationship, the die may well be cast. The two economies will continue their growing articulation, barring a dramatic explosion triggering a completely new direction in policy from one side or the other. Increased integration of the economies was underway even before NAFTA. For example, Mexico launched the Border Industrialization Program in 1965, fostering the *maquiladora* industry, which established a system of production sharing between the two countries. Mexico's adherence to GATT (now the World Trade Organization) in 1986 signaled another important step toward binational economic integration. From another perspective, the expanding number of U.S.–owned firms in Mexico implies ever-larger amounts of intrafirm trading between companies in the United States and their subsidiaries in Mexico.

Even if American protectionism runs amok, a limited number of important Mexican products would certainly continue to be welcomed in the United States. Mexican petroleum is a case in point. A number of Mexican minerals are also crucial to U.S. industry. Of course, winter vegetables and fruits of all varieties have a secure place in the U.S. market.

Even if that part of the binational balance evolves as outlined here, the future promises increasing stresses and strains, occasionally exploding into open conflict. The Zedillo administration is less dedicated to rapid reconversion than its predecessor. The rebellion in Chiapas triggered a growing demand to cushion the agony of social dislocation wrought by the modernization program. Intertwined with the natural complexity of administering NAFTA, the Mexican government's adjustment of its domestic policies creates a context fraught with potential for friction.

On the U.S. side, the expanding tide of nativism and antimigration sentiment is bound to become worse before its gets better. Many in Mexico (and the United States) deplore the contemporary anti-Mexican tone of the debate. Prodded by public concern and/or political ambition, local officials, state legislators, governors, and federal officials crowd the antimigration bandwagon to proclaim their position against the supposedly deleterious consequences of undocumented workers. Several governors have filed suits to gain financial support from the federal government. Such actions have, intentionally or not, inflamed public opinion. Electoral rhetoric brims with schemes and counterschemes to solve the "problem" of the *indocumentados*. As the argument heats up, proposals to toughen sanctions against employers mix with the fever to construct higher and sturdier walls and to employ even more military men with even more firepower.

The Immigration and Naturalization Service, the Border Patrol, the U.S. Customs Service, some elements of the military, and other border-related bureaucracies also play on the theme of migration. They claim all kinds and degrees of nefarious ramifications of the Mexican poor seeking gainful employment in the United States. They also advertise their ability and readiness to combat the danger. In the process, of course, they petition budgetary increases to expand their personnel and/or hardware.

In mid-1994, the inevitable surfaced when several U.S. federal representatives declared that scotching the flow of undocumented workers was an imperative of national security.[9] To paraphrase Dr. Samuel Johnson, the specter of a threat to national security seems to be the last recourse of stymied policy makers. If arguments of social progress or economic advantage fail to convince the public, the image of a threat to national security may succeed. Although Mexican friends of the United States hope fervently that xenophobic nativism does not take the same destructive turn that it has in some European countries, the tendencies are cause for concern.

WHAT IS TO BE DONE?

Several strategies appear to be appropriate for Mexicans and Americans as they face the increasingly passionate issue of undocumented migration. The first is applicable to both nations; the second and third are more germane to Mexico and the United States, respectively, although elements may be relevant for both.

First, both Mexicans and Americans need to fathom the entire process of undocumented migration, from its original causes through its several effects in both countries. Informed citizens and policy makers must seek to understand the positions of both sides, especially the other side. Beyond grasping the socioeconomic nuances of the issue, it is also imperative to understand the political possibilities and limitations that inform policy makers. One definition of politics is "the passionate pursuit of the second best." In that sense, it may be that politically feasible or acceptable policies in Mexico City and/or Washington will be viewed as second best in the other capital. That is the nature of the political process.

Second, the Mexican government needs to undertake several policies and programs as part of a joint effort to alleviate the negative dimensions of undocumented migration to the United States. Clearly, Mexico must push for economic growth to diminish labor outmigration. It must repudiate its premodern social, economic, and political structures and processes and nurture the evolution of a modern system designed to produce more goods and services, distribute them more equitably, and establish norms for socioeconomic activity within a participatory, democratic political arrangement. In the long run, that system will encourage Mexico's young, productive, and vibrant workers to remain in their country and contribute their considerable talents and energies to a more successful Mexico. Such reforms will defuse criticism and opposition in the United States as the numbers of Mexicans moving north decrease.

But Mexican policy makers need to realize that the rate of the demolition of the old cannot exceed the rate at which the new processes and institutions are created and mature. Social and economic modernization do not emerge with the formal act of signing a decree, but rather result from slow, difficult, and sometimes painful incremental progress. Training traditional peoples for industrial work, for example, requires profound changes in sociocultural values. Those changes, in turn, evolve from rethinking the theory and practice of education and, perhaps, the very bases of social organization. A social organization that nurtures the emergence of free men and women may be even more challenging. A civic culture that gives rise to the practice of participatory democracy may be the most difficult creation of all.

Eloquent speeches or artistically designed legal norms form only a minute part of the larger modernization process. If a government promotes educational reform but resists the revision of premodern, corporative political structures or panics at the thought of independent social organizations, it is pursuing contradictory policies destined for failure.

As a fallout from the shock of the Zapatista rebellion and the 1994 election campaign, the Zedillo *sexenio* promises to be more socially oriented than that of President Salinas. With hindsight, it is obvious that the urban and rural poor paid too high a price for the "reforms" of the 1980s and early 1990s. Moreover, Salinas' social development program, Solidarity, proved to be too little, too late, if not basically flawed from the outset.

Third, U.S. citizens and policy makers need to understand the larger context of Mexican undocumented migration. This is no perverse scheme designed to threaten the United States. On the contrary, the migration follows a natural and impeccable logic. It reflects the desire of relatively poor people to improve their lot. Furthermore, Mexican undocumented migrants make a significant contribution to the U.S. economy.

Given these realities, two U.S. strategies may reduce and/or more efficiently manage the movement of labor. The first is based on a recognition that relative poverty is the most important push factor encouraging Mexicans to move to the United States.[10] Therefore, a reduction in relative poverty will reduce the temptation to leave. NAFTA supporters hit hard on that issue and probably overplayed it, but the general point is valid. In the same context, the United States should sympathize with sociopolitical reform fashioned to reduce the inequities of Mexico's maldistribution of wealth. The lesson of Chiapas proves that economic change is only part of a more global process of profound, comprehensive change.

A second set of strategies revolves about efforts to manage migration more effectively. It is time once again to manage and institutionalize labor movement through a guest worker program. The Bracero Program (1942–1964) suffered from many shortcomings, but it also counted significant advantages for the U.S. and Mexican economies. A guest worker program for the 21st century should accentuate the positive dimensions of that experience and others and work to reduce the negatives.

Undocumented migration is a complex issue. It is not clear that these prescriptions will be successful in responding to its fundamental causes or resolving its vexatious effects. But some efforts are mandatory. From the Mexican perspective, it is frighteningly evident that xenophobic nativism is on the rise in the United States, threatening to trigger a crisis in Mexican–U.S. relations.

NOTES

1. See George Vernez and David Ronfeldt, "The Current Situation in Mexican Immigration," *Science,* March 8, 1991, pp. 1189–93.

2. *El Financiero,* February 2, 1993.

3. See "Steel Dispute Heats Up," *El Financiero Internacional,* Mexico, D.F., February 15, 1993.

4. See, for example, a report on increasing unemployment in *El Mañana* (Nuevo Laredo), May 11, 1993.

5. Grupo de Economistas y Asociados, Mexico, D.F., 1993.

6. Banamex-Accival, *Review of the Economic Situation of Mexico,* March 1994, p. 112.

7. Banamex-Accival, *Review of the Economic Situation of Mexico,* February 1994, pp. 61, 93; March 1994, p. 112.

8. See "Trade Balance" and "Capital Flight Ahead of Repatriation," *Latin American Weekly Report,* February and June 1994, pp. 58, 260.

9. Stephen Green, "House OKs Plan to Put Troops on the Border," *San Diego Union-Tribune,* June 9, 1994.

10. See the Report of the Commission for the Study of International Migration and Cooperative Economic Development, *Unauthorized Migration: An Economic Development Response,* Executive Summary, 1990.

10

The Zapatista Revolt and Its Implications for Civil–Military Relations and the Future of Mexico

Stephen J. Wager and Donald E. Schulz

The 1994 New Year's celebration in Mexico started with a bang. A mere hour into the year, the Zapatista National Liberation Army (EZLN) assaulted and captured four cities in the Los Altos region of Chiapas, Mexico's southernmost state. The *Ejército Zapatista de Liberación Nacional* shocked the Mexican people and most of the world. Although Mexican political and military leaders denied that they were caught off guard, they were in fact totally surprised by the magnitude of the assault.

As events unfolded, the reasons behind the seizure of San Cristóbal de las Casas, Las Margaritas, Altamirano, and Ocosingo became apparent. The Zapatistas called for a nationwide movement for "jobs, land, housing, food, health, independence, freedom, democracy, justice and peace." Unlike traditional guerrillas, they did not seek to destroy the state, but rather to shift "the balance of forces in favor of popular and democratic movements, thereby isolating and ultimately defeating anti-democratic tendencies" within the PRI, the state, and the rest of society.[1] Whether or not the Zapatistas will be able to accomplish their goal of making government more accountable to the people and establishing fair representation for all Mexicans remains to be seen. However, almost a year after the initial uprising, the movement has prompted some visible changes, including some positive ones. In fact, the Zapatistas may have done more to accelerate democratization than the previous five years of dramatic economic reform engineered by President Salinas.

As the government responded to the crisis, one point became clear: The rebellion was not a "military problem." Instead, it can most properly be viewed as a concatenation of the many endemic economic, political, and social problems not only in Chiapas but in most of rural Mexico. Nonetheless, the army's involvement in restoring order has in some ways changed a long-standing civil-military equation. To understand this change, one must examine the military's response in light of other recent problems confronting the armed forces. This chapter will look at that reaction within the context of the institution's response to the transition to democracy. We will also analyze the implications of this increasingly rapid democratization for the Mexican army.

THE ROOTS OF THE CONFLICT

The contrasts between Chiapas and the rest of Mexico are both striking and sobering. In Mexico as a whole, only 29 percent of the populace lives in rural areas; in Chiapas the figure is 60 percent. Although the Mexican illiteracy rate is 13 percent, for *chiapanecos* it is 31 percent. A third of the households in Chiapas are without electricity, 41.6 percent are without drinking water, and 58.8 percent lack drainage. (The figures for all of Mexico are 12.5 percent, 20.6 percent, and 36.4 percent, respectively.)[2] Moreover, the data for Ocosingo, Altamirano, and Las Margaritas—three of the cities captured by the Zapatistas—highlight even greater contrasts. In Altamirano, 75 percent of the households lack electricity, and the figures for Ocosingo and Las Margaritas are almost as large. In Las Margaritas, 72.7 percent are without drinking water.[3] The farther into the countryside, the fewer such amenities are to be found.

Yet Chiapas is a rich land. The region contains fertile farmlands, pastures, and forests and an abundance of petroleum. It is a major source of the nation's coffee as well as three-fifths of its electricity. The problem is that the wealth is maldistributed. The gap between rich and poor is probably as great as anywhere in the hemisphere. A little over a hundred people—just 0.16 percent of all coffee farmers—control 12 percent of the coffee lands. Some 6,000 families hold over 3 million hectares of cattle land—the equivalent to almost half the territory of all of the state's rural landholdings.[4]

These elites have access to the best land and infrastructure and most of the credit. Over the years, they have acquired their properties by fair means and foul. The system dates back to Spanish colonial days, when many of their ancestors received grants of land, labor, and tribute from the Crown. Ever since, the members of this "Chiapas Family" have been able to dominate the local power structures and assure that their interests would be protected. In alliance with local PRI political bosses, they have been able to manipulate the legal system by bribing officials and securing delays and exemptions while assuring that the letter of the law would be applied to those without money or influence. Many of their estates were created illegally, through the violent seizure of *ejido* and national lands, and maintained by private armies and the complicity of local judges, sheriffs, and military commanders. A sign which as recently as 1971 hung in the Ocosingo Lions Club said it all: "In the Law of the Jungle it is willed that Indians and blackbirds must be killed."[5]

Although the rebellion caught the government by surprise, it had been brewing for years.[6] In the decades prior to the uprising, a wide variety of groups had been active in promoting peasant organizational activities. As early as the late 1960s, Catholic priests and catechists, inspired by Liberation Theology, had begun to engage in politically oriented pastoral work, especially in the Diocese of San Cristóbal de las Casas. During the 1970s, other organizations (among them, the Proletarian Line, People United, the Socialist Workers Party, and the Independent Organization of Agricultural Workers and Peasants–Mexican Communist Party) also became involved. Beginning in 1979, moreover, a broad-based revolt of the state's primary and secondary school teachers led to the formation of a "democratic teachers' movement," which embraced the *campesinos'* cause and became an interlocutor with the state government on their behalf.

By then, major socioeconomic, ecological, and demographic changes had begun to aggravate the already precarious existence of the peasants. The oil boom of the late 1970s had triggered social polarization, which was accelerated by the debt crisis of the early 1980s. After the boom ended, many highlanders who had left their homelands for more lucrative opportunities in nearby oil fields returned, bringing with them capital and new technology. They introduced modern farming methods, including fertilizers and herbicides, which allowed more intensive and extensive cultivation of the land. Unfortunately, these changes led to a dramatic increase in soil erosion and a loss of fertility, which sapped the land's ability to sustain the human population. They increasingly polarized communities as the new entrepreneurs expanded their wealth, often at the expense of those at the bottom of the socioeconomic pyramid. As peasants were pushed off the land by more powerful agro-export farmers and cattle ranchers, many drifted to urban areas or the agricultural frontiers in the Lacandona lowland.

Social tensions were further aggravated by rapid population growth (the rate in Chiapas is 4.5 percent, which means that the population doubles every sixteen years)[7] and the arrival of some 100,000 Guatemalans, most of whom were fleeing bloody counterinsurgency operations in their own country. Furthermore, after August 1982 Mexico entered into a period of financial crisis and economic stagnation unprecedented since the Great Depression. Over the next half-dozen years, unemployment and inflation soared, while real wages and per capita GNP plummeted. In response, the de la Madrid administration adopted a neoliberal economic strategy. Government spending was slashed, and the bureaucracy reduced. The poor and the middle class were hardest hit.

In short, a combination of factors had produced a milieu that was ripe for alienation and political organization. Grassroots intellectuals, religious catechists, Marxist organizers, and other proponents of change (including federal development agencies, such as the National Indigenous Institute) helped raise the political consciousness of Chiapas' peasants and Indians, encouraging them to organize to defend their interests. The upshot was a proliferation of *campesino* groups, the most important being the Union of Ejido Unions (UU), the Independent Central of Agricultural Workers and Peasants (CIOAC), and the Emiliano Zapata Peasant Organization (OCEZ). As *campesino* militance increased and calls for agrarian reform and political change intensified, so did violence. When peasants began seizing land, the ranchers unleashed paramilitary squads. *Campesino* leaders were killed, and entire villages were threatened and in some cases burned to the ground. Local authorities, as usual, sided with the cattlemen.

Under the Salinas administration (1988–1994), the situation deteriorated further. A collapse of coffee prices devastated local producers, causing both productivity and total output to fall by about 35 percent between 1989 and 1993. On average, small growers suffered a 65 to 70 percent drop in income. Many were forced to abandon production.[8]

Meanwhile, the administration was accelerating and extending the economic policies of its predecessor. Article 27 of the constitution was revised and a new Agrarian Law passed. These measures formally ended the government's moribund land distribution program. *Ejido* members now acquired the right to sell their lands. At the same time, however, they had to cope with reduced agricultural subsidies, privatization of state enterprises, and liberalized trade policies. When import licenses were removed, many peasants found themselves unable to sell their crops because of the sudden influx of cheaper grains from the United States. Although corn and beans continued to be subsidized, under NAFTA all tariffs and import quotas were to be phased out gradually. In combination with the *ejido* reform, these measures raised the prospect that landlessness and rural inequalities might soon grow much worse, as millions of *campesinos,* unable to compete with foreign imports, were forced off the land. The resulting insecurity and confusion fueled discontent throughout rural Mexico, providing the Zapatistas with a base of support on which to launch their rebellion.

Not even Solidarity, President Salinas' much-lauded social development program, ameliorated these fears and realities. During Salinas' first five years in office, federal spending in Chiapas increased more than tenfold. Solidarity funding grew 130 percent in 1989–1990, 50 percent in 1990–1991, 20 percent in 1991–1992, and a further 1 percent in 1992–1993.[9] But much of this money ended up in the pockets of local political bosses. Meanwhile, these same authorities frustrated the efforts of poor Indians and *campesinos* to pursue their interests within the system. It was symptomatic that some 30 percent of Mexico's unresolved land petitions came from Chiapas.[10]

Salinas was the most modern of Mexican presidents. Yet in spite of pledges of reform and democratization, in Chiapas he chose to work with the existing retrograde power structure. Indeed, he depended on these elements—and on others like them throughout rural areas of the country—for his own political fortune. In the 1988 election, this system had delivered between 85 and 90 percent of the state's vote. In the 1991 federal elections, the PRI had won 100 percent of the vote in fifty municipalities, many in precisely those areas most affected by the insurrection.[11]

In short, the first five years of Salinas' term brought few changes in the state's governance. The new "reform" governor, Patrocinio González Garrido, continued the repressive practices of his predecessor. Electoral fraud continued unabated. By 1990–1991, social conflicts were sharply on the rise. As land invasions and protest movements proliferated, the authorities cracked down. So harsh was the repression that the Bishop of San Cristóbal de las Casas, Samuel Ruiz García, set up a diocesan human rights center to document the abuses.

In October 1992, moreover, an extraordinary demonstration took place in San Cristóbal. During a celebration commemorating 500 years of popular resistance, thousands of peasants took to the streets, toppling and smashing the statue of conquistador Diego de Mazariegos, a symbol of white domination. For some, this was an important psychological turning point, crystallizing what many already felt: that violence was the only way to achieve Indian demands.

KNOWING THE ENEMY

One of the tenets of a sound military operation is to know the enemy. On January 1, 1994, Mexican government officials were forced to scramble to identify the insurgents. Ironically, the Zapatistas provided some immediate assistance. Subcomandante Marcos burst onto the national scene with the now famous "Declaration of the Lacandona Jungle," which declared war on the Mexican army, called for the repudiation of President Salinas, and demanded the establishment of a transitional government. The masked commander gained immediate notoriety as well as hero status in the eyes of many Mexicans, including many marginalized peasants and members of the middle class throughout the country. Marcos projected the image of a Robin Hood defending the rights of the downtrodden against an unjust and repressive government. His physical appearance added to his aura. Although a black ski mask remained a permanent part of his uniform, one could detect his handsome features and light complexion. Over the course of the next few months, he became a celebrity. Marcos dolls became the craze in Mexico City, and many women treated him like a matinee idol.

The identity of Marcos remains unknown, as do many other details about these rebels who call themselves Zapatistas, in honor of the famous

Mexican revolutionary, Emiliano Zapata, who gave his life for the cause of agrarian reform. Recent Mexican military estimates suggest that the EZLN has about 1,500 well-armed fighters with several thousand others poorly armed and trained.[12] The Zapatista army was born in the Lacandona jungle in 1983. According to some of its leaders, it has been recruiting and training there and in small, indigenous communities in central Chiapas ever since. Initially, the movement was led by a handful of "northerners"— apparently city folk of mestizo and caucasian extraction—who served as a disciplined cadre and provided military organization and training for the indigenous irregulars. Gradually, however, these outsiders were co-opted by their hosts.[13] Although the relationship between Indians and non-Indians remains unclear, at least some of the latter (most notably, Marcos) are still among the EZLN's leaders. As for the indigenous, they seem to be comprised not of the "most backward, or even the poorest, campesinos of Chiapas . . . but, rather, the innovators: adventurous frontiersmen and women who were convinced that they could make a new world."[14]

Beyond this, there is not much hard information. Although the historical underpinnings of the movement were Maoist, it has come a long way since then. Today, the ideology is much broader and more flexible, containing substantial doses of democracy as well as populism and socialism. The group's military resources are modest. According to Marcos, the guerrillas have obtained arms from the peasants themselves (obsolete rifles, shotguns, machetes, and so on) and, from the police, military and *guardias blancas* (the cattlemen's hired gunmen) through the black market.[15] Some suspect that the EZLN is getting money and weapons from other sources as well— for example, from terrorists, the Central American arms market, and kidnappings and ransoms.

The roots of the EZLN may extend as far back as October 1974, when San Cristóbal de las Casas hosted an Indigenous Congress in honor of the 500th anniversary of the birth of Fray Bartolomé de las Casas, Spain's staunchest defender of Indian rights. The convention provided a major impetus to peasant efforts to organize. This mobilization, supported in part by Liberation Theologians from the Catholic Church, led to the development of the three major campesino organizations mentioned earlier (UU, CIOAC, and OCEZ), which in turn started a struggle for rights to Indian lands and against repression. From that base, the Zapatista cadre had a ready source of recruits. Subsequently, the OCEZ and a Zapatista mass organization calling itself the National Independent Emiliano Zapata Peasant Alliance (ANCIEZ) joined together to take over the movement begun by the "northerners."

There is little information on the structure of the EZLN. Marcos has emphasized that he is not the leader of the movement but is subordinate to a Clandestine Revolutionary Indigenous Committee, which makes the major decisions after polling the organization's membership. It is believed that there is a national directorate above the clandestine committee, but little about the structure has been confirmed. Reports have circulated that the EZLN hierarchy has maintained a liaison with the Revolutionary Workers Clandestine People's Union Party (PROCUP), a longtime umbrella organization for subversive political and guerrilla groups. Mexican army sources released a schematic of the EZLN's organization, which shows clandestine committees for each of the major indigenous groups in the region and has the EZLN subordinate to those committees. According to this, there are also local militias and popular assemblies at the community level. In short, the organization is more a political-military body than a purely military one. Some captured documents indicate that the military wing of the EZLN is organized along lines similar to the Mexican army, especially with regard to unit and rank designations and military regulations.[16]

The EZLN trained at both special camps and within local communities. In some cases, whole villages participated, the women preparing food while recruits trained and elderly people tended to chores. Bases were set up in isolated areas and rugged terrain. After a decade of preparation, the group was ready to take a major step. Because it was not well armed, surprise was critical. Employing that principle of war, along with sound discipline and small-unit tactics, the Zapatistas launched their attack at San Cristóbal de las Casas, a picturesque colonial city with an international flavor. In addition to a Catholic Church strongly supportive of indigenous demands, there were many Protestant groups and nongovernmental organizations (NGOs) in the city. This would help the movement gain extensive national and international attention, one of Marcos' major aims. During the first week of January, the NGOs played a key role in disseminating information about the uprising.[17]

At first, Marcos declared freedom as the movement's goal. Although he soon moved to articulate his objectives more precisely, there remained some confusion as to the group's ideology. Although the Declaration of the Lacandona Jungle stated that the Zapatistas were fighting for socialism, Marcos did not demand a socialist government but merely a transitional one. In the second EZLN communiqué on January 1, 1994, the rebels made ten demands. The first five (jobs, land, housing, food, and health) were socioeconomic in nature, while the second five (independence, freedom, democracy, justice, and peace) were distinctly political. These demands served as a basis for negotiation after the government declared a unilateral ceasefire on January 12. As the political phase of the conflict progressed, it became apparent that the rebels were trying to force the regime to negotiate a democratic opening rather than take power themselves. Had their uprising produced a chain reaction in other states, perhaps this goal might have been altered to allow them to compete for power at the national level. But with their severely limited resources, such a course of action was simply not viable.

THE GOVERNMENT'S RESPONSE

The government responded to the events in Chiapas with great uncertainty. The Salinas administration was caught completely off guard. Official sources initially tried to downplay the situation and deflect criticism by declaring the rebellion to be the work of external influences trying to destabilize Mexico. The government blamed Central American guerrillas, the drug cartels, and, as a last resort, the Catholic Church. Even when the causes of the crisis became apparent, the official media attempted to suppress them. However, word spread rapidly via telephone, computer traffic, and the NGO network, and government radio and television stations had no alternative but to report it.

Patrocinio González Garrido, the interior minister and former governor of Chiapas, initially dismissed accounts of armed groups in the four towns that were eventually captured. The rebels held San Cristóbal for over twenty-four hours before moving on to attack the garrison of the 31st Military Zone in Rancho Nuevo. With that, the army asked for and received authorization to counterattack. By midday on January 6, military forces had dislodged the rebels from all towns and villages previously occupied, forcing most of them to flee into the Lacandona. Nevertheless, the garrison at Rancho Nuevo was subjected to intermittent attacks and sniper fire until January 12.

The conflict had two phases. The first was a military phase that virtually concluded on January 12, when President Salinas declared a unilateral ceasefire. By then, the army's presence in the region had swelled from 2,000 soldiers to over 14,000, more than enough to cordon off the Zapatistas' stronghold in the Lacandona jungle. Under those circumstances, the EZLN probably welcomed the ceasefire. At that point, the second or political phase began, and it has continued ever since. On January 10, Salinas had fired Patrocinio González because of his ineptitude and his ties to the longstanding repression in Chiapas, and replaced him with Jorge Carpizo MacGregor, the attorney general and former president of the National Commission on Human Rights. He followed that move by appointing Manuel Camacho Solís, the foreign minister and former presidential contender, as his principal peace negotiator. On January 19, Elmar Setzer, the governor of Chiapas, resigned. The next day, Congress passed an amnesty decree, clearing the way for meaningful negotiations.

By mid-January, the army had received considerable criticism for its slow response to the hostilities. Media reports described it as ill prepared and poorly equipped to carry out a successful jungle campaign. Military leaders privately fumed over these allegations. Many felt the political leaders had taken away their prerogative to complete their operations.[18] In actuality, unfavorable international attention was pushing the government toward a ceasefire. On January 4, a photo of five cadavers near the marketplace in Ocosingo hit the national and international wires. The dead men had their hands tied behind their backs and had been shot in the head, execution style. Accompanying stories placed the blame on Mexican soldiers. After this, the government could no longer withstand the pressure. Accordingly, it sought the most expeditious way to end the fighting.

Although the military served as an initial scapegoat, it soon became evident that Mexican political leaders had blundered by underestimating the size of the threat and ignoring a series of warning signs. Among the latter was a public statement by an opposition congressman that the army and Interior Ministry had information about an armed movement in Chiapas. In March 1993, the bodies of two junior officers had been found hacked to pieces and buried in a shallow pit outside an Indian village in the Los Altos region. Army and police forces ransacked two villages and tortured some of the inhabitants in search of the guilty parties. This incident was followed in May by a firefight between Mexican soldiers and a group of armed men outside Ocosingo. For months thereafter, rumors abounded of guerrillas roaming the countryside. A colonel from the 31st Military Zone reported that his unit had been conducting reconnaissance missions in search of training camps. A Jesuit priest declared that insurgents had been active for the past eight years. As late as October, residents reported seeing soldiers in numerous communities around Ocosingo and hearing gunfire at night. Nevertheless, the government issued a steady stream of denials.[19]

As events unfolded in January 1994, it became evident that the government had been following a specific agenda in attempting to cover up the guerrilla presence. It needed to put on its best face for the impending U.S. congressional vote on NAFTA. NAFTA was the key piece in Salinas' economic reforms, and Mexico could not risk its defeat by drawing attention to potentially destabilizing developments. According to one insider, a representative of the *Centro de Investigación y Seguridad Nacional* (Center of Investigation and National Security, or CISN), which is a combination Federal Bureau of Investigation and Central Intelligence Agency, had visited Chiapas on three separate occasions in May 1993 in response to the trouble there. He added that the intelligence failure was attributable to the government rather than the army. The latter had been reporting on these activities and recognized the potential for an uprising, but government officials believed that the *focos* (guerrilla units) were small and could be easily controlled. These developments were kept secret so they would not prejudice the vote on NAFTA or the presidential campaign of Luis Donaldo Colosio, the assumption being that corrective action could wait until after the August 1994 election.[20]

This suggests not so much the inadequacy of the government's response to the rebellion but a gross failure of its intelligence apparatus. It should come as no surprise that military leaders were disgruntled. They felt that blame had been unjustly placed on their own shoulders.

THE MEXICAN MILITARY TAKES THE OFFENSIVE

From a military perspective, the Zapatista uprising was unique because, unlike any time in the recent past, the army found itself in the eye of a political hurricane. One U.S. official in Chiapas during the first days of the rebellion reported that its leaders had been privately voicing displeasure at the ineffective and poorly planned political strategy that they were being asked to carry out. On one occasion, General Miguel Angel Godínez Bravo, commander of the 31st Military Zone and of all army forces in Chiapas, told reporters that the best course would be to go on the offensive and wipe out the Zapatistas. The next day he suggested that he had been mis-quoted and that he supported wholeheartedly the government's strategy of a negotiated settlement. There were also other indications of discontent. Army leaders reportedly were annoyed at the new peace commissioner, Camacho Solís, when he called for a ceasefire and asked the military to withdraw from certain communities. Moreover, although the army had traditionally been the principal administrator of humanitarian aid, during the conflict the government was pressured into replacing it with the Red Cross and assorted NGOs.[21]

Not since 1968 had the armed forces been subjected to such harsh public criticism as during the first few months of 1994. For that reason, Chiapas represents a kind of watershed. Prior to the Salinas administration, the military had always been looked on as an *intocable* or untouchable. The golden rule for journalists and writers had always been that everything was subject to criticism except the president, the army, and the *Virgen de Guadalupe* (Virgin of Guadalupe). On those few occasions when the military was the subject of criticism, the president had always spoken out in its defense. But the Salinas *sexenio* witnessed the end of the army's mythical status.

The increasingly irregular relationship between the military and the president was ironic in light of the first few months of Salinas' term. Back then, with the legitimacy of his electoral victory still in question, army leaders had organized a parade on inauguration day in support of the new president. Shortly thereafter, Salinas had called on the military to apprehend a corrupt and well-armed labor leader. He later asked for the army's help in tracking down the nation's leading drug trafficker. Those actions were followed by preemptive measures to prevent a violent strike at a copper mine in northern Mexico. Nonetheless, after relying on the army to get off to a solid start, Salinas fell uncharacteristically silent in its defense toward the end of his term.

The flood of criticism began in 1989, when numerous reports implicated former Secretary of Defense (SECDEF) General Juan Arévalo Gardoqui in high-level narcotics trafficking. At the time, President Salinas had remained silent. Then, in November 1991, soldiers killed seven federal narcotics agents at a remote landing strip in Veracruz. Instead of allowing an in-house investigation, the president ordered the National Commission on Human Rights to look into the crime, and as a result five officers were imprisoned. In September 1992, the Ministry of Public Education distributed textbooks to public schools which described soldiers as having fired on innocent students during the 1968 student movement. When army leaders took exception, the textbooks were recalled, but Salinas never publicly disavowed their content.

By 1993, the public attacks had accelerated. It seemed that the army had fallen victim to democratization. In April, its deteriorating relations with the Catholic bishop in Chiapas received considerable publicity, and most reports sided with Bishop Ruiz. (The latter had irked General Godínez by trying to stop the army's searches of Indian villages. In addition, Godínez had been accused of collaborating with former Governor González Garrido to expel or jail two priests.) Some implied a military role in the assassination of Cardinal Juan Jesús Posadas Ocampo by drug traffickers in Guadalajara that May. Others used the incident to criticize perceived army ineffectiveness in the national antinarcotics campaign. With the 25th anniversary of the October 1968 student deaths at Tlatelolco, moreover, many groups lobbied for the release of classified documents related to that affair. This opened old military wounds. A *Comisión de la Verdad* (Truth Commission), comprised of prominent citizens and intellectuals, many of whom had been university students in 1968, was set up to investigate the events at Tlatelolco. When the final report was presented, the army found itself again having to defend itself from accusations of complicity in the killings.[22]

Finally, the case of General José Francisco Gallardo Rodríguez has proved nettlesome. Gallardo has been imprisoned since November 1993, ostensibly for defaming the military's reputation. The general had committed the sin of publishing an article stating that the army had frequently violated the rights of soldiers and officers; he suggested creating an ombudsman to help rectify the situation. The case has captured the attention of both Mexican and U.S. human rights groups, which have been pressuring the army for Gallardo's release. Although official sources insist that the case is more complex, army leaders have been made to appear as the guilty party.[23]

The Chiapas uprising added more fuel to the fire. The army has had a much more difficult time in fending off accusations from human rights organizations than it had in forcing the Zapatistas back into the Lacandona jungle. Since the beginning of hostilities, it has been subjected to a barrage of criticism. The picture of the five dead bodies in Ocosingo opened the floodgates. In the face of these accusations, the SECDEF, General Antonio Riviello Bazán, has remained steadfast in his defense of the army. General Godínez in Chiapas has also denied that any of his troops were guilty of violations.[24]

The army has not been without its defenders. The director of the principal human rights center in Chiapas stated that, while some soldiers may have engaged in abuses, there existed no systematic pattern of violations. Speaking for a group of nonpartisan legislators, a Mexican senator declared that the military's behavior had been beyond reproach. A group of almost 500 grateful citizens from Ocosingo demonstrated in favor of the army and denounced human rights organizations said to be unjustly tarnishing its reputation.[25]

More recently, however, Physicians for Human Rights and Human Rights Watch/Americas have issued a report detailing serious violations by both the military and the EZLN. Among the Mexican army's reported abuses were summary executions, arbitrary arrests, prolonged incommunicado detentions, and torture. According to this study, neither the federal attorney general's office nor the National Commission on Human Rights did an adequate job of investigating and prosecuting these abuses: The former often showed "a greater interest in protecting the Mexican army's reputation than in conducting independent and thorough investigations," while the latter seemed reluctant to speak out even when aware of credible eyewitness testimony or other evidence.[26]

Whatever the merits of the accusations, President Salinas generally chose not to dispute them. After the first few weeks of the conflict, General Riviello recognized that the army could no longer depend on the president, so the military began defending itself. The SECDEF took the first step in establishing a new public relations modus operandi in a speech commemorating the anniversary of the Loyalty March of February 9, 1913. Fed up with seeing Subcomandante Marcos and the Zapatistas glorified by the press, the SECDEF spoke aggressively in defense of the army. He proclaimed that the military had not digressed from its best traditions of loyalty to the president and the Constitution, or to its mission of guaranteeing internal order. He said that Mexican soldiers had been the victims of aggression by the EZLN, and he added that the army stood firmly behind the government's efforts at peace and reconciliation. He followed up that speech with another on Army Day, in which he reiterated the institution's commitments and described it as "an army in search of peace."[27]

General Riviello clearly understands the new rules of the game that are being established in countries making the transition to democracy. He appointed a public relations expert to deal with the press. The SECDEF set up meetings with journalists and academicians who had been critical of the army and made overtures to establish a more open dialogue. But the criticism did not stop. Perhaps the press views the military as a target that had long been off limits and senses a public interest in learning as much as possible about it. In February, army sources had to refute unsubstantiated allegations that the leadership was trying to obtain U.S. military aid in order to escalate the conflict in Chiapas. A few months later, it was reported that the army had obtained at least two dozen armored riot-control vehicles in anticipation of increased violence. The most recent uproar concerns overtures made to the United States to buy AH-1 Cobra attack helicopters. Some journalists implied that there would soon be a step-up of repression.[28] (In turn, a high-ranking officer explained the riot-control vehicles and attack helicopters as part of the army's ongoing modernization program. With regard to the former, he remarked that water was a lot safer than rifles. As for the latter, he seemed surprised that the request for only three helicopters would create such a reaction.[29] In the end, the request for the Cobras was denied.)

Looking back over the last few years, army leaders acknowledge that the political–military situation has begun to change significantly. Although the army continues to adhere to its sacred traditions—loyalty to the president and the Constitution and unwavering defense of the nation's sovereignty— the Mexican people's perception of the institution has probably changed forever. Public relations reforms are just the beginning. Greater changes lie ahead. The challenge of adapting to an increasingly democratic society will be a difficult one.

CHIAPAS AND THE FUTURE OF THE MEXICAN MILITARY

After examining recent events, the prescient observer might ask whether the Mexican military is at a crossroads. In fact, there are indicators that it may soon undergo significant changes. Some analysts anticipate substantive alterations in its mission and structure. At this point, political leaders are beholden to the military for its response to the Zapatista threat. At the same time, accusations of army human rights abuses have helped to take some of the pressure off already overburdened political leaders who have been trying to rectify their flawed strategies.

Political leaders will most likely try to compensate the military with increased salaries (which have remained at uncharacteristically low levels during the Salinas years) and new equipment. The latter has already been evident in the attempt to buy U.S. attack helicopters. A new military zone has been established in the state of Tabasco, and some new battalions have been added to the army's inventory.

Some have suggested that the military may soon begin a new professionalization process to shore up its deficiencies. It will likely try to improve its counterinsurgency and jungle-operations capabilities. As recently as February 1994, rumors surfaced concerning Mexican requests for U.S. support in counterinsurgency training.[30] Another area that begs for improvement is human rights instruction. If nothing else, Chiapas proved that the army is no longer immune from criticism. Political leaders, including the president, have become increasingly involved with deflecting media attacks and no longer possess the credibility or influence to defend the military. The army has been introduced rather rudely to the long-neglected field of public relations, and one means of reducing unfavorable press is to pay closer attention to human rights. The first step should consist of mandatory human rights training at all levels. The military has transitioned, somewhat reluctantly, into a new and highly competitive environment, and its leaders now find themselves scurrying to defend its interests. They must expeditiously formulate a strategy to function effectively in this transitional period. If they fail to do so, the institution could be seriously weakened. The recent improvements in public relations suggest that the leadership now understands the need for change.

There are also strong indications that relations between the PRI and the military may undergo substantive alteration. The irregular relationship during the Salinas years points to a distancing of the two institutions. Uncontrollable events brought on by accelerated democratization seem to be forcing military leaders into a more neutral corner with respect to politics. In the past, the Constitution has served as justification for the army's unique relationship with the party. Since the president was head of both the legitimate government and the PRI, the military invariably favored the latter. Given the weakness of the opposition, this relationship was seldom questioned. The past decade, however, witnessed the growth of more viable opposition parties, and this has led the SECDEF to declare repeatedly that the army would remain at the margin of the presidential succession and would uphold the results of the August 1994 election. In addition, he denied his partiality for the PRI candidate.[31]

At the same time, military leaders have probably questioned the allegiance of the president and the PRI to the armed forces. Here one has to understand how a Mexican officer thinks. The institution's ideology stresses six core concepts—revolutionary heritage, loyalty, discipline, patriotism, nationalism, and apoliticism—which comprise a creed by which an officer lives.[32] Since the 1920s, the army has maintained steadfast loyalty to the president and the institutions of government. Yet the president's "silence" at numerous times during the Salinas *sexenio* has raised doubts about the system's loyalty to the armed forces. As a result, the army has become less willing to bail the government out of problems emanating from failed and heavily criticized economic, political, and social policies.

Since the 1968 student movement, the military has been extremely reluctant to engage in repressive actions against the Mexican people. Army leaders learned their lesson the hard way at Tlatelolco. Many of the junior officers who faced the students on that occasion now serve in the upper echelons of the armed forces. The conflict in Chiapas once again forced the military to take up arms against the people, and one of the casualties was the military's reputation. Army leaders can dismiss their current dilemma as unavoidable, but they do not want to be forced into similar situations in the future. In recent months, there has been a fair share of private expressions of dissatisfaction over government policies. The military has grown increasingly disenchanted with having to clean up after politicians' mistakes. Consequently, one anticipates that its leaders may become more assertive on national security issues that have a direct impact on their institution.

There is no easy solution for Mexico's military leaders. But in a truly democratic system, the army will no longer be able to take sides. Some of its leaders have begun to understand this, and they seem to fear the opposition less than in the past.

Despite the winds of change, however, there are indicators that suggest a high degree of continuity for the military. Alterations in its structure and budget may prove temporary once Chiapas is resolved. In this era of downsizing, it would be difficult for Mexico, which has traditionally had one of the poorest armed forces in Latin America, to justify a major buildup. Improvements will be made in counterinsurgency capabilities, but the mission of the army will not change drastically. Rather, it will gradually return to antinarcotics operations (primarily crop eradication) and civic action on a full-time basis, with the latter being the preferred mission.

Chiapas may eventually be viewed as a brief distraction from the army's traditional missions. In 1980, then secretary of defense General Félix Galván López became the first military leader in years to speak out on national security, which he defined as "the maintenance of social, economic and political equilibrium guaranteed by the armed forces."[33] That has become the accepted army definition, and it suggests that military force is not a solution to national problems. The Mexican approach has been and will continue to be negotiation, thereby obviating the need for large, totally modern armed forces. In their present state, those forces could not be seriously challenged by any internal opposition group.

As in most military institutions, leadership in the Mexican army is a function of hierarchy. Since the 1950s, the position of SECDEF has been filled by men well into their sixties. After over forty years in uniform, these leaders have lost any aspirations for political power they may once have had. They have become consumed with ensuring that their organization adheres to its proud traditions of loyalty to the institutions of government and service to the Mexican people. Only in that way can each SECDEF hope that his legacy will be favorably judged. In addition, most SECDEFs view their position as the achievement of a life-long dream and would never consider ruining their good fortune by becoming embroiled in political struggles. This system of military succession has become well entrenched. At present, there is no move to modify it by bringing in younger leaders who might seek an active role in politics.

Because the Zedillo *sexenio* has just begun, it is hard to speculate about the future. As with the political system itself, the military experiences a major internal transformation every six years. The direction in which it moves will depend principally on its new leader. As of this writing, President Zedillo has been in office for only a few months. Thus far, relations between the military and Zedillo have been a bit tense. The new president will have to mend some fences, for both his past actions and his recent moves in Chiapas (see chapter 1) have not endeared him to the armed forces. Zedillo was the minister of education who authorized publication of the textbooks that accused the military of repressing the student movement in 1968. Early in his career, he worked for the army's bank, and after leaving that position, he made some untoward and imprudent remarks about the military's efficiency.

All this suggests that there will be some changes in civil-military relations. How the new president and SECDEF proceed in the months ahead will go a long way toward determining whether the relationship only needs a minor tune-up or whether a major overhaul is in order. At this point, it seems likely that Zedillo will try to quickly win back the support of the armed forces, since the military remains one of the crucial pillars on which the entire system rests.

WAR OR PEACE?

What of the Zapatistas? In the months prior to the August elections, they had repeatedly warned that a PRI victory, if fraudulent, would lead to a resumption of hostilities. The EZLN had retained its weapons during the ceasefire. Indeed, Subcomandante Marcos claimed to have been contacted by "armed groups in the four corners of the country." There were reports of guerrilla activity in Guerrero, Oaxaca, Jalisco, Nayarit, Durango, Veracruz, Puebla, Hidalgo, Michoacán, and Chihuahua.[34] The image being cultivated was that of a peasant army ready to resume the offensive not only in Chiapas but throughout rural Mexico.

At the same time, Zapatista leaders gave few indications that they were willing to temper their militance or abandon their more unrealistic demands. When the government offered sweeping socioeconomic concessions (including land redistribution, aid to impoverished farmers, the creation of new industries, job-retraining programs, schools, and roads) designed to ameliorate the hardships and inequities of Chiapan society, the terms were rejected. Nothing less than fundamental political reform on a national level would do. The rebels renewed their call for Salinas' resignation and the formation of a transitional government to organize "democratic and free elections." In addition, they demanded an end to central government control over indigenous communities and a renegotiation of NAFTA.

Not even Cuauhtémoc Cárdenas, the major presidential candidate most supportive of the rebels' demands, seemed pure enough to merit their support. In May, Cárdenas had journeyed to Chiapas in search of favorable publicity, hoping to bask in the glow of Subcomandante Marcos' charisma. Instead, he was publicly humiliated. Marcos accused Cárdenas' party of pursuing the same economic policies and undemocratic practices as the PRI. The candidate was subjected to staged harangues by guerrilla commanders. In the end, the photo opportunity turned into a nightmare, undermining the campaign (which was already shaky) of the contender most likely to come to terms with the rebels.

Since March 1994, there has been a growing sense of unreality and irrelevance about the Zapatistas. With the March assassination of the PRI presidential candidate, Luis Donaldo Colosio, the selection of his successor, Ernesto Zedillo, and the relaunching of the election campaign, public attention was increasingly diverted from Chiapas. Whereas during the first months of the crisis Marcos' communiqués had been front-page headlines, by spring they were largely being consigned to the back pages of Mexican newspapers. Meanwhile, the government moved to undermine the rebels' support through massive social spending. In less than six months, over $220 million was poured into the state's social development and infrastructure projects, a 44 percent increase over what had been budgeted. By far the largest recipients were San Cristóbal, Altamirano, Ocosingo, and Las Margaritas. By now, too, the military's treatment of the Indians had improved, and the latter were becoming more vocal about the hardships and abuses (especially forced recruitment) of guerrilla rule. For their part, the Zapatistas seemed increasingly divorced from those whom they purported to represent. After May, they virtually dropped their socioeconomic demands, calling instead on "civil society" to rise up and demand national political reform.[35]

The culmination of this shift was the convocation of a "National Democratic Convention" in Chiapas in early August. The gathering, part of which was held in Marcos' jungle hideout, was attended by several thousand representatives from a spectrum of left-wing groups. Proclaiming the PRI "the common enemy of us all," the delegates called for a nationwide campaign of civil disobedience to push the ruling party from power.

On election day, however, the voters cast their ballots for Zedillo and the PRI. Although the process was not free from irregularities, the magnitude of the victory was such that it left little doubt about who had won. Mexicans might be unhappy with the PRI's long record of authoritarianism, corruption, and violence—or, for that matter, with the weak state of the economy—but they were unwilling to risk more instability and violence by turning power over to the opposition. The preceding eight months had left deep insecurities in the national psyche. Mexicans were not yet ready for such a transition.

The election results left the Zapatistas in a difficult position. Obviously, the Mexican people did not reject the existing system and did not support the kind of violence that the EZLN represented, even when they were sympathetic to many of its proclaimed objectives. (Significantly, the presidential candidate favored by most delegates to the "National Democratic Convention"—Cárdenas—had finished a poor third. Moreover, in Chiapas the PRI gubernatorial candidate had handily defeated the candidate favored by the Zapatistas. Subsequently, the EZLN refused to recognize the validity of that election and threatened to resume fighting if the governor-elect assumed office.) For the moment, at least, the PRI had snatched the cloak of legitimacy away from the rebels, and it was by no means clear that they could recapture it.

The question that remains unanswered is whether the Zapatistas will carry out their threats to resume fighting. Certainly, it would be difficult— if not impossible—for them to regain the moral high ground they held the previous January. (Many supporters balked at the leadership's militant challenge to the gubernatorial election results.) Nor would they any longer have the advantage of surprise. Over the preceding months the Mexican army, with some 20,000 troops in Chiapas,[36] had carefully surrounded the Zapatista forces in the Lacandona jungle, leaving the Guatemalan border as the only escape route. Given the limited resources of the guerrillas, a resumption of their offensive would likely prove suicidal.

As for the threat of "other Chiapases" in states like Veracruz and Guerrero, where there have been reports of guerrilla activity, one can only speculate. Most accounts are sketchy. The numbers and viability of these groups remain in doubt. Where they exist at all—and some are probably nothing more than rumor—they appear to be small, based on local land disputes, and lacking a national political agenda.[37]

So we are left with a classic Mexican standoff. Thus far, at least, the military has been willing to play a waiting game and avoid more accusations of human rights violations. It continues to stand behind the government's negotiation strategy and seems unlikely to attack the Zapatistas unless provoked. The latter have also exhibited caution. Notwithstanding their rhetoric, they clearly understand that they are in a very weak position militarily. Thus, their shift away from a military strategy to a political strategy based on public relations and popular mobilization.

The problem, however, is that the strategy does not seem to be going anywhere. The rebels are increasingly isolated and trapped. Unable to move forward and unwilling to surrender, they risk being indefinitely consigned to limbo. However, as long as the deadlock continues, the potential for violence remains. There is a streak of martyrdom in the Latin American political culture that could be activated by prolonged frustration. Moreover, the army and the guerrillas are not the only potentially explosive elements in the equation. Since January 1994, local elites have seen their properties and power threatened as never before. They are angry, afraid, and prone to violence. Many are not above taking the law into their own hands to recapture stolen cattle or occupied properties. Some may even be tempted to provoke a resumption of fighting in the hope that the army may help them retrieve their losses.

Thus, there is a need to defuse the conflict by bringing the rebels in from the cold. One of the priority tasks of the Zedillo administration should be to explore ways to co-opt the Zapatistas and their supporters, both economically and politically. On the one hand, that means fulfilling the promises to alleviate the poverty and desperation that drove so many *chiapanecos* to support the guerrillas. On the other, it means reforming state and local power structures to assure the rule of law and the access of those who have been shut out of the system. Nor are these requirements limited to Chiapas, for there are many other areas of rural Mexico with comparable problems which, if neglected, may lead to social explosions.

Finally, it is imperative that the process of national political reform be deepened and consolidated. On this point—even if not on all their specific demands—the Zapatistas are right. Without democratization, other gains will prove ephemeral, since what can be so easily given can also be taken away. Here then may be the rebels' ultimate contribution: that at a critical moment in Mexican history, they forced reform on a reluctant president and an even more reluctant political system. On the other side of the ledger, the Mexican army has done its part to keep the system afloat and restore an environment of stability and security. But whether these developments will be enduring or merely a passing illusion remains to be seen. On that issue rests the future of Mexico.

NOTES

1. Neil Harvey, "Rebellion in Chiapas: Rural Reforms, Campesino Radicalism, and the Limits to Salinismo," in *Transformation of Rural Mexico*, No. 5 (La Jolla: Center for U.S.–Mexican Studies, University of California, San Diego, 1994), pp. 1–2.

2. Instituto Nacional de Estadística, Geografía e Informática (INEGI), *Anuario Estadístico de los Estados Unidos Mexicanos* (Aguascalientes: INEGI, 1991); INEGI, *XI Censo General de Problación y Vivienda, 1990* (Aguascalientes: INEGI, 1992).

3. Consejo Nacional de Problación, cited in *La Jornada*, January 3, 1994.

4. Luis Hernández Navarro, "The New Mayan War," *NACLA Report on the Americas*, Vol. 27, No. 5 (March–April 1994), p. 6.

5. Ibid., pp. 6–7.

6. For more detailed treatment of the origins of the rebellion, see George Collier and Elizabeth Lowery Quaratiello, *Basta! Land and the Zapatista Rebellion in*

Chiapas (Oakland, Calif.: The Institute for Food and Development Policy, 1994); and John Ross, *Rebellion from the Roots: Indian Uprising in Chiapas* (Monroe, Maine: Common Courage Press, 1995).

7. Andrew Reding, "Chiapas Is Mexico: The Imperative of Political Reform," *World Policy Journal,* Vol. 11, No. 1 (Spring 1994), p. 16.

8. Harvey, "Rebellion in Chiapas," p. 11; Luis Hernández Navarro, "The New Mayan War," p. 9.

9. Human Rights Watch/Americas, *Mexico, The New Year's Rebellion: Violations of Human Rights and Humanitarian Law During the Armed Revolt in Chiapas,* Vol. 6, No. 3 (March 1, 1994), p. 5; Carlos Salinas de Gortari, *Quinto Informe de Gobierno,* Annex, 1993.

10. Luis Hernández Navarro, "The Chiapas Uprising," in *Transformation of Rural Mexico,* p. 44.

11. Human Rights Watch/Americas, *Mexico, The New Year's Rebellion,* p. 5; Reding, "Chiapas Is Mexico," p. 17.

12. Andrés Oppenheimer, "Mexico Rebel Leader: I Am a Poet, Not a Politician," *Miami Herald,* July 28, 1994.

13. Collier and Quaratiello, *Basta!,* pp. 81–83; Ross, *Rebellion,* pp. 278–79.

14. Alma Guillermoprieto, "Zapata's Heirs," *The New Yorker,* May 16, 1994, p. 54.

15. Collier and Quaratiello, *Basta!,* p. 84.

16. Untitled document, dated January 8, 1994, prepared by the Mexican Interior Ministry, pp. 15–18. See also Raymundo Riva Palacio, "Guerrillas en México," *El Financiero,* February 4, 1994; Miguel Angel Ortega, "Características de Partido en los Organos de Dirección de la Guerrilla," ibid., February 28, 1994; and Miguel Pérez, "Tiene EZLN Reglamento Militar," *Reforma,* March 2, 1994.

17. Raúl Benítez Manaut, "El Desafío de las Guerrillas," *Nueva Sociedad,* No. 130 (March–April, 1994), pp. 24–26; "La Guerrilla Zapatista, una Mezcla de Ambición y Mesianismo," *Epoca,* January 10, 1994, pp. 8–9; Interview with U.S. Embassy official, March 1994.

18. March 1994 interview with Mexican government official who had talked to army officers in Chiapas.

19. Armando Guzmán and Rodrigo Vera, "Militares y Sacerdotes Se Enfrentan por el Caso de los Dos Oficiales Asesinados e Incinerados en Chiapas," *Proceso,* April 12, 1993; Guillermo Correa, "Infantería, Tanquetas, Helicópteros y Paracaidistas, en los Combates de Ocosingo," ibid., June 7, 1993; Julio César López and Rodrigo Vera, "Hay Noticias de Gente Armada en Chiapas, Pero No de la Iglesia," ibid., September 20, 1993; Arturo Cano and Daniel Moreno, "La Guerrilla que No Exista," *Enfoque,* January 9, 1994; "La Realidad que Nadie Quería Ver: la Guerrilla," *Epoca,* January 10, 1994, pp. 13–14.

20. Interview with Mexican official having close ties to CISN, March 1994; interview with high-ranking Mexican military officer, March 1994; and Raymundo Riva Palacio, "Entremés Dominical," *El Financiero,* January 23, 1994.

21. Interview with U.S. Embassy official, March 1994; Elena Gallegos and Emilio Lomas, "Se Integrarán en Guarniciones de Plaza las Tropas en Chiapas," *La Jornada,* January 21, 1994; Riva Palacio, "Entremés Dominical"; and Rodrigo Vera, "Al Tono Negociador del Gobierno Civil, El General Godínez Sobrepone La

Agresividad: 'Ni Son Ejército Ni Son Zapatistas . . . Son Unos Delincuentes,' " *Proceso,* February 14, 1994.

22. Armando Guzmán and Rodrigo Vera, "Militares y Sacerdotes Se Enfrentan por el Caso de los Dos Oficiales Asesinados e Incinerados en Chiapas," *Proceso,* April 12, 1993; Carlos Puig, "Ante la Incapacidad Policiaca, Salinas Adoptó como Suya Estrategia de Reagan: Militarizar la Lucha Antinarco," ibid., July 5, 1993; Rodrigo Vera, "Acusa el Clero al Ejército, Adultera Documentos y Se Divide ante las Marchas," ibid., July 5, 1993; Alberto Aguirre and Ignacio Ramírez, "El General Riviello Aceptó que en el 68 el Ejército Fue Utilizado Mas Allá de Sus Atribuciones," ibid., December 27, 1993; and Manuel Robles and Rodrigo Vera, "Ocurrencias, Contradicciones y Mentiras, los Recursos del Gobierno para Cerrar Archivos del 68," ibid., January 3, 1994.

23. See, for example, Roberto Zamarripa, "Autoritarismo, Impunidad y Ejercicio Irracional del Poder dentro del Ejército, Ponen en Riesgo la Seguridad Nacional," ibid., December 13, 1993; and Octavio Rodríguez Araujo, "El Caso Gallardo," *La Jornada,* December 23, 1993.

24. Juan Manuel Venegas, "Godínez: Apoya el Ejército una Solución Negociada y Política," *La Jornada,* January 28, 1994; and Amparo Trejo, "Responde Ejército a CNDH," *Reforma,* March 9, 1994.

25. Sergio Aguayo Quezada, "Comprender a los Militares," *La Jornada,* February 16, 1994; Jesús Aranda and Oscar Camacho, "Las ONG, Injustas con el Ejército: Riviello en Reunión con Legisladores," ibid., February 23, 1994; and José Reveles, "Manifestación en Apoyo al Ejército y al Gobierno en Ocosingo," *El Financiero,* January 15, 1994.

26. *Waiting for Justice in Chiapas* (Boston: Physicians for Human Rights, December 1994), pp. 114–17.

27. "México Cree en la Lealtad, la Práctica y la Reconoce Como Valor: Riviello Bazán," *La Jornada,* February 10, 1994; and Amparo Trejo and Julieta Medina, "Somos un Ejército para Lograr la Paz," *Reforma,* February 20, 1994. One incident, in particular, angered military leaders. On February 21, Subcomandante Marcos had his picture taken with Peace Commissioner Camacho Solís, with each man holding one end of the Mexican flag. Army leaders consider the flag sacred and resented the sight of the Zapatista leader posing as a patriot. See Ciro Gómez Leyva, "Molestó a Militares el Episodio de la Bandera Nacional," *El Financiero,* February 23, 1994.

28. Scott Morrison, "Come the Crackdown," *Mexico Insight,* May 29, 1994; Andrés Oppenheimer, "Mexico Wants U.S. Attack Copters," *Miami Herald* (International Edition), June 11, 1994.

29. Interview, July 1994.

30. See "Ninguna Dependencia del Gobierno Ha Solicitado Ayuda Militar a EU," *La Jornada,* February 11, 1994.

31. Carlos Ramírez, "Indicador Político," *El Financiero,* February 18, 1994.

32. See chapter 3 of Stephen J. Wager, "The Mexican Army, 1940–1982: The Country Comes First" (Ph.D. dissertation, Stanford University, 1992) for a detailed analysis.

33. Stephen J. Wager, "The Mexican Military Approaches the 21st Century: Coping with a New World Order," Strategic Studies Institute, U.S. Army War College, February 21, 1994, p. 3.

34. See, for example, Andrés Oppenheimer, "Mexico Rebel Leader: I'm a Poet, not a Politician," *Miami Herald,* July 28, 1994; Andrew Reding, "For Mexico's Rulers, Reform Is Risky," *Washington Post,* August 7, 1994.

35. See the Second Lacandona Jungle Declaration, in Foreign Broadcast Information Service, *Daily Report: Latin America,* June 14, 1994, pp. 21–25; Tod Robberson, "Mexico Takes the Initiative from Rebels," *Washington Post,* July 6, 1994.

36. According to official figures. Anthony DePalma, "Rebels Say Mexican Army Is Breaking Terms of Truce," *New York Times,* September 18, 1994.

37. Oppenheimer, "Mexico Rebel Leader."

11

Through a Glass Darkly: On the Challenges and Enigmas of Mexico's Future

Donald E. Schulz

Once again we are faced with the question: Whither Mexico? During the 1993 debate over NAFTA, many supporters of the agreement painted a portrait of a country rapidly vaulting into the 21st century, modernizing economically, democratizing politically, creating a more prosperous and equitable society for its citizens while curtailing northward migration, maintaining political stability, and entering a new era of harmonious co-operation with the United States. Others, however, were more pessimistic: Economic modernization, it was argued, would not necessarily spill over into the political realm or, if it did, it might have unanticipated effects. Thus political reforms, for instance, might be designed to co-opt critics and contain dissent while the system was being streamlined and transformed into an even more effective mode of authoritarianism. The destructive side effects of NAFTA—including socioeconomic displacement, unemployment, increased migration (both to the cities and to the United States), and ac-celerated environmental degradation—might well produce a "new" Mexico in which the gaps between rich and poor would be even greater than they already were. Neither would economic development necessarily lead to po-litical stability. As this is being written, the rebellion in Chiapas serves as a reminder that development and modernization can often have highly de-stabilizing results.

Nor could it be assumed that Mexico's relations with the United States would be conflict free. Closeness does not always translate into amity. Historical antagonisms and conflicts of interest would persist, and so would Mexican nationalism. Mexicans would continue to have ambivalent feel-ings about *gringos,* and greater U.S. involvement in their social, economic, and political life could well generate a backlash. At the same time, illegal migration to the United States was already producing political reactions in border states like California. The real questions were how serious these backlashes would be on both sides, and how well each would handle them.

This concluding chapter briefly addresses some of these challenges and enigmas. Specifically, it deals with the prospects for democratization, socioeconomic development, political stability, and U.S.–Mexican relations. All of these issues are multidimensional and interrelated, and since all are currently in rapid flux this analysis must be preliminary and speculative. All that can be said with confidence is that Mexico is passing through a watershed. But whether the result will be development or decay remains to be seen.

THE DIALECTIC OF DEMOCRATIZATION

The first point to be made is that although the August 1994 elections were an important step forward on the road to democracy, the process remains incomplete and the gains are by no means irreversible. That Zedillo committed himself to relatively fair elections in one instance does not necessarily mean that he will do so in the future. Neither is it clear how far he will be willing to push other democratic reforms, especially those that might undermine his own authority and power. The circumstances of the 1994 campaign, after all, were fairly unique. The confluence of a variety of pressures, both domestic and foreign, made it difficult for Salinas and Zedillo to resist democratization in the short run. But whether the latter will continue to push the issue once those pressures ease and/or new ones arise is anybody's guess.

Within the PRI, the "dinosaurs" still have a strong foothold, and they will try to protect their power and spoils by obstructing reforms by all means possible, both fair and foul. During the campaign, Zedillo was forced to embrace them for the sake of party unity and victory. The question now is whether—or to what extent—he will be willing and able to free himself from their grasp so that reform can be continued, or even accelerated.

Make no mistake about it, democratization poses serious risks and costs for both the PRI and the president. It will likely lead to the further erosion of the party's political dominance and all the benefits that go with it. At some point, the PRI might become just another party, one of several contending for public office. This is a prospect that even PRI technocrats cannot be comfortable with, since their power and perquisites are also at stake. Technopoliticians ("technopols") are still politicians. In the short run, at least, they will continue to be dependent on the "dinosaurs" for their own survival. Even after the Old Guard has lost its political usefulness—and this is gradually occurring, as privatization and other reforms undercut its patronage power and control over traditional constituencies like organized labor—the "technopols" can be expected to try to limit democratization by preventing the emergence of a truly level playing field.

By the same token, democratization holds very real dangers for Zedillo. If he pursues it too vigorously, he risks the same fate as Colosio and Ruiz Massieu. Even if he avoids that ultimate sanction, a too rapid erosion of *presidencialismo* would weaken his ability to govern, including his capacity to promote further democratization should he choose that course. Indeed, there is already strong evidence of such erosion in the resistance of business and labor to Zedillo's requests for price and wage restraints in the aftermath of devaluation.

Here, both an irony and a paradox: Under Salinas, democratization was largely dependent on the president's willingness to use his autocratic powers on its behalf. Strong presidential leadership is still necessary to constrain electoral and human rights abuses and corruption and guide the country farther down the path of democracy. Thus, "an abrupt, premature dismantling" of the presidentialist system might actually "doom future democratization efforts."[1] On the other hand, if this is the case, then Mexican democracy will remain precariously dependent on the goodwill and determined commitment of Zedillo and his successors. Given the historical record of Mexican presidents, this is not a particularly reassuring thought.

There is also the fear of losing control and descending into violence. There is a danger that democratization could unstick the glue that has held Mexico together for the past six and a half decades. The end of the single-party hegemonic system could lead to an authority vacuum, political immobilism, and perhaps chaos. The decline of the PRI would almost certainly be accompanied by an erosion of party discipline. If the bitterness between the governing party and the opposition should greatly increase with the growth of real competition, multipartisan cooperation might become impossible. In that case, it is entirely possible that no single party or coalition would be able to govern effectively. The resulting deadlock, combined with the increasing demands accompanying rapid democratization and growing resistance to reform both within and without the PRI (from narcotraffickers, for instance), could lead to the wholesale breakdown of the system.

None of this is to suggest that such a scenario is probable, but it is certainly a possibility. Thus, there is a temptation to limit, halt, or reverse the reform process. There is a great deal of ambivalence about democracy in the Mexican political culture. There is an attraction based on an idealized notion of democracy and the benefits often associated with it, but there is also a deep fear of the unknown and the destruction of a political arrangement that has maintained order and security for a very long time. Personal security is not something that people risk easily. If the violence wracking Mexico should continue to grow, the ability of democracy to provide order and security may be called into question. At some point,

President Zedillo or his successor may feel it necessary to make peace with the "dinosaurs" and the mafiosos for the sake of national stability. That would probably mean an authoritarian restoration, with the president trying to rule as a *caudillo* (strong man) while federal, state, and local authorities increasingly relied on repression to maintain order.

Another important variable in this scenario, of course, is economic. If the economy should continue to decline, social discontent would grow, making governability even more problematic. If this occurred in conjunction with an upsurge in political violence, the prospects for an authoritarian restoration would significantly increase.

One of the most important social bases of Mexican democracy has been the middle class. Yet, under current conditions of economic crisis, that sector is being pulverized. Will middle-class Mexicans continue to support democracy when they are no longer middle class? The danger of a prolonged, agonizing socioeconomic crisis is that it can destroy the legitimacy of the democratic model by exposing its inability to solve the country's social and economic problems. And the bottom line for most Mexicans—as for most human beings—is economic. Democracy may be desirable, but food, clothing and shelter are essential.

All this makes probable a continuation of the present trend toward greater social and political violence. Labor unrest, guerrilla activity, and terrorism are likely to get worse. Middle-class protest movements, composed of small and medium businessmen, credit card debtors and other desperate members of the bourgeoisie, will become more widespread and angry. At the same time, there are signs that the threat from narcotraffickers is entering a new stage: The danger is no longer confined to the economic penetration of political and bureaucratic structures (i.e., bribery). As in Colombia, the cartels seem to be increasingly waging violence against the state itself. That may well be part of the larger meaning of the Colosio, Posadas, and Ruiz Massieu assassinations.

Finally, there is the role of the United States. The historical record does not lend much support for the assumption that the U.S. government will take a strong and concerted stand on behalf of democracy and human rights in Mexico. In the past, Washington has almost always valued stability over democracy. Neither the Bush nor the Clinton administration included political issues in the NAFTA negotiations. Only in the aftermath of the Zapatista uprising and the Colosio assassination, when Mexico's political stability seemed in jeopardy and a fraudulent balloting in the August 1994 elections would have posed major problems for U.S.–Mexican relations (including NAFTA), did the Clinton administration really press Salinas on the issue of democracy. Once Washington's political needs have been satisfied and Mexico disappears from the front page of the *New York Times,* one suspects that there will be a return to business as usual.

In short, the future of Mexican democracy remains problematic. Although progress has been made, the country still has a long way to go. On the positive side, President Zedillo has moved quickly to accelerate the reform process. The entire Supreme Court has been replaced; efforts are being made to bring the opposition into the political process; new elections have been promised in Chiapas. Moreover, pressures for reform have acquired a momentum of their own and will not soon disappear. This is not simply a matter of the Mexican president occasionally pressing for democratization. The political culture is in flux. Economic modernization is spilling over into the social and political realms. New forces have been unleashed which are eroding the dominance of traditional structures and interests. There has been an enormous growth of civil society, including a proliferation of Mexican and international NGOs (nongovernmental organizations) that have pushed for political reform and monitored its progress. These elements have become important transmitters of information to the outside world. As long as NAFTA remains a priority, the Mexican government cannot afford to ignore its international image.

Although it is possible that this concern with foreign—especially U.S.—opinion may fade once the current economic crisis abates, the opening of the Mexican economy and society to U.S. and Canadian influences will probably continue the subtle nurturing of democratic values. (On the other hand, this is not a sure thing. If U.S.–Mexican relations deteriorate, the opposite could happen.) Considerable progress has already been made in developing real opposition parties and a competitive party system. With a less erratic but still attractive candidate (Vicente Fox, perhaps), the PAN might become an even more formidable foe in 2000 than it was in 1994. Even the PRD, if it could find a dynamic new leader and improve its internal unity, could stage a comeback. The economic crisis unleashed by the December 1994 devaluation of the peso has already produced a strong political backlash. There are signs that 1995 may be a bellwether year. A series of state elections are scheduled in which the PRI is likely to be challenged as never before. Although it is far too early to tell, it may well be that we are witnessing the birth of a genuinely competitive multiparty system.

In sum, the outlook is mixed. The political milieu continues to be swept by strong cross-currents. This can be detected even in the behavior of President Zedillo. Thus, even as he was pledging to encourage democratization within the PRI by pushing for internal elections or representative conventions, he limited that promise to the period prior to his inauguration. After that, he said, he would become a "passive" member of the party and would not "interfere in any way" in the candidate-selection process.[2] One has to wonder how meaningful promises of reform are if the president is not willing to follow up on them aggressively.

Similarly, while Zedillo sought to signal his support for political and judicial reform by appointing the PAN's Antonio Lozano attorney general, he simultaneously bowed to the Old Guard by making Ignacio Pichardo Pegaza secretary of energy. This was the same Pichardo who had been accused (whether justly or not has not been determined) of impeding the investigation of the Ruiz Massieu assassination. Needless to say, the appointment raised questions about how far the president was really willing to go in terms of weeding out corruption and promoting political reform. In the wake of the peso's devaluation, moreover, the credibility of the "technopols" has been seriously damaged. Old Guard representation in the cabinet has been strengthened, casting further doubt about the government's direction.

A comparable ambivalence surrounds the January agreement between the Mexican government and the four leading political parties, providing for additional democratic reforms and the defusing of the crises in Tabasco and Chiapas through new elections. No sooner was the ink dry on this "historic" pact than the government changed direction on Chiapas, adopting a new hard line and sending the army into guerrilla territory. This prompted the PRD to declare that the accord had been shattered.

In light of the extreme ambivalence and fluidity associated with Mexican democratization, the best that can be said is that the Zedillo *sexenio* will witness a continuation of the ongoing struggle for the soul of the nation. In part, this will assume the form of a dialectical conflict between those forces that want to accelerate democratization and those that are bent on derailing it. Under these circumstances, the most likely outlook is for a long, drawn-out process that will take years—and perhaps decades—to complete. This process is unlikely to be linear. There will be setbacks as well as successes. It is hoped that there will be more of the latter than the former, but there are no guarantees. Nor can one discount the possibility of an authoritarian restoration.

THE PITFALLS OF ECONOMIC RECOVERY

To appreciate fully the tenuous nature of the democratic transition that is underway, one must take into account the closely related challenges of socioeconomic development and political stability. In a country like Mexico, where there has been a serious erosion of regime legitimacy, economic performance assumes increasing political significance. In effect, a deal has been struck with the Mexican public: Economic and political modernization has been presented as a strategy for accelerating economic growth in order to create new wealth that will "trickle down" to the masses and raise living standards. If the plan is successful, the legitimacy of both the government and the political system may be strengthened. Precisely because that legitimacy has become so dependent on performance, however, economic setbacks are potentially more destabilizing than ever. If the strategy is unsuccessful, it risks being discredited and so, by implication, does democracy.

What are the prospects for economic development? In late 1993, the future seemed assured. NAFTA appeared ready to usher in a new era of growth that would catapult Mexico into the ranks of the developed nations. (Or so it was argued by some treaty enthusiasts.) Indeed, for most of 1994 there was some evidence to justify such hopes. In spite of severe political turmoil, roughly $2 billion a month in foreign capital flowed into the country during the first half of the year. U.S. exports to Mexico reached a record $24.5 billion, up 17 percent from the previous year. (By May, U.S. exports to Mexico were exceeding those to Japan on a seasonally adjusted basis. In addition to being the United States' third largest trading partner, Mexico had become the second largest customer for U.S. goods.) Similarly, Mexican exports to the United States were up nearly 21 percent, to $23.4 billion. At the same time, inflation remained about 7 percent (down from the triple-digit figures of the 1980s), even as the economy was picking up momentum. By the time of his State of the Nation address in November, President Salinas was predicting an economic growth rate of almost 3 percent for 1994 (and nearly 4 percent for the last half of the year).

Then, in December, the bottom dropped out of the peso. Delirious optimism gave way to bottomless gloom. Yet, in perspective, the collapse should not have come as such a shock. The warning signs had been clear: Mexico was living far beyond its means, purchasing foreign goods and services much faster than its economy could create the wealth to pay for them. The peso was overvalued. The country was running a huge current account deficit, which could be financed only through a massive influx of investment. To make matters worse, the U.S. Federal Reserve was now repeatedly raising the discount rate, making U.S. investments much more attractive. Obviously, investor confidence was critical. Rather than devalue earlier, when it might have been possible to make a soft landing, Salinas (for political reasons) chose to pretend that the problem did not exist. Even after the elections, he refused to make the hard decision that was necessary. (He had been warned by key advisors that a devaluation could lead to a stock market crash. By then, moreover, he was running for the presidency of the World Trade Organization and did not want to hurt his chances by admitting that his economic policy was flawed.) Instead, he gambled that investors would continue to pour money into Mexico, even in the face of continuing political turmoil.

The fallacy of that assumption is now painfully evident. Between the end of 1993 and mid-December 1994, Mexico's foreign currency reserves fell from $28 billion to $7 billion. Throughout the year, foreign investors, nervously eying Mexican political stability and increasingly tempted by the improving investment opportunities in the United States, had been shifting money from peso-denominated notes to lower-interest dollar-denominated securities (*tesobonos*) that allowed them to withdraw their funds more easily. At the same time, the Mexican Central Bank was frantically using its increasingly scarce dollars to buy pesos in order to prop up the latter. When Salinas revealed the state of Mexico's declining reserves in his State of the Nation address in November, it only accelerated the problem. In November and December, billions of dollars fled the country. When on December 19 the Zapatista rebels announced (falsely) that they had slipped through the military's cordon and occupied thirty-eight municipalities in Chiapas, investors panicked, dumping Mexican stocks and bonds and prompting the government to spend billions more of its rapidly evaporating reserves in a short-lived and futile effort to maintain the value of the peso.[3]

At this point, the administration reluctantly accepted the inevitable: Zedillo devalued the peso and, when that failed to stem the flow, allowed it to float. An Economic Emergency Plan was hurriedly put together, and an $18 billion international credit line provided. But even that did not suffice. Some $28 billion in short-term Mexican treasury bills were scheduled to fall due in 1995, and it was clear that most of these would be redeemed. As the peso and stock market continued to fall, along with investor confidence, the specter of a full-scale panic mounted. If Mexico was forced to default on its obligations, it would likely plunge into a depression, with ominous implications for political and social stability. In turn, a Mexican default could trigger massive capital flight from other Latin American and developing countries and come back to hit the United States, which depended on those areas for about 40 percent of its exports.

In the end, the Clinton administration and the international bankers stepped in and saved the day. When his efforts to win approval for a $40 billion loan guarantee package ran into heavy congressional opposition, President Clinton acted on his own authority to offer Mexico $20 billion in U.S. government short-term loans and loan guarantees from the federal Exchange Stabilization Fund. Along with some $30 billion in commitments from the International Monetary Fund, the Bank for International Settlements, and other sources, this brought the total global commitment to Mexico to over $50 billion.

This rescue effort seemed to stabilize the situation, but whether the economy had hit bottom or was merely resting on a ledge, poised to resume its downward plunge at some point in the future, could not be predicted. In purely economic terms, the problem appeared manageable. Major structural changes had been made. Trade had been broadened. NAFTA had given Mexico enormous advantages over its Latin American neighbors in terms of access to North American trade and capital. By early 1995, moreover, the devaluation had reversed the country's trade deficit with the United States. Mexicans were selling more and buying less; their goods were more competitive. If they could establish a massive trade surplus, it would reduce their need to import foreign capital. At the same time, efforts were being made, through the imposition of high interest rates, to convince investors to keep their money in Mexico. If the economy could be restabilized and put on a sounder footing, the prospects for a gradual recovery might be good, so long as political turmoil and a wage and price spiral could be avoided.

The problem is that it might not be possible to meet these requirements. Though in narrow economic terms the current crisis may not seem to be of the same magnitude as in 1982, the domestic social and political ramifications are much greater, and these in turn feed the economic crisis and make it even more dangerous. Political stability, in particular, will be a key variable. If the crisis in Chiapas continues or spreads to other states, if there are more political assassinations and scandals (not to mention kidnappings, drug trafficking, social violence, and electoral turmoil), then the crucial psychological preconditions for economic recovery may not be established. Investors are reluctant to invest in politically unstable, risky environments.

Furthermore, both the current economic crisis and its solutions are severely aggravating the country's enormous social problems. Mexico is now in a recession, unemployment is rising fast, and Zedillo's recovery program, with its emphasis on reduced spending, high interest rates, and more privatizations, will only make the pain worse. Moreover, notwithstanding efforts to hold down price increases, inflation is expected to exceed 40 percent in 1995. Real wages will decline sharply, and labor unrest will grow, making it unlikely that social turmoil will diminish. It may, indeed, get worse, which would make it even more difficult to attract and retain investment capital.

Moreover, international loan guarantees are not unlimited. As of May, half of the $20 billion U.S. emergency loan package has already been used, and another $8.5 billion is expected to be paid out by September. According to one source, Mexico may have to spend as much as $59 billion on foreign debt payments in 1995 alone.[4] If this estimate is in the ballpark, then the current international commitment—large as it is—may not be enough.

To all this one must add such other factors as an emerging banking crisis; a wavering U.S. ally whose continuing financial support remains uncertain; cultural norms that value short-term gratification/consumption over saving/ investment; and a possible new era of volatile global markets, marked by the speed with which investors can withdraw their funds and the ease with which such moves can trigger a domino effect, inducing economic crises in countries far removed from those in which the process began.

Some of these pitfalls, to be sure, are problematic. The U.S. strategy, for instance, is based on the assumption that the Mexican crisis is the product of bad policies, rather than a new era of unstable markets, and that the economy can be turned around by making the right policy adjustments.

This may be so, but there are enough unfavorable or uncertain variables in the equation that one cannot be very sanguine about the future. At best, the economy seems likely to sputter along in a recession for another year before resuming modest growth. Equally probable, however, is the prospect that Mexico will become caught in a bind: Political and social instability will continue to undermine the recovery, while government policies designed to stabilize the economy will produce more political and social instability. If this is indeed the case, then the most likely outcome is a lengthy period of recession/stagnation or, in the worst case, a resumption of a descending economic spiral. If international support for Mexico should falter, then the latter would become an increasingly probable scenario.

SOCIOECONOMIC DEVELOPMENT IN MEXICO: A CONTRADICTION IN TERMS?

Yet the current crisis is only part of the problem. A potentially more serious danger lies in the implications of Mexico's economic strategy for social development. Economists and politicians often overlook the fact that there is much more to socioeconomic development than economic growth: There are also the implications of that growth for the living standards and quality of life of the populace. It can no longer be assumed—as it once was—that the generation of economic wealth will automatically "trickle down" to the masses. It is entirely possible to have economic development and social decay occurring simultaneously—as, for instance, in the case of a growing economy that does not create enough jobs to absorb the expanding labor force, or, equally to the point, an economic growth that produces *greater* socioeconomic inequality. Wealth created in highly inequitable societies gets distributed inequitably. The crucial question is this: Who benefits?

In Mexico, the beneficiaries of structural adjustment have been mainly the upper class, especially the super rich. One statistic is particularly striking: In 1991, Mexico had just two billionaires; by late 1994, there were twenty-eight. (Only three countries had more.)[5] Although some members of the middle class have also prospered, the farther one moves down the socioeconomic ladder, the fewer beneficiaries are to be found. The upshot has been a significant increase in inequality and poverty.

One need only mention in passing some of the factors that have produced these changes: the reversal of the agrarian reform (the emasculation of Article 27 of the Constitution), the elimination of most tariffs and food price controls and subsidies, the opening of the economy to the large-scale importation of food and feed, and the privatization of credit, technical assistance, and state corporations. The result has been growing unemployment, underemployment, landlessness, and land poverty. Nor is there any end in sight. Under NAFTA, thousands of uncompetitive Mexican businesses will be forced to close. Tariffs and import quotas on maize and beans will be phased out, along with corn subsidies. With the reform of Article 27 now permitting the sale of *ejido* lands, it appears highly probable that inequality and land concentration will become much worse, as peasants, unable to compete with cheap foreign imports, come under growing pressure to sell out to large agro-export producers. Although the number of peasants and agricultural workers affected cannot be confidently calculated, former Mexican undersecretary of agriculture Luis Tellez has revealed that it was the Salinas administration's intention to encourage the emigration of over 13 million people from rural areas by the end of the century.[6]

It may be, of course, that the impact will be much less than intended. But even so, there will be major displacement. Those no longer able to make a living in the countryside will flock to the cities. Unless the economy grows extremely fast, and in a way that is labor intensive rather than just capital intensive, it is not likely to produce enough jobs to absorb this influx. The current oversupply of labor will grow, and wages will be depressed. The poor will continue to migrate to the United States; indeed, the flow will probably increase. How many will come, no one can say. A number of studies have estimated that the combination of NAFTA and other policy changes could bring in up to several hundred thousand additional immigrants annually in the short to medium run.[7] But that was before the current economic crisis triggered fears of a larger influx.

In the longer run, the flow may well decline. Demographic factors (decreasing rates of population growth) suggest as much. Once the current crisis and the socioeconomic disruption caused by it and by Mexican policy decisions are past, the economy may pick up, creating more jobs and better wages. But this is problematic. There are too many unknown or uncontrollable variables in the equation to be sanguine about the ultimate outcome.

THE SYNDROME OF VOLATILITY AND ITS IMPLICATIONS FOR MEXICAN POLITICAL STABILITY

All this obviously carries implications for political stability. First, however, it must be placed within the larger context of the syndrome of volatility. As 1994 so dramatically illustrated, Mexico has become one of the most volatile countries in Latin America. Given its long record of political stability, this came as a shock to both Mexicans and foreign observers. Yet the symptoms could be traced back at least as far as 1968 and the bloody suppression of the student movement. In the 1970s and early 1980s, they were manifested in the form of a guerrilla conflict in Guerrero and, much more potently, the boom–bust cycle of the economy, as oil-generated prosperity gave way to debt shock and recession. Less obvious, but also symptomatic, was the "curse" of Mexican presidents: Beginning with Díaz

Ordaz in the 1960s, every presidency has turned sour in the last year or so of office. Salinas was simply following the established pattern. In recent years, we have seen wild swings between political crisis (1988) and political triumph (1991–1993), followed by crisis (early 1994), triumph (August 1994), and once again crisis (December 1994 to the present).

The symbolism of Popocatépetl could not be more apt. The volcano (Mexico) has been bubbling for some time; recently, the eruptions have been growing more frequent and in some cases more intense; the question is whether there will be a full-scale explosion or whether the cauldron will continue to engage in midscale eruptions before cooling back down to a simmer.

If political instability should worsen, what form would it take? Perhaps the least likely scenario would be a *golpe de estado* (coup d'état). The Mexican army is not a stereotypical Latin American military. There are no indications that it is interested in seizing power. On the contrary, it seems content with its established place within the existing political system (which it played a major role in creating) and would not want to be saddled with the responsibility of governing, especially under tumultuous circumstances. In the unlikely event that it does intervene, it will do so very reluctantly— as a last resort in response to an acceleration of the current crisis for the purpose of "saving the nation" from wholesale disintegration.

Unfortunately, the possibility of such a breakdown can no longer be dismissed. The Soviet example underscores the danger of pursuing major political and economic reforms simultaneously, especially when the country lacks a solid economic base. In Mexico, economic liberalization and political democratization have threatened powerful interests. The emerging alliance between narcotraffickers and reactionary elements in the PRI will almost certainly lead to more violence and assassinations if Zedillo accelerates the reform process. Already, the president's attempts to intervene in the state elections in Tabasco and Chiapas have produced a backlash within those local power structures, and it is by no means clear that he has enough authority to impose his will à la Salinas. Rather, the impression one gets from Zedillo's first months in office is that the system of *presidencialismo* may be history.

At the same time, the PRI seems weaker than ever. The party's victory in the August 1994 elections was largely due to the belief of millions of voters that the PRI could maintain political and economic stability. That confidence has been dealt a severe blow in recent months by the Ruiz Massieu assassination, the turmoil in Chiapas and Tabasco, and the devaluation of the peso. The latter is especially damaging, since it has become public knowledge that Salinas knew that the crisis was brewing yet did nothing to avert it. That failure—which is widely viewed as a betrayal of the public interest—has seriously undermined the legitimacy of the regime and the new administration and is likely to haunt the president and the PRI for years to come. In 1995, the ruling party will face major challenges in a flock of state elections, including those in Jalisco, Michoacán, Baja California, Guanajuato, and Yucatán, where the opposition has launched strong campaigns of civil disobedience in recent years. One anticipates that both the quantity and intensity of this kind of turbulence will increase during this *sexenio*. As a result, Zedillo may well face a no-win situation: If he tries to placate the PAN and the PRD by intervening in disputed elections, he will further alienate the "dinosaurs" in his own party. Yet a failure to intervene will further antagonize the opposition. Either way, conflict—and probably violence—are more likely to grow than abate in the years ahead.

This will probably also be the case with regard to agrarian unrest. At this writing, the crisis in Chiapas remains unresolved. Although neither side wants a renewal of the fighting, the issues separating them will be difficult to settle. Although Zedillo has promised a new election, it is not clear that state and local PRI authorities will accept such an intervention. (In neighboring Tabasco, where the president has also sought to intervene, they are in open revolt.) Even if a new balloting is held, it may not result in an opposition victory. Would the Zapatistas and the PRD accept another PRI win? Or would they once again cry fraud and renew their campaign to make the state ungovernable? Nor is the government any longer in a position to fulfill its promises of social development. The peso crisis will force it to cut back spending, limiting its ability to provide programs that might alleviate the discontent that produced the uprising in the first place.

Even if war can be avoided, the most likely prognosis is for continuing turmoil and violence. Chiapan politics is a zero-sum game, or at least it is perceived as such. Since January 1994, peasants have seized over 50,000 hectares of privately owned cattleland and farmland. The previous owners/occupants want it back and have threatened to resort to force unless the government acts. In many cases, they have already unleashed their *pistoleros* (gunmen). Thus, notwithstanding the recent reopening of peace talks, the local situation has become more polarized since the August elections. Land occupations have spread beyond those areas in which the EZLN has operated. Now, moreover, there are at least two other armed groups in Chiapas sympathetic to but not controlled by the Zapatistas.

The greatest danger, of course, is that the contagion may spread. A renewal of the fighting in Chiapas would spark antigovernment protests in many areas of Mexico, including those with large Indian populations. Some of these would probably be violent. There have already been media reports of guerrillas in other states. Although some are no doubt false or inflated, they cannot all be dismissed. The most likely candidate for a serious guerrilla movement is probably Guerrero, which hosted an insurgency in the 1970s. Recently, wall slogans there have announced the presence of the Revolutionary Workers Clandestine People's Union Party (PROCUP), an ultra-leftist group which claimed credit for bombings in Acapulco and Mexico City in January 1994. There is also a guerrilla organization calling itself the Armed Force for the Mexican Revolution, which claims a thousand armed followers (no doubt an exaggeration). Reportedly, there are also other groups operating in the state, some of which are thought to be receiving advice from the EZLN.[8]

Most of these movements are still in their nascent stages of development, but they have considerable potential for growth. Agrarian unrest is mounting and will continue to increase in the years ahead—in large part because of the government's own actions: The agricultural modernization program—including the revision of Article 27, NAFTA, the elimination of quotas, tariffs, subsidies, credits, and so on—is creating the socioeconomic conditions for insurgency. The current economic crisis may be expected to add fuel to what are still (with the exception of Chiapas) scattered bonfires. The Zapatistas have provided inspiration for hundreds of thousands of peasants, some of whom have already begun to seize lands for themselves. Some of the new guerrilla groups are clearly trying to emulate the EZLN. Whether these fires will spread, and how far and how fast, is impossible to say, but it would be foolish to ignore them.

Beyond this, the United States, both through its actions and inactions, could also fan the flames. Congressional and public resistance to President Clinton's $40 billion loan guarantee plan suggests a willingness in some circles to let Mexico go down the drain. Should those sentiments somehow become policy, turmoil will increase even further, perhaps to the point of explosion. At the same time, the temptation on the part of some members of Congress to place humiliating conditions on U.S. assistance has already led to a backlash in Mexico. That country will be experiencing a painful period of austerity in the months ahead. Inevitably, there will be resentment on the part of those who will have to bear this burden. An excessive intervention in the internal affairs of Mexico could generate an intense nationalistic reaction that could severely damage U.S.–Mexican relations and undermine the Zedillo government, which could become identified with the "imperialist penetration" of Mexico, the violation of national sovereignty, and the onerous austerity measures required to stabilize the economy. The upshot could be more instability.

U.S. immigration policy could also worsen the problem. Economic crisis and neoliberal economic policies will mean hardship for labor and the middle class, as well as the peasantry. In the short run, at least, recession and rural-to-urban migration will mean higher unemployment. That, in turn, will create more pressure to emigrate. Mexico's northern border has long served as an escape valve to siphon off socioeconomic frustration. Indeed, this has been one of the keys to the country's political stability. Now, however, growing anti-immigrant sentiment in the United States has led to stepped-up efforts to stem the flow of illegal aliens. Operation "Hold the

Line" in El Paso and "Gatekeeper" in the San Diego area have brought a sharp decline in arrests at those key entry points. Inspired by these results, the Justice Department is talking about reducing the number of illegals crossing the border by 90 percent.

There are serious doubts about the feasibility of such plans. A 2,000-mile border will be extremely difficult, and perhaps impossible, to patrol, and measures designed to halt crossings at selected points may simply increase the flow at others. The effort may be likened to squeezing a balloon; push in at one end and it swells at the other. Already, Nogales seems to have become a new preferred crossing spot. But assuming for a moment that the objective can be attained, what would be its implications for Mexico? A successful illegal immigrant-reduction program would worsen socio-economic conditions and bottle up frustrations at precisely the moment when such tensions are dangerously on the rise. It would also be likely to strain relations with the United States and undermine NAFTA and hence the prospects for Mexico's future prosperity. In a worst-case scenario, it could contribute to a social explosion.

This will probably not happen. Apart from the question of whether the United States has the capability to reduce greatly the flow of illegal immigrants, one should not underestimate those factors that have maintained stability in the past. The foundation of the Mexican system, although seriously eroded, is still in large part intact. The regime retains a considerable capacity to co-opt, contain, or repress its enemies and potential enemies. The military is still loyal; the corporate controls and powers of patronage, while weakened, are still formidable. At the same time, the political opposition remains badly divided. One of the PRI's greatest strengths is the weakness of its enemies. Lacking a single, unified opposition party, the anti-PRI forces are divided between the right-wing PAN and the left-wing PRD, making it difficult for either to amass enough votes to defeat the PRI on the national level.

Nor do the prospects of the revolutionary opposition look all that good. The success of a revolutionary counterelite would require leadership, organization, unity, financial resources, arms, and a mass following, all of which are either absent or in short supply at present. Subcomandante Marcos might have the charisma and intelligence to provide national leadership, if he can escape capture or assassination, but whether he could unify the proliferation of small guerrilla groups that is emerging into a single, large organization is questionable. Without that, the revolutionary movement is more likely to resemble a scattering of small, isolated brushfires than a nationwide conflagration.

In any case, President Zedillo is aware of the danger and is trying to defuse the Chiapas crisis by promising new elections. For their part, the Zapatistas are clearly reluctant to renew the fighting. They remain surrounded on three sides and very weak militarily. For them, a full-scale war would be disastrous. For this reason, there is still a good chance that it can be avoided.

In short, the prospects are for a very troubled *sexenio*. Mexico is experiencing a classic syndrome of rising expectations (generated by Salinas and NAFTA) followed by sharp economic decline, which in turn has created enormous frustration and anger. Although this will probably not lead to a wholesale, violent revolution à la 1910–1920, it does presage continuing lower-level violence and instability, along with an accelerated erosion of the PRI's political control. In effect, Salinas and Zedillo have partially dismantled the old political system without replacing the discarded parts with solid new structures. Until a more coherent system can be formed, the turmoil will not abate.

At the same time, Mexico finds itself trapped between the requisites of economic development and social development. How does one get the country's financial house in order without creating more Zapatistas? By the same token, if political instability and social unrest continue or increase, as seems probable, economic recovery will take longer and will be more painful and less bountiful than most U.S. and Mexican government analysts are predicting.

Nevertheless, barring the unexpected (a complete economic collapse, for instance), there will be no grand explosion. There is even a chance, if the economy picks up, that the PRI may rebound politically. It has done so before, and it may do so again. One should never underestimate this extraordinarily resilient organization.

One final point in the form of a cautionary: Zedillo's initial approach to governing seems to be based on the premise that the solution to the problem of political instability is more democracy. One hopes that this assumption is correct, but one must be coldly realistic: Democracy does not always work, and in any case it is not a cure-all. In this instance, democratization might actually weaken Zedillo's ability to govern by subverting his authority and encouraging the opposition to undermine his policies and further spread civil unrest. Can a democratic president command the respect of his authoritarian predecessors? Or will he be regarded as weak and less worthy of support? If the latter, the country could slide toward ungovernability. Under those circumstances, the response might well be to try to seize back the powers that have been lost. That could mean an attempt to restore *presidencialismo* or, in an extreme situation, the resort to a Fujimori-style *autogolpe* (self-coup) with the support of the military.

THE UNITED STATES, MEXICO, AND THE FUTURE: THE UNEASY SYMBIOSIS

The United States has few foreign policy concerns more profoundly consequential for its national interests than the welfare and stability of Mexico.

Yet U.S. political leaders and the public at large have only recently begun to realize that. Indeed, many *gringos* still take their southern neighbors for granted. That is no longer possible, however. Mexico has entered a "Time of Troubles," and precisely because its economy and citizens have become so intertwined with those of the United States, we cannot ignore this. Greater interdependence means that Mexico's problems are increasingly becoming U.S. problems. From this, there is no escape.

Thus, there is a need to inject a dose of realism into U.S.–Mexican relations. U.S. political leaders have a tendency to oversell their policies, and Mexico is a glaring example. In effect, NAFTA was presented as a cure for most of Mexico's ills and many of our own. It was to lift that country out of underdevelopment and into the ranks of the advanced industrial nations, in the process assuring political stability, fostering democracy, protecting the environment, creating more jobs, raising living standards, solving the nettlesome (for the United States) problem of illegal migration, and paving the way for a new era of U.S.–Mexican cooperation and harmony. Although some of these benefits may still accrue to one extent or another, others will not. In some cases, problems will grow worse *because* of NAFTA and the larger neoliberal economic strategy associated with it.

Nowhere is this ambivalence more apparent than in the evolving U.S.–Mexican symbiosis. That the two countries have entered a new era of much closer, more intense relations is clear. But closeness does not necessarily mean harmony. In a complex relationship, marked by serious conflicts of national interest and a long history of suspicion and resentment, intensity could as easily lead to greater hostility as amity. At minimum, strains and conflicts will continue, and one must be prepared to deal with them. The danger of overselling your product is that you may become the victim of your own propaganda. With respect to Mexico, two U.S. administrations became so enamored with their vision of the future and the strategy necessary to attain it that they were lulled into a false sense of optimism. This, in turn, made it difficult to anticipate or head off emerging problems. When early signs that the Mexican economy was in trouble began to appear, U.S. leaders engaged in denial rather than warn investors or take measures to avert the crisis. When those realities finally hit full force, the response was shock, confusion, and indecision—exactly the wrong messages to send frightened investors.

Another problem, of course, is that false optimism can lead to disillusionment and isolationism. This, in turn, could seriously damage U.S.–Mexican relations and aggravate the very problems that it is so much in the U.S. interest to ameliorate. To its credit, the Clinton administration has resisted that impulse, although the heavy congressional resistance to its loan guarantee program is one more indicator of the anti-Mexico backlash that has been growing in the United States in recent years.

These criticisms, of course, apply to Mexico as well. Rather than facing

the country's emerging economic crisis courageously and taking the politically painful measures needed to contain it, Salinas pretended that the
problem did not exist. Similarly, Zedillo's handling of the situation ("5
weeks of bumbling," in the words of one observer) only worsened the crisis
of confidence among both foreign investors and Mexicans. There are plenty
of other examples. Among other things, the Mexican government still
seems not to fully understand or care about the social crisis that its economic policies have unleashed.

Thus, realism will be needed on both sides of the border. The most immediate challenge for U.S.–Mexican relations (aside from that of restabil-
izing the Mexican economy) will be to contain the backlash. It is not simply
that U.S. investors have been burned; they feel (with good reason) that they
have been manipulated and betrayed. Mexican leaders knew that a potential crisis was brewing, yet they led U.S. investors on, reassuring them of
the stability of the peso even on the eve of devaluation. The bitterness and
mistrust sown by that deception will not soon dissipate. At the same time,
U.S. efforts to come to Mexico's rescue will fan the resentment of those
who believe (in part correctly) that irresponsible Mexican leaders and Wall
Street speculators are being bailed out at taxpayers' expense.

At the same time, U.S. rescue efforts will receive a mixed welcome from
Mexicans. For many nationalists, the enormous package of loans and loan
guarantees will seem to confirm their worst fears and suspicions of the
"Colossus of the North." In the words of one, "I think you [the United
States] should be very happy; you're now the proud owners of Mexico."[9]
If perceptions of U.S. economic penetration should fuse with other emotion-
laden perceptions—for example, that the United States is interfering in
Mexico's internal affairs and violating its sovereignty, that it is inflicting
onerous economic pain on ordinary Mexicans so that U.S. investors might
profit, and that this aid will not solve Mexico's problems but merely increase its indebtedness—then the nationalistic backlash could threaten the
entire relationship.

The point is that, in highly interdependent systems like the United States
and Mexico, what happens on one side is likely to have an effect on the
other. A backlash south of the border could easily fuel a backlash to the
north, and vice versa. The issue of illegal immigration has already started
such a process. The question is whether it will gain momentum from other
resentments.

No doubt the U.S.–Mexican symbiosis will survive in one form or another. It may even blossom, as NAFTA's advocates envisioned. But that
remains to be seen. In the final analysis, the extent to which relations will
be constructive or destructive, friendly or hostile, trustful or suspicious will
be up to the leaders and citizens of both countries. That needs to be kept
in mind as the United States and Mexico go about the tasks of coming to

terms with what will be one of their greatest challenges in the 21st century: their relationship with each other.

NOTES

1. Wayne A. Cornelius, "Mexico's Delayed Democratization," *Foreign Policy,* No. 95 (Summer 1994), pp. 68–69.

2. Foreign Broadcast Information Service, *Daily Report: Latin America,* August 5, 1994.

3. R. Jeffrey Smith and Clay Chandler, "Peso Crisis Caught U.S. By Surprise," *Washington Post,* February 13, 1995.

4. Jane Bussey, "Nagging Question Remains: Will Aid Plan Be Enough?," *Miami Herald,* February 1, 1995; Tod Robberson, "While Peso Stabilizes, Investors Hold Back," *Washington Post,* May 22, 1995.

5. More recently, the economic crisis has taken a toll. There are now only ten billionaires in Mexico. Sam Quinones, "Broken Promises, Broken Dreams," *New York Times,* January 12, 1995; Joel Millman, "Mexico's Billionaire Boom," *Washington Post,* November 27, 1994.

6. David Barkin, "The Specter of Rural Development," *NACLA Report on the Americas,* Vol. 28, No. 1 (July–August 1994), p. 32.

7. Philip L. Martin, *Trade and Migration: NAFTA and Agriculture* (Washington, D.C.: Institute for International Economics, 1993), pp. 4–5.

8. Canadian Security Intelligence Service (CSIS), "Mexico: Prognosis for Stability," No. 52 (December 1994), p. 7.

9. Quoted in Tod Robberson, "Mexicans Wary of Bailout's Fallout," *Washington Post,* February 2, 1995.

Selected Bibliography

Bailey, John J. *Governing Mexico: The Statecraft of Crisis Management.* New York: St. Martin's Press, 1988.

Barkin, David. *Distorted Development: Mexico in the World Economy.* Boulder, Colo.: Westview Press, 1990.

Camp, Roderic Ai. *Generals in the Palacio: The Military in Modern Mexico.* New York: Oxford University Press, 1992.

Collier, George A., with Elizabeth Lowery Quaratiello. *Basta! Land and the Zapatista Rebellion in Chiapas.* Oakland, Calif.: The Institute for Food and Development Policy, 1994.

Collier, Ruth Berins. *The Contradictory Alliance: State–Labor Relations and Regime Change in Mexico.* Berkeley, Calif.: International and Area Studies, University of California, 1992.

Conroy, Michael E., and Amy K. Glasmeier. "Unprecedented Disparities, Unparalleled Adjustment Needs: Winners and Losers on the NAFTA 'Fast Track.'" *Journal of Interamerican Studies and World Affairs,* Vol. 34, No. 4 (Winter 1992–1993): 1–37.

Cornelius, Wayne A. "Mexico's Delayed Democratization." *Foreign Policy,* No. 95 (Summer 1994): 53–71.

———, Judith Gentleman, and Peter H. Smith, eds. *Mexico's Alternative Political Futures.* San Diego, Calif.: Center for U.S.–Mexican Studies, University of California, San Diego, 1989.

———, Ann L. Craig, and Jonathan Fox, eds. *Transforming State–Society Relations in Mexico.* San Diego, Calif.: Center for U.S.–Mexican Studies, University of California, San Diego, 1989.

Cook, Maria Lorena, Kevin J. Middlebrook, and Juan Molinar Horcasitas, eds. *The Politics of Economic Restructuring in Mexico.* San Diego, Calif.: Center for the Study of U.S.–Mexican Relations, University of California, San Diego, 1994.

Cothran, Dan A. *Political Stability and Democracy in Mexico: The "Perfect Dictatorship?"* Westport, Conn.: Praeger, 1994.

Hufbauer, Gary Clyde, and Jeffrey J. Schott. *NAFTA: An Assessment.* Revised Edition. Washington, D.C.: Institute for International Economics, 1993.

———. *North American Free Trade: Issues and Recommendations.* Washington, D.C.: Institute for International Economics, 1992.

Lustig, Nora. *Mexico: The Remaking of an Economy.* Washington, D.C.: Brookings Institute, 1992.

Martin, Philip L. *Trade and Migration: NAFTA and Agriculture.* Washington, D.C.: Institute for International Economics, 1993.

Roett, Riordan, ed. *Political and Economic Liberalization in Mexico: At a Critical Juncture?* Boulder, Colo.: Lynne Rienner Publishers, 1993.

Smith, Peter H. "The Political Impact of Free Trade on Mexico." *Journal of Interamerican Studies and World Affairs,* Vol. 34, No. 1 (Spring 1992): 1–25.

Index

Agrarian conflicts, 9–10, 13, 16, 165–74, 177–83, 199–202

Agrarian reform, 8–9, 108, 168, 170, 196

Agricultural modernization, 8–9, 144, 158–59, 168, 196–97, 200

Alemán, Miguel, Jr., 34

Altamirano, René, 101

Arévalo Gardoqui, General Juan, 175

Aridjis, Homero, 56

Armed Forces for the Mexican Revolution, 200

Army, 10, 12, 24–25, 34, 36, 59–74, 102, 165–66, 171–83, 198, 201–2; arms purchases, 67, 70–71, 177; Cananea mine affair, 68–70; Chiapas and the, 12, 24–25, 36, 41, 69, 165–66, 171–83; civic action, 60–66, 73, 102; corruption, 65–66, 70, 73, 75–76 n.31, 175; counterinsurgency training, 178–79; crisis management, 61, 67, 69–70, 178–79; criticism of, 66, 70, 172–79; democratization and the, 166, 175–80; discontent in the, 172–80; human rights violations, 69–70, 173, 175–77; ideology, 59, 61–62, 71–72, 178–79; internal security, 60–70, 178–79; "1La Quina" affair, 68, 94

n.13; leadership, 179–80; likelihood of a coup, 71–73, 198; modernization of the, 67–69, 72–73, 177–79; organic laws, 60, 63; public perception, 70, 177; public relations, 176–78; relationship with the political leadership, 59–62, 66, 70–73, 173–80; relations with the PRI, 34, 59, 71, 178; relations with the U.S. military, 70–71, 73, 177; relations with Zedillo, 180; reorganization, 67, 73, 177; roles and missions, 59–67, 71–74, 177–79; structure, 67–69, 73, 177, 179

Article 27 (of the Mexican Constitution), 8–9, 158, 159, 168, 196–97, 200

Authoritarianism, 2, 6, 34, 40, 49–50, 81, 92, 126–30, 181, 187; NAFTA and, 127–30

Authoritarian restoration, 127–30, 133, 187, 189–90, 192

Auto industry, 89–90

Avendaño Figueroa, Amado, 19, 21

Barrio, Francisco, 49

BECC (Border Environmental Cooperation Commission), 148

Borderlands, U.S.–Mexican, 64, 103,

About the Editors and Contributors

RODERIC AI CAMP is a Professor of Political Science at Tulane University. He has written over a dozen books on Mexico, including *Intellectuals and the State in Twentieth Century Mexico, Generals in the Palacio: The Military in Modern Mexico, Who's Who in Mexico Today, Politics in Mexico,* and *Mexico's Political Stability.*

MARÍA LORENA COOK is an Assistant Professor of Collective Bargaining, Labor Law, and History at Cornell University. She is the author of a forthcoming book entitled *Organizing Dissent: Unions, the State, and the Democratic Teachers' Movement in Mexico* and coeditor of *The Politics of Economic Restructuring in Mexico.*

STEPHEN P. MUMME is a Professor of Political Science at Colorado State University. He is coauthor of *Statecraft, Domestic Politics and Foreign Policymaking: The Chamizal Dispute.* His articles have been published in *Latin American Perspectives, Journal of Borderlands Studies, Western Political Quarterly,* and the *Journal of Interamerican Studies and World Affairs.*

AL I. PÉREZ is a veteran Foreign Service officer with the U.S. Department of State. He has served as Deputy Director of the Office of Southern Cone Affairs in the Bureau of Inter-American Affairs and has been deeply involved with U.S. political, economic, and development policy concerns, including the Caribbean Basin Initiative and the Enterprise for the Americas Initiative.

DONALD E. SCHULZ is a Professor of National Security Affairs at the Strategic Studies Institute, U.S. Army War College. He has coauthored and coedited books entitled *The United States, Honduras, and the Crisis in Central America; Cuba and the Future; Revolution and Counterrevolution in Central America and the Caribbean;* and *Political Participation in Communist Systems.*

ISIDRO SEPÚLVEDA is the Coordinator of Political Development in the State Government of Nuevo León, Mexico. He has published various government studies on political, social, and economic aspects of Mexican life.

JESÚS TAMAYO is the Director of the Center for Social Research on Regional Development and a researcher in the Department of Economics at the Centro de Investigación y Docencia Económico (CIDE) in Mexico City. Among his publications are *Documentos de Trabajo: Las Áreas Expulsoras de Mano de Obra del Estado de Zacatecas* (coauthor) and "Urbanization and Development of the United States–Mexican Border" (in Lawrence Herzog, ed., *Changing Boundaries in the Americas*).

STEPHEN J. WAGER is an Associate Professor of History at the U.S. Military Academy at West Point. His articles have appeared in the *Journal of Borderlands Studies* and *Hemisphere* and in David Ronfeldt's *The Mexican Military: A Reassessment.* He is currently writing a book on the Mexican military.

EDWARD J. WILLIAMS is a Professor of Political Science at the University of Arizona. Among his best-known works are *Mexico's Central American Policy, The Rebirth of the Mexican Petroleum Industry, Latin American Political Thought,* and *Latin American Politics: A Developmental Approach.*

ISBN 0-313-29518-2

90000>

EAN

9 780313 295188

HARDCOVER BAR CODE